The Accidental Soldier

The Accidental Soldier

Owain Mulligan

HODDER &
STOUGHTON

First published in Great Britain in 2025 by Hodder & Stoughton Limited
An Hachette UK company

2

Copyright © Owain Mulligan 2025

Illustrations © Marianne Waite 2025

100% of the author's royalty earnings (expected to be at least £20,000) from
sales of the book in the UK & Commonwealth will be given to War Child (a
registered charity, charity number 1071659) and its wholly owned subsidiary War
Child Trading Limited (a registered company, company number 05100189).

A CIP catalogue record for this title is available from the British Library

Hardback ISBN 9781399737050
ebook ISBN 9781399737074
Trade Paperback ISBN 9781399737067

Typeset in Sabon MT by Hewer Text UK Ltd, Edinburgh
Printed and bound in Great Britain by Clays Ltd, Elcograf S.p.A.

Hodder & Stoughton policy is to use papers that are natural, renewable
and recyclable products and made from wood grown in sustainable
forests. The logging and manufacturing processes are expected to
conform to the environmental regulations of the country of origin.

The authorised representative in the EEA is Hachette Ireland, 8 Castlecourt
Centre, Dublin 15, D15 XTP3, Ireland (email: info@hbgi.ie)

Hodder & Stoughton Limited
Carmelite House
50 Victoria Embankment
London EC4Y 0DZ

www.hodder.co.uk

To Marianne

Contents

Glossary

2 LANCS – 2nd Battalion, the Duke of Lancaster's Regiment
2/4/10 – 2nd Battalion, 4th Brigade, 10th Division of the Iraqi
   Army
3/4/10 – 3rd Battalion, 4th Brigade, 10th Division of the Iraqi
   Army
ARF – Airborne Reaction Force
BDU – Battle Dress Uniform
CAN – Camp Abu Naji
CO – Commanding Officer
CP – Close Protection
DBE – Department of Border Enforcement
DFID – Department for International Development
EFP – Explosively Formed Projectile
HME – Home Made Explosive
IDF – Indirect Fire
IED – Improvised Explosive Device
IFV – Infantry Fighting Vehicle
JAM – Jaish al-Mahdi
LEC – Locally Employed Civilian
MiTT – Military Transition Team
MoD – Ministry of Defence
NCO – Non-Commissioned Officer
NVG – Night Vision Goggles
OC – Officer Commanding
OPTAG – Operational Training and Advisory Group
PDT – Pre-Deployment Training

PIC – Provincial Iraqi Control
PIR – Passive Infra-Red sensor
PKM – Soviet Machine Gun
PRR – Personal Role Radio
PTSD – Post-Traumatic Stress Disorder
PWRR – Princess of Wales's Royal Regiment
QM – Quartermaster
QRH – Queen's Royal Hussars
REME – Royal Electrical and Mechanical Engineers
RiP – Relief in Place
RLC – Royal Logistics Corps
RMP – Royal Military Police
RPG – Rocket-Propelled Grenade
RSM – Regimental Sergeant Major
RSOI – Reception, Staging and Onward Integration
RTA – Road Traffic Accident
RV – Rendezvous Point
SAF – Small Arms Fire
SITREP – Situation Report
SQMS – Squadron Quartermaster-Sergeant
SSM – Squadron Sergeant Major
TA – Territorial Army
VCP – Vehicle Check Point
VP – Vulnerable Point

Author's Note

This is a story about British soldiers on active service. It is compiled from diary entries, emails home, hurried scrawls in a notebook, and my own imperfect memory to fill in the gaps. Names have been changed, and some details glossed over when they have either been shunted out of my hippocampus by nineteen years, two children and the name of every single one of the *Paw Patrol* characters, or to respect people's privacy. But if it wouldn't win any prizes for official history, it is as close a reflection of the spirit and characters of those times as I could make it.

I have tried to tell it like it was (or at least, how it looked to us). As such, certain passages in the book may offend; British soldiers are many things, but Regency-era debutantes they are not. If anything you read does make you uncomfortable, then I can only apologise and offer up the defence of authenticity. And reassure you that it's probably not half as uncomfortable as when your editor, sitting opposite you in a brightly lit office buzzing with impossibly glamorous publishing types, carefully clears his throat and observes, 'There's rather a lot of . . . masturbation in the book, isn't there?'

Finally, a word to the Iraqi Army. I have managed to eke out over 300 pages from my eyeblink of a seven-month tour. Their stories, from twenty years (and counting) since the invasion, would fill the British Library. The ones we worked with were simultaneously maddening, corrupt, brilliant, crafty, ingenious, inept, brave and lazy. But when it really mattered, they delivered. And two years after we had left Basra, they stepped up and retook a city the British Army had lost. As much as it's for anyone, this book is for them.

1

The Great Escape

The militia gunman is the other side of that door.

I can hear him clearly through the breeze-block wall that separates us – roaring defiance between long bursts on the machine gun which caught half the troop in the open, five minutes ago. He must know his time is nearly up. He must have heard the shouts as we pounded up the stairs to the second floor, searching for the window where the sudden four-leaf clover of his muzzle blast had come from. But he doesn't care. He's got what he came for. The evidence for that is lying face down and motionless in the street below.

I plant the butt of my rifle in my shoulder and glance at the soldier beside me. He's blinking over and over again. Either the sweat's dripped into his eyes or he – like me – can't comprehend what's happened to our quiet, early morning patrol. But when I nod, he will put his boot straight into that lock. And I will clear the room. I will kill whoever's behind that door. I feel for the small metal nub of my change lever and click it down. A for Automatic. Then I take one last shuddering breath. And nod.

The door explodes open and I am in the room before the gunman can even register the movement. He's crouched by the window, cradling the machine gun as it leaps and judders, one hand feeding a long, copper-coloured belt of ammunition into its hungry breech. Then his head whips round towards me. But it's too late. It's a lifetime too late. Because I am five yards away, and I have him cold.

I pull the trigger.

Click.

The dead man's click.

The whole world seems to drop away. And all I can see is the face of the gunman, framed by a tattered, red-and-white *keffiyeh*. His lip curls in a slow smile of realisation. Then he stares straight at me.

'Oh. My. God . . . you absolute *wanker*! Fuck me, mate, you should see your face . . .'

Later on, after a withering debrief from the Directing Staff – complete with sarcastic congratulations on the first attempt in British Army history to clear a room using telekinesis – I worked out that I'd bollocksed up my magazine change. Do it right, and you'll burst into the gunman's eyrie with thirty rounds of deadly 5.56mm in your rifle and one already in the chamber. Do it the way I did, and you may as well kick in the door and point a copy of *HELLO!* at him. Thank God it was only an exercise.

On the long drive back from Salisbury Plain to London and our Territorial Army (TA) Centre, I thought about whether I'd rather take on a real-life enemy machine-gunner with a rifle that went *click*, or go back to work tomorrow. But it was no contest really; I'd have stormed Omaha Beach with a Nerf gun if it meant avoiding another Monday morning at my job. I was a teacher, and I hated it. No, scratch that. I *loathed* it.

My short career had been an ocean-going disaster from day one. The school was like *The Hunger Games* and I was the worst teacher there. Possibly anywhere. It wasn't the kids' fault; lots of them had the kind of home lives that meant it would have been a minor miracle if they *weren't* sociopaths. But that's pretty scant comfort when you're the one picking the Pritt Stick out of your eyebrows for the third time in a week.

My one outlet was TA weekends like the one I'd just finished. After endless cortisol-soaked days of frantically trying to persuade eleven-year-olds that nailing your neighbour's hand to their desk with a compass wouldn't actually make you feel any better, it was quite ironic that spending a weekend bayonetting straw-filled dummies and screaming did such wonders for my own mental health.

And now it looked like it might even get me out of teaching for good. Several members of my TA regiment had recently come back from Iraq. They appeared – on the face of it, anyway – happy and whole, with *Love Island* tans and a seemingly endless supply of cool stories, which I was pretty sure would knock the socks off the kinds of girls who normally just ignored me at parties (i.e., all of them). I wasn't particularly interested in fighting anyone, but long-range desert patrols and bustling bazaars straight out of *Arabian Nights* were starting to sound a lot more appealing than another year in Enfield confiscating Nokia 3210s and being reminded I was a 'fucking bellend' five times a day. It also looked like the Army would need the manpower.

With an impressive disregard for the fact that Iraq wasn't so much teetering on the brink of a civil war, as it was standing in thin air ten feet clear of the brink and staring comically at the camera, Wile E. Coyote style, the British government had just made a very hefty troop commitment to Afghanistan. Judging by the number of mobilisation letters now going around the TA, we were well past barrel-scraping territory. In fact, it seemed a lot like the barrel was now upside down and being banged hopefully on the bottom to see if any dregs fell out. It was clear that if I wanted, I could be one of those dregs.

I made my mind up the very next day. It was a dank December morning and I was teaching a Year 8 class on Henry VIII. I wasn't really, of course. I was shouting something about monasteries while thirty-odd twelve-year-olds variously carried on animated conversations, flicked spit wads at each other, or simply sat there quietly devouring all the Blu Tack. Then it all kicked off at Dillon and Curtis' desk.

As with any good blood feud, the original reason behind Curtis and Dillon's implacable enmity had long since been lost in the mists of time. Unfortunately, that didn't stop them trying to take each other apart like Frazier vs Ali every time they entered the same classroom. By the time I scurried over clucking, Dillon had bypassed all the usual pleasantries, removed the protective guard, and pushed the big red button marked 'Your Mum'. As any schoolboy knows, there is no verbal escalation possible beyond this point. I could already see Curtis reaching for Dillon's shirt collar.

I was saved by the arrival of the Head of Music, who rapped on the door and brightly announced it was time for Curtis to come and collect his violin. For a moment I was confused; this was a bit like asking Genghis Khan to come and pick up his easel. Then I remembered that as one of its regular Hail Mary plays to turn things round, the school had started dishing out free musical instruments to some of its more obvious headcases.

The idea was that music might soothe their troubled souls, or at least reduce the rate at which they were vigorously flushing their peers' heads down the toilet. Privately I doubted Curtis had a musical bone in his body, but it wasn't my idea and if it got him out of the classroom they could let him lead the London Philharmonic string section for all I cared. Prising him apart from Dillon, I thrust him gratefully towards the door and he wandered off down the corridor to collect his prize.

Peace descended for the next twenty minutes or so, at which point Curtis returned, violin in hand. I am no musician, but it looked like a beauty, all sinuous lines and richly coloured whorls. Curtis seemed thrilled with it, clutching it so hard his little fingers were white, while his other hand stroked its glistening surfaces. Even Dillon stared, Curtis' mum temporarily put aside. As it were.

'What a lovely violin, Curtis,' I said, as he returned to his desk. 'When will you start your lessons?'

Curtis beamed, still standing, and shrugged wordlessly. A great sigh of happiness seemed to consume his small body, and as he breathed out he lifted his violin high above his head, as if to show it to the world. Then, still smiling beatifically, he brought it thundering down and broke it clean in two over Dillon's head.

I volunteered for Iraq that afternoon.

Thursday, 5 January 2006 – London

Mobilisation paperwork arrived today; a big brown envelope marked 'On Her Majesty's Service' hits the doormat with a *thunk* that sounds like freedom. If this was a film, I'd spend the rest of the day smoking pensively while it sat unopened on the kitchen table. But I've just spent several months being worked over by Enfield's answer to *Children of the Corn*, and this envelope is my get-out. So instead I more or less float to work and tender my resignation before morning break. In a mark of the deep esteem in which the school holds my teaching abilities, it's accepted before lunchtime.

The paperwork itself is light on detail, but there are a few clues; I will deploy to Iraq in April, on Operation TELIC 8,[1] with a regiment called the Queen's Royal Hussars (QRH). They are based in Sennelager, Germany, and I am to get myself out there to join them for pre-deployment training as soon as possible. Finally, I am assured that my mobilisation arises only after 'much careful thought by the Secretary of State for Defence'. I bet they say that to all the girls. At least I hope they do. Otherwise the war effort's in a lot more trouble than I'd thought.

Tuesday, 10 January 2006 – Sennelager

I fly to Hanover in the evening, and find a bored trooper from the QRH waiting to give me a lift to Sennelager ('Probably the worst lager in the world, sir . . .'). We're in a decrepit Army minibus, so even the slow lane on the autobahn feels like entering hyperdrive in the Millennium Falcon, and we don't arrive until well after midnight.

The QRH's barracks is a collection of low huts, set deep in a freezing cold pine forest, with all the cheery ambience of a Siberian logging camp. It was put up as temporary accommodation immediately after the war by the British occupation authorities, who would presumably be quite surprised to see 500 soldiers still bitching endlessly about having to live there some sixty years later. I find a note in the Officers' Mess telling me to report to B Squadron in the morning.

I've had some time to do a bit of research on the QRH since getting the mobilisation paperwork, and am beginning to feel a healthy sense of imposter syndrome. They are an armoured cavalry regiment, which means they go to war in Challenger 2; 75 tons of Main Battle Tank with a 120mm barrel on the front.

In my TA unit, by contrast, we use arthritic 1970s Land Rovers and shoot pencil flares out of the window when we're pretending to fire the main gun. Which isn't actually a gun, it's a broomstick covered in black gaffer tape and tied to the roof with bungee cords. And the QRH have been to Iraq before. Not to mention Kosovo, Bosnia, and Northern Ireland before that. In fact, they are probably one of the most operationally experienced units in the Army today.

I think back to my four weeks of panicked TA officer training at Sandhurst. We'd gone through the motions – patrols, ambushes, platoon attacks – basically the full warfighting menu. But a month is not that long to learn how to be a soldier. Particularly not when you're spending a lot of your time discreetly trying to check whether you've got your helmet on backwards, or remember where you were in this particular forest when you last saw your rifle. Our instructors, seasoned infantry veterans with a daysack full of stories from Crossmaglen and Sarajevo, had obviously despaired of us, and spent most of our post-exercise debriefs informing us that we were all living proof that evolution can go backwards, while angrily kicking nearby saplings to death.

Quite how the Army has concluded that this blink-and-you'd-miss-it level of professional training qualifies me for active service is a mystery. But there isn't a great deal I can do about it now. As I stare at the ceiling of my room in the Officers' Mess, listening to the wind battering the pine trees, I reassure myself that the grown-ups will have a plan. They will have combed through a big manila personnel file stuffed with meticulous records of everything I've done in the TA. Whatever it is they want me to do in Iraq, it will be fully in keeping with my very limited military skills.

Probably something in the operations room. Or maybe some kind of liaison job. After all, I'm with the Regular Army now. They'll know what they're doing.

Wednesday, 11 January 2006 – Sennelager

I will be leading a fighting troop in Basra.

My new squadron leader, a small, ebullient major called Jonty, delivers the news as if he's telling me I've won the Thunderball draw. I goggle blankly at him and try not to be sick in my mouth. Apparently B Squadron are short of an officer, so I'm now Third Troop Leader. I suppose you can see why Jonty is expecting me to be thrilled. This is exactly what officers are supposed to join the Army for; to lead men, be the tip of the spear, deliver cold Sheffield steel to the Queen's enemies and all that.

And it's not like I haven't led a troop before. But that was cosplaying around Wiltshire with half a dozen TA soldiers, all of whom would go back to being accountants or electricians on

Monday morning, no matter how many times I got them 'killed' doing something stupid. It's a long way from being given sole charge of twelve professional soldiers on a real-life operational tour.

This is a very grave business. And quite likely to put a few people *in* one if I fuck it all up. In fairness to Jonty, it isn't like he doesn't recognise the seriousness of what he's asking. After giving me a quick rundown on the troop, he cheerfully informs me that 'if you turn out to be shit, I'll just sack you.' Which has to be the most stirring vote of military confidence since some unnamed Israelite handed David his slingshot and asked, in a roundabout kind of way, what size sandals he took.

I walk to the tank park to meet the troop, and busy myself with a quickfire round of catastrophising on the way over. What if they ask about my actual experience? What if I make a total tit of myself during the training? What if they demand a proper troop leader instead of a TA one? By the time I get over there, I have more or less resigned myself to meeting a wall of soldiers coming towards me with their arms linked and singing 'Give Peace a Chance', on their way to telling Jonty that they're not going to Iraq after all.

A gaggle of soldiers stands behind a tank with '3–0' written on the back. I walk towards them with what I hope is a purposeful, martial stride, but which on reflection probably just makes me look like I'm recovering from a scrotal tuck. A man the approximate size of a JCB backhoe loader introduces himself as Sergeant Mason and gets the soldiers on parade.

With a rictus grin on my face I introduce myself as their new troop leader (glossing over the fact that last week, Matthew, I was a humanities teacher from North London), stammer a few details about the next months' training that Jonty has just told me, then ask if there are any questions. Not exactly Henry V before Agincourt. And the troop don't look remotely inspired; I'm not expecting anyone to leap onto a chair and start shouting, 'O Captain! My Captain!', but these lads are showing all the visceral emotion of pensioners who've fallen asleep listening to *Test Match Special*. On the other hand they don't look visibly mutinous either. And I haven't thrown up all over my shoes. So I'm counting it as a win.

Sgt Mason takes me to his small office and makes me what he calls a 'Julie Andrews'.[2] Then he talks me through Third Troop's soldiers; who the drivers are, who's good on a machine gun, who's generally reliable, and who has Platinum Elite status at the Sennelager garrison cells. He is straight out of central casting, six foot one with the torso of Goliath's harder brother, hair shaved to the skull, and a voice like aggregate being crushed. I am very aware that getting our relationship right will be the making – or breaking – of me.

Ideally you want it to be a neat symbiosis; a partnership for the common good. Like those clownfish that can live snugly inside poisonous sea anemones, and in return defend the anemones from other fish trying to eat them.[3] The troop leader makes the tactical decisions, reads the maps and occasionally murmurs, 'Very good, carry on,' like David Niven when they're not sure what to do next. The troop sergeant looks after the equipment and the administration, and channels Captain Bligh on the *Bounty* if any of the boys step out of line.

But while you'd be a special kind of idiot not to listen to the man with the decade-plus of experience, the troop leader is ultimately in charge. If anything goes wrong – we lose a weapon, a vehicle gets trashed, the boys desert *en masse* and join a passing circus – it's my feet that will be in Jonty's in-tray. Even so, I have heard several discomfiting stories about newly arrived young officers being told by their troop sergeants to pipe down and keep their sticky little hands to themselves. Luckily Sgt Mason seems to have a much more modern approach to parenting, and we agree that I will make the decisions, while he will only intervene if it appears that someone is about to lose an eye.

2

Tin City

Thursday, 19 January 2006 – Sennelager

Pre-deployment training – PDT – starts today. And it's clear we need it.

When I first joined the Army, I'd been very impressed by a recruitment brochure which described soldiers as being like Premier League footballers; finely honed athletes ready to go at a moment's notice. That's what they'd like you to think. In reality, between operational tours (and particularly straight after Christmas leave), many soldiers more closely resemble a League Two player-manager with a fucked ACL and a forty-a-day Superkings habit.

As I watch Third Troop stumble wheezing over the line after Jonty's 7 a.m. 'welcome to PDT' five-mile run, like something out of the Bataan Death March, it's clear that the QRH is no exception. Trooper Buxton, who is a good two stone the other side of 'big boned', looks like he's about to die right there on the pavement. This is actually a bit of a positive. Ever since mobilisation I have been thrashing myself silly in the gym. I might have the operational experience of a Brownie, but I am at least fit.

B Squadron will go through PDT alongside 1st Battalion The Princess of Wales's Royal Regiment (1 PWRR), who are in charge of our battlegroup.[4] Despite the somewhat dainty name, they are a hard-nosed armoured infantry regiment of about 500 men. They recruit mainly from London and the South-East, and as we walk onto their snow-covered tank park on the first day it's like being in the middle of an *EastEnders* Christmas special. Everyone seems to be calling everyone else a 'fackin' caaaaaahnt', and I also hear at least one 'sling yer hook', which until now I've always assumed was only ever said on telly.

The PWRR were last in Iraq two years ago, on what is by now a legendary tour. They were based to the north of the British area in a province called Maysan. It had traditionally been quite restive, and shortly after the PWRR's arrival the local militias had decided they definitely wanted it back. The PWRR had demurred, and charged around Maysan like tanked-up Millwall fans on Derby Day, fighting a series of epic battles over several months, doubtless with the regimental battle cry on their lips ('fackin' 'ave some of that, you caaaahnts').

They'd finished the tour with a brace of Military Crosses, a few Distinguished Service Orders, and a Victoria Cross for a Warrior armoured vehicle driver called Beharry, who hadn't let the small matter of an RPG (*rocket-propelled grenade*) to the head stop him from driving through a nasty ambush. At the moment they are about the most lionised unit in the British Army, and will presumably be very useful to show us around those bits of southern Iraq that they didn't raze to the fucking ground the last time they were there.

This bit of PDT will take place in 'Tin City'. It's a purpose-built training facility with all the houses, shops, schools and so on that you can expect to see on operations. Providing, that is, that you're going on operations in a small Northern Irish border town. In the 1970s. But the Army isn't worried about details. Even details like the Central Mosque (itself a rather *bouji* Roman Catholic church with 'Central Mosque' spray-painted on it) being directly next door to a large pub called the Crown and Shamrock. They have simply relabelled the pub – with the kind of breathtaking cultural sensitivity that makes you suspect they think *Aladdin* is a documentary – as 'Ali Akbar's Kebab Emporium'.

Tin City itself is 'populated' by a small contingent of German Iraqis (who must be getting paid through the nose to sit around in unheated pretend houses in a Sennelager winter), and a company's worth of Liverpudlians from 2 LANCS, the 2nd Battalion the Duke of Lancaster's Regiment (who will be getting paid exactly what they always get paid). Their role is to act variously as both townsfolk and enemy.

The Army is clearly a big believer in the Stanislavski Method approach to acting, because the 2 LANCS lads have been living here a month already, fully immersed in their new lives as Adil the Toyota mechanic or Hashmat the deranged jihadi. They all wear costumes that look like a party shop Arabian sheikh outfit, and are very probably on the verge of mutiny by this point.

The whole thing is run by a small cadre of external instructors from OPTAG(I) (Operational Training and Advisory Group(Iraq)), who are, in theory at least, bang up to date on all the tactics being used in theatre right now. They wear yellow fluorescent jackets and have whistles they can blow if things ever get out of hand (e.g., you find your skull being rhythmically bounced off the pavement by a sixteen-stone corporal from 2 LANCS, who has been here so long he genuinely believes he's a Ba'ath Party *fedayeen*).[5]

As we file into our accommodation for what will probably be the last good night's sleep in a while, I can't help but wonder whether spending several weeks in a Northern Ireland training facility, populated almost entirely by Scousers and currently covered in six inches of snow, is going to be particularly useful preparation for a summer tour of southern Iraq. They say Waterloo was won on the playing fields of Eton, but at least they were both technically a grass surface. That said – and in common with 99 per cent of things that the Army does to you – it's not like I can do much about it now.

Monday, 23 January 2006 – Tin City

Urban patrolling today. The concept sounds pretty simple: wherever you're going, you make sure you've got some of the troop going there, some of the troop covering them, and whoever's left just lurking around unpredictably. It makes for slow going, but the theory is that nothing will give an enemy sniper pause like the nagging feeling that if he does open fire, those soldiers he last saw twenty minutes ago wandering off in completely the wrong direction will pop up unexpectedly from behind a wall and shoot him in the face. He will soon become Confused and Demoralised, and with any luck eventually just stop being a sniper and open an artisanal bath salts pop-up or something. It's a technique honed over many painful years in Belfast and Londonderry, but has been working well in Basra, too.

That's the theory, anyway. Add in four hours' sleep the night before, a constant stream of chatter from Jonty on the radio asking where the fuck you are, and a sketch map of Tin City that appears to have been drawn by rolling a blind spider in ink, and very quickly you can find yourself with a troop which is – as one OPTAG instructor puts it to me balefully – 'all over the place like a mad woman's shit'. On the other hand, as the boys tell me happily while we trudge back to the accommodation, if the idea was to Confuse and Demoralise then job done, '. . . because we were confused as fuck, sir . . .'

Thursday, 26 January 2006 – Tin City

No patrolling today – it's indoor lessons instead. We're in the Tin City lecture theatre, which is warm, dry, and thus after about ten minutes also doubling up as the biggest sleeping bag in the British Army.

We start with a cheery PowerPoint presentation from a medic on all the various horrific diseases we're probably going to catch. All the old favourites are there – cholera, hepatitis of both A and B varieties, typhoid, yellow fever, malaria and TB. We're only really missing monkeypox and ebola. There are also half a dozen that I've never even heard of until today, each one of which immediately makes me wish it had stayed like that.

Like leishmaniasis, which will apparently at best leave some nasty scars, and at worst turn your spleen into custard. It's 'spread by sandfly bites' according to the slide. Which then goes on to soberly advise us: 'so don't get bitten by sandflies'. This may top the leaderboard of 'technically correct but completely fucking useless' bits of advice the Army has given me so far. And it is shaping up to be a competitive field.

Before leaving the stage, the medic tells us not to worry, because at some point we'll get up-to-date vaccinations against most of what they've just described. This is a bit concerning for a couple of reasons; firstly, because being 'vaccinated against most of these diseases' feels a bit like putting on a condom that 'can handle the majority of these flesh-eating STDs'. And secondly, because the last time the Army started sticking needles in people they were sending to the Gulf, they ended up having a whole syndrome named after them.

Next up is language and culture. It's a classic *écoutez-et-répétez*-style lesson with Mo, a British Iraqi who has been flown to Germany for the express purpose of spending several weeks listening to hundreds of squaddies butchering his native language. He could double for Saddam Hussein's even hairier younger brother, but he is the sweetest man. He is also clearly desperate to impart as much knowledge as he can in the forty-five minutes that OPTAG have decided should probably be enough to cover 8,000 years of civilisation and the basics of one of the planet's top five most complex languages.

I watch Mo pluck fretfully at his enormous moustache as he carefully enunciates a basic greeting. B Squadron listen, digest, and then respond as if they're inpatients in a Crimean War TB ward. Mo smiles weakly and pronounces it 'very bad'.

Not to worry though, because there's a laminated booklet to go with the lesson. It is rather grandly titled a 'cultural aide memoire', and is chock-full of what could charitably be described as somewhat niche factoids. If I'm ever facing the last question in the *Who Wants to Be a Millionaire?* chair, I may yet be grateful that I now know a *turbah* is a small, circular piece of clay used in Shia prayers. Or that the Iraqi Chaldeans entered full communion with the Holy See in 1552. But right now they strike me as somewhat odd choices to include in a booklet for people whose main job will be to walk slowly around southern Iraq carrying machine guns.

The booklet also contains a few cultural dos and don'ts. Some are quite handy, and the kind of nuanced local practices we might well have missed otherwise. 'Don't admire an Iraqi's personal belongings; he may feel obliged to give them to you,' or, 'Do expect to see blood on the front of a house; this represents a religious celebration and blessing,' (which suggests there has been at least one impromptu meeting between a size eleven desert boot, an Iraqi's front door, and a very emotional mother of the bride). Others are breathtakingly patronising: 'Don't put your open palm in someone's face – this is rude.' 'Don't fart in public – this is very rude.' I bet they are, but then again I'm not sure they're exactly considered the high-water mark of civilisation on the Charing Cross Road either.

The last page of the booklet is headed 'Helpful Orders and Questions', with the Arabic on one side and its doubtless mangled phonetic equivalent in English on the other. Mo takes us through the phrases, the smile gradually sliding off his face as we murder each one in turn. The page starts in an encouragingly bombastic fashion: 'Stop', 'Do not move', 'Drop your weapon'. Your everyday commands for the confident British Army soldier who's on top of his brief. We then enter more tentative territory: 'Who are you?', 'What has been happening?', 'When did you last see them?', and so on.

At the end there is a section that should probably be retitled, 'Things to Say When It's Gone Completely Up the Fucking Swanny'. To wit: 'Where did they come from?', 'Who is in charge?', 'Calm down', and finally – and I assume you don't so much say this one as babble it through all the tears and snot – 'Can you get us out of here safely?'

I'm not sure whether to be impressed at the author's diligence, or aghast that they think we might actually need to ask the locals to MacGyver us out of the shit. Either way, Mo – probably wisely – elects not to practise that one.

Saturday, 28 January 2006 – Tin City

More patrolling. This morning I discovered they've installed compressed air jets on some of the street corners; linger next to one for too long and it does a very good impression of an AK-47 round parting your hair. You, in turn, do a very good impression of a rescue cat seeing a toaster pop for the first time, trip over the kerb in a blind panic, and neatly brain yourself on a postbox.

Third Troop's patrolling is getting there; we're not SEAL Team Six[6] by any stretch, but on the other hand we don't seem to be any worse than the rest of the squadron. And we're gelling together as a team. You can see it in the way we're starting to anticipate one another as we move across the ground, the new brevity of our radio messages, and the familiar little rituals we go through before patrols. My worst fears – that Jonty will decide I'm the biggest military fuck-up since Suez and sack me before we've even finished PDT – are starting to subside.

They're being replaced just as quickly by some fundamental worries about what I'm letting myself in for. PDT has started to feel, to put it mildly, a little bit spicy. Today alone Third Troop have staggered dazedly from a small-arms-shoot, to bomb-in-a-culvert, to previously-friendly-stallholder-peremptorily-tries-to-stab-me-in-the-neck-during-a-chat-about-watermelons. We are constantly reminded by the OPTAG staff that everything they're putting us through has happened in Basra in the last six months. Well, yes lads, I want to say, but presumably not all to the same person, and not all on the same afternoon?

It's not just the number of incidents, it's their sheer intensity too. According to what we can glean from the PWRR, a lot of real-life shooting incidents are quite inconclusive. Even if you can work out where your gunman is hiding (which'll be about one time in ten, they reckon), he's unlikely to hang around once he has made his point. If you're in a vehicle, you may be several hundred metres down the road before you've even registered the shot. Or no one may notice it at all. Which must be a rather deflating experience for the gunman, who has presumably been looking forward to his moment in the sun.

That's not how they do it on PDT, though. Here every contact[7] seems to be a balls-out gun battle of epic savagery against a fanatical enemy, who is more often than not standing in the middle of a main road wearing a Tommy Cooper fez and screaming at the top of his lungs. And it ends not with him quietly melting away into the crowds, but only after you've fire-and-manoeuvred halfway across Tin City, cornered him in the Kebab Emporium, and filled him, snarling, with a magazine full of blanks. Or in First Troop's case, kicked in the door to the next-door building and noisily laid waste to what the OPTAG staff will later sorrowfully inform them was supposed to be a meeting of local sheikhs about girls' education. While the PWRR assure us this is all 'faaackin' ridiculous', I can't help but wonder.

Whatever the case, we're taking 'casualties' at a rate to make Kitchener wince. The benign gods of OPTAG let us respawn after every scenario, which is just as well, because by my own count we've been through the squadron's manpower at least twice already. I've personally been 'killed' five times; shot twice, blown up twice, and in what feels like one particularly vindictive scenario, lengthily immolated in a burning Land Rover.

Being killed isn't all bad – they let you lie down for a bit at least – but it's not doing loads for my morale. As Jonty remarks one evening after his O (*Orders*) Group, Iraq *had* better be a sight gentler than PDT. Or we're going to need a lot more soldiers.

Friday, 3 February 2006 – Tin City

The Army has a drill for absolutely everything. From how to salute while on a bicycle (return rear firmly to saddle, and brace arms straight on the handlebars) to how to conduct an emergency burial service in the field (ensure the hole is at least six feet deep if you don't want your departed brother-in-arms to be dug up by a badger, and for Christ's sake write down where you put him). In fact the Army's drill manual alone runs to something like 400 pages. It should therefore come as no surprise that they've also got a drill for what to do if someone sets you on fire.

B Squadron's cheerfully titled 'Fire Inoculation' lesson takes place in a blustery car park the other side of Tin City. We patrol there for the novelty, and get killed a couple of times on the way over. Then we start nervously fitting visors to our helmets and hefting the six-foot plastic shields that the OPTAG instructors have doled out.

The Army doesn't issue any kind of actually fireproof kit (although this isn't a total surprise for an organisation which has only recently cracked the concept of everyone getting a set of body armour each). But we are told to wear our thermal long johns as an extra layer of protection. Not the issue fleece though, because that will melt into your skin if exposed to naked flame. Of course it will. I try not to look at the scorch marks on the tarmac. Presently our instructor arrives, a chipper Gurkha colour sergeant called Gurung.

A lot of people drift through this world doing what society expects, living the 'paint by numbers' version of life, but never working out what it is that makes them truly happy. Others find their passion and revel in the sheer naked joy of it for the rest of their days. It quickly becomes clear that CSgt Gurung is in the latter category. And that his particular passion is throwing petrol bombs at people.

'Today, gennlemen, we practise what to do when there is riot, and petrol bomb is thrown,' he announces happily. 'Yes. First of all, very important that no panic. Petrol bomb is hot. Yes. Very hot. Burn you all over. But, if you panic, run around with hands in air shouting, "Aaaaaaaah!", not helpful. Burn even hotter!'

Gurung giggles delightedly. His audience stares back at him, aghast. He is oblivious.

'So, petrol bomb is thrown. Smash! Whoomp! Fire is all around. Yes. Fire come between your legs, up your front, up your back.' He pauses, thoughtfully. 'Also up your face. But no panic. Yes. First you must protect your face.' He drops his chin to his chest in exaggerated fashion. 'Then, you must tell everyone that you are on fire and there is problem. Say, "I am on fire," like this . . .' He draws breath. ' "I AM ON FIRE!" '

I see the boys glance at each other. Presumably they are wondering, like I am, whether the fact that the soldier standing next to you has just gone up in an enormous ball of flames wouldn't be enough of a clue that 'there is problem'.

'Then take one step to the backwards, and you must stamp your feet. Stamp stamp stamp, like this.' His feet drum a tattoo on the tarmac. 'Also you must bang your shield. Bang bang bang. Then petrol fall off! It just fall off!' He beams, inviting us to share in this marvellous phenomenon. 'Then you just say, "Back in," like this . . .' Another breath. ' "BACK IN!" and then you carry on with riot. Yes. Yes. I need a volunteer.'

The boys, lulled by Gurung's pyromaniacal monologue, have been leaning in to get a closer look at his demonstration, but at hearing this they lunge back as one man. Gurung's shining eyes range over us, practically hopping with excitement at the thought that he is shortly going to get to immolate someone again. Eventually Jonty resigns himself to the inevitable and steps forward. Thirty seconds later he is a roaring five-foot-eight ball of flame, and has to be put out with a fire extinguisher.

Of course, we all do it in the end, with Nepal's answer to the Human Torch hurling his milk bottles full of petrol at our feet and clapping his hands with maniacal glee. When my own time comes, I am surprised to find that the drill actually works. I adapt it slightly – adding a whispered litany of *'fuckfuckfuckfuckfuck'* while waiting for the explosion, and shouting 'BACK IN!' with my helmet still on fire – but otherwise it's more or less as described. There is an initial unpleasant burst of heat as the flames billow up your body, but with sufficient stamping and banging (and I would have given the cast of *Riverdance* a run for their money), the burning gobbets of petrol do fall off.

Our lesson over, we patrol away to do a bit more practice at getting killed, and one of the PWRR companies takes our place. We can still hear the cries of 'Argh, you *caaaahnt*, I'm on faackin' *fire*!' the other side of Tin City.

Monday, 6 February 2006 – Tin City

This morning we are back in the lecture theatre for a lesson on the Law of Armed Conflict. There have been a number of recent incidents in Basra where it's clear some major lines were crossed. Lines like 'Don't blindfold detainees and make them simulate oral sex on you, jump up and down on top of them while they're lying handcuffed on the floor, or indeed tie them to forklift trucks and drive them around camp'. While it's equally clear that the blame lies with a very small minority, the Army has evidently now concluded that inside every British soldier there resides a tiny roaring *SS Sturmscharführer*, who cannot wait to get out to theatre and start lining villagers up against walls. So this is about the fifth such lesson we've had in the past month.

First off is a re-introduction to Joint Services Publication 398, or as it's known by its snappier title, Card Alpha. This is a small piece of white paper that lays out in helpful detail when exactly you're allowed to shoot someone. Broadly speaking, it's only when there's a threat to life. The card is very explicit that threats to property don't count, suggesting that at least one squaddie has come over very UKIP Party Conference about someone nicking his brake lights at some point.

The card also reminds you that before shooting someone, you must shout, 'British Army, stop or I fire' – or, somewhat coyly, 'words to that effect'. This will ensure that whoever you're about to blow away gets fair warning in a language they probably don't understand. Most importantly of all, you *must* make sure you carry a copy of Card Alpha at all times. If you don't have one and you do happen to shoot someone, then in the words of the hitherto prim Army lawyer giving the lesson, you are 'turbo-infinity-fucked'.

This is absolutely classic Army. You could pore over Card Alpha until your eyes bled and you were able to recite the whole thing in Esperanto, but if you're not carrying a physical bit of paper when you do shoot someone, they will instantly assume you have never so much as glanced at it and nail you to the wall. Conversely, you could read it once and then stuff it down the front of your body armour for seven months, which is probably what most of B Squadron will do, and you're golden.

The lawyer then plays us a training video shot from the point of view of a soldier on patrol, and invites us to put up our hands when we think you could legally open fire. It is beyond naff, with the camera panning slowly from three men in balaclavas setting up a mortar to a small child riding their bike unsteadily down the road. Soldiers love it when people try to patronise them, so B Squadron ignore the mortar crew and collectively decide that Tiny Tim is going to fucking get it. Perhaps sensing that she's losing her audience, the lawyer moves us swiftly on to detainee handling.

Given recent events in Basra, I can see why we're doing this. But I have my doubts that a set of PowerPoint slides read out with all the pizzazz of a Belgian's eulogy is going to get to the root of whatever has been going on. The Army plainly disagrees, though. As far as they're concerned, if a soldier in Iraq has been caught tying detainees to a forklift and rallying them around, then it's nothing to do with that soldier's own innate sociopathy, an unhealthy code of *omerta* among small units of fighting men, or any other more deep-seated issues. No, it's because there was no lesson in PDT entitled, 'Forklifts and Iraqis; So What *Are* The Rules Here?'

Eventually the lawyer's slides run out and we emerge blinking into the daylight. I can't help but feel like the whole thing is infinitely better summed up by Sgt Mason's simple advice to the troop before we head off for lunch: 'Don't be a cunt to people who aren't being a cunt to you.'

3

Having a Riot

Wednesday, 8 February 2006 – Tin City

There is an edge to the atmosphere in Tin City today; a crackling tension in the crisp winter air. It is the day of the battlegroup riot.

We've already been through what OPTAG call 'minor aggro' training. Most of the time we should just ignore it, they tell us; no one's ever died from a bit of spittle-flecked chesty-pokey by an angry local. More to the point, if you try to square up to everyone who has a go at you then you'll be there for ever because, cheeringly, 'everyone fucking hates us'. If things ever do get out of hand, though, the recommended drill is to form a 'Ring of Steel'.

It's much more impressive than it sounds; basically the boys form a ragged circle around me and Sgt Mason, and shepherd us solicitously out of trouble like Secret Service agents protecting the President. Except in this case the Secret Service are getting relentlessly battered by deranged Liverpudlians. It's safe to say the boys don't *love* it, particularly after Sgt Mason tells them that if they had wanted to be on the inside of the circle all snug and safe like him and the troop leader, as opposed to on the outside getting filled in by 2 LANCS, then they probably should have tried harder at school.

The battlegroup riot will take minor aggro up a notch. This time it's the 1 PWRR Battlegroup against 120 of Merseyside's finest, quite a few of whom probably aren't total novices when it comes to large-scale collaborative violence. We've got six-foot shields and plastic batons, they've got several hundred chunks of two-by-four, meant to 'represent' bricks; and milk bottles full of petrol, which do a lot more than just 'represent' Molotov cocktails. Jonty pairs up Third Troop with Second Troop and sends us to one of the main roads leading out of Tin City's central square.

The square is already full of a baying mob. Some of the OPTAG staff are visibly nervous. Soldiers love beating the snot out of their colleagues – it's a regular Saturday night event in most garrison towns – and riot training can spin out of control at the best of times. I just hope OPTAG know what they're doing. If the red-faced Scouser I spot wearing a cocktail dress and jumping up and down on top of a phone box shouting something about George Bush is anything to go by, then 2 LANCS are well and truly through the fucking looking glass.

The plan is simple: push the rioters out of the town square and down a pre-designated route to the edge of Tin City. The tactics are pure Roman legion; the boys stand in a baseline and batter the enemy with their batons and shields, while their troop leaders stand ten yards behind them and send positive vibes. I ask Godders, the Second Troop leader, what he reckons about turning our rank slides around so that the 2 LANCS rioters can't see that we're officers.

Godders is dark, tall and has a degree from UCL, which by the Army's standards renders him some kind of lisping, Viennese café-society intellectual fop. I suspect he would sooner come out as a jihadi. He scowls and tells me it would show a disgraceful lack of moral courage. Which he is personally fine with, he explains, but there's no point because they'll be able to tell we're officers anyway since neither of us are carrying shields.

It is a worry though. There are only two occasions on which soldiers can stick one on an officer without any fear of repercussions. One is in the boxing ring, and the other is in training exactly like this. I've heard several stories from the old days about hapless troop leaders being pulled out of the baseline to be stripped, gagged, and Scotch-taped to the front of Land Rovers. Frankly, I can think of better days out.

We listen to the OPTAG staff issue their spectacularly unreassuring final instructions to the rioters through a megaphone. ('No gouging, biting, scratching or using anything you find on the ground as a weapon. If one of the staff tells you he's had enough, he's had enough. Other than that, go for your life, fellas.') Then someone blows a whistle, and it's go time.

The first clue that things aren't going to plan is when Godders takes a piece of two-by-four straight to the dick and folds neatly in half with a sound like a blue whale's grieving call. The second is when the entire mob in the central square immediately rush us like fucking Vikings. Within seconds we've lost three shields and the baseline is a scrum of bodies. The front rank are giving it back to 2 LANCS in spades, but we are definitely starting to go backwards.

I see a couple of the boys dishing out some highly illegal overhead baton strikes and think about saying something. Then I remember that they're about the only thing between me and a ride round Tin City as a bollock-naked hood ornament, and decide that they can use chainsaws if it keeps 2 LANCS off me. To top it all off, Gurung has arrived and is now busy setting absolutely everyone he can see on fire.

I get Jonty on the radio, tell him we're in trouble, and ask what we should do next. He sounds a bit annoyed and tells me to 'stop fucking flapping and push them back'. Presumably it's that kind of tactical gem that they pay him the big bucks for. I may as well have rung the speaking clock, and immediately resolve not to bother asking him next time.

If there is a next time. More shields have gone now; in fact I have to duck as one of them is hurled straight back at us, crashing to the ground a couple of feet behind me. I can also see Trooper Cameron, who must be about nine stone soaking wet, being pulled by the arms into the crowd. His mates have got his legs in a death grip, but they don't have the numbers and he's slowly disappearing. Meanwhile Gurung is having the time of his life and there are burning puddles of petrol everywhere. Godders and I are clucking encouragement, but we are definitely losing this fight. Then, just as I'm starting to wonder whether the Scotch tape will take my pubes off with it, I hear the roar of a Warrior behind me.

The 2 LANCS boys react exactly as you'd expect them to when faced with a 30-ton armoured vehicle driven by someone who can't really see what he's doing, and run for it. We part to let the Warrior through, along with an amped-up platoon from the PWRR, who start chasing the rioters back up the street, screaming like Cockney berserkers. Then the rest of the battlegroup lob themselves bodily into the fray and it's all over in about twenty minutes.

It's then that I realise, quite suddenly, that I have spent the last half an hour being afraid. It wasn't adrenaline; this was the real deal. Genuine, honest-to-goodness, 95 per cent ABV human fear.

Intellectually, of course, I knew it was an exercise, and that at some point someone was going to blow a whistle and we'd all go back to being on the same team. But more viscerally, it's still bodies slamming into a shield wall, a roaring mob who want to hurt you, and soldiers staggering backwards in sheets of flames. I'd been able to pummel the fear down; it's not like I'd been close to turning round and running away or anything. But I could certainly feel the icy fingers of panic plucking at the edges of me.

This is a bit of a concern. Judging by the latest news from theatre, the battlegroup riot is basically tea at the vicarage compared to what's actually happening in Basra. And if 2 LANCS have put the wind up me, then presumably a real encounter with an Iraqi intent on turning my testicles into furry dice is going to see me hyperventilating like a claustrophobic in a broken lift.

Just as I've started to think I might have the right brain to be a troop leader, I'm suddenly a bit worried about whether I've got the backbone.

Saturday, 11 February 2006 – Sennelager

The battlegroup riot marks the end of PDT's urban phase. We're getting a couple of days off, but Jonty makes it clear in his O Group that he'll crucify anyone who takes advantage. Our ORBAT (*Order of Battle*) is settled now, and the last thing he needs is to find another driver because someone's been caught setting a Stella Artois-sponsored land-speed record on the autobahn outside camp.

I already quite like Jonty, and it's clear the squadron do too. Despite the fact that they got rid of all the horses about seventy years ago, there are nonetheless a few officers in the cavalry who still believe they're living in a *Flashman*-esque era of raffish adventurism. Often they do no more harm than looking a bit of a twat wearing a cravat in uniform, or taking a set of clubs on operations so they can bray about playing golf in a minefield.

Just occasionally though, it goes too far, and these characters genuinely start to wing it. Soldiers are understandably not very keen on this kind of thing; no one wants to end up splattered all over the inside of their Land Rover because their squadron leader was dicking about trying to channel some guy who landed on D-Day playing the bagpipes.

Jonty isn't like that. In fact he's the opposite; detail-oriented, careful and methodical. To the point that there's a half-believable rumour that he issues a set of convoy orders when he takes his kids to school. But no one minds. As Sgt Mason reminds me gravely as we leave the O Group, 'Believe you me, sir, you'll be glad the boring old bastard's in charge when we're out there.'[8]

Monday, 13 February 2006 – Tin City

Today we start learning how to operate in rural areas. Sgt Mason, who has been to Iraq before, calls this the 'Gifa'. For a while I assume this is some romantic, pidgin version of the local name that all the old hands use, the way soldiers in India used to say *dhobi* or *baksheesh*. Until he tells me that it actually stands for the 'Great Iraqi Fuck All', and all my Kipling-esque fantasies come crashing down around my ears.

This phase of PDT is also our first proper introduction to the Snatch Land Rover. Now, when it comes to equipment I do understand that – as Mick, Keith and Ronnie would put it – you can't always get what you want. In fact if the Army had a theme tune, that would probably be it. I also understand that the history of British military equipment fuck-ups is a long and storied one; all the way from handing out unopenable ammunition boxes at Isandlwana, to sending aircrew to the Gulf War in green flying suits, because the RAF had sold all the desert ones the year before to (yes, you've guessed it) the Iraqi Air Force. But nonetheless, to all those venerable generals and august civil servants who decided that Snatch Land Rovers were the perfect vehicle for operations in Iraq, I can say only this: 'Lads, were you fucking *high* or something?'

We gather round one in the same car park where Gurung tried to immolate us all, for a briefing by one of the OPTAG instructors. The Snatch looks like what it is: a Land Rover Defender with a box on the back to put soldiers in, and a hole in the roof so they can stick their heads out and see what's going on. The instructor tells us that Snatch was originally introduced in the early nineties for patrolling 'low threat' areas in Northern Ireland. Which is a curious opener for an audience who are about to take it to what is turning into a fairly energetic 'civil war' in southern Iraq.

The armour, which looks a lot like MDF and comes away in flakes if you pick at it, is some kind of composite. According to our instructor, it'll stop a pistol round 'on a good day', but 'won't even slow down' an AK. Marvellous. In the unlikely event that we come up against someone plinking away at us like Doc Holliday, we may be alright. All we really need to worry about is the fact that there is precisely zero protection against the single most ubiquitous assault rifle on the planet.

It gets better. Next, the OPTAG instructor pops the bonnet and shows us the engine. It's a V8, but apparently the vehicle is so heavy that it may as well be out of a Fiat Punto. And while he doesn't want to put us off, he continues, it's also very prone to overheating. He needn't worry; by this point half the squadron are wondering when he'll show us the button that makes all the doors fall off and fills the Snatch with bubbles. He concludes with a few words on the extensive 'desertification' programme that this Snatch has been through – essentially just painting it yellow – then wanders off. Presumably to tell some passing five-year-olds that the tooth fairy doesn't exist and that one day their parents are going to die.

We spend the next couple of hours exploring our new ride, and quickly conclude that the Snatch may actually be even worse than Captain Morale has suggested. For starters it is extraordinarily top heavy; turn the steering wheel at more than fifteen miles an hour and the whole thing feels like it's a single, violent sneeze from toppling over like a pub drunk.

It's also underpowered. Horribly, arthritically, wheezingly underpowered. From a standing start, the acceleration is like one of those World's Strongest Man competitions where huge Scandinavians try to drag an articulated lorry for fifty yards. In short, I'd rather go to war in a Reliant Robin.

Eventually darkness falls and I hitch a lift to the accommodation in the Snatch. It breaks down halfway there, so we walk the rest of the way back.

Sunday, 19 February 2006 – Sennelager training area

Vehicle drills today. There are literally dozens of these, all the way from how to deal with a blown tyre, to how to get someone out of an upside-down Snatch (if it's Sgt Mason, send for a block and tackle and an A-level physics textbook). It's key that we know them all off by heart and follow them to the letter. Firstly, because if anything does happen it'll mean we can react with slick, flowing synchronicity. And secondly, because something about being in Snatches is clearly fucking with our radios, so it looks like the only way we're going to be communicating on the move is by wrapping a written memo round one and lobbing it at the vehicle behind us.

The OPTAG instructors are in the vehicles with us, crouching in the back like malevolent gnomes as we chug across the snowbound training area. Occasionally they tap the commander on the shoulder and say, 'Your vehicle has broken down,' or 'You have spotted a suspicious object by the side of the road.' Or, hearteningly, 'You have been shot in the neck and you're bleeding out.' We then carry out the relevant drill (respectively: 'assume all round defence and wait for recovery', 'stop short and dismount to investigate', 'paint the inside of the windscreen in Dulux Arterial Scarlet, then die'). Then we wait for the OPTAG instructor to drop his face into his hands and make us do the whole thing all over again.

The single most important drill they teach us is Vulnerable Point crossing. A VP is in essence anything that is not the open road; most often a junction, bridge or culvert. They're called VPs because they're all very popular spots for getting blown to smithereens by an IED (*Improvised Explosive Device*). According to OPTAG, IEDs are by now the weapon of choice for the enemy, who didn't take long to work out that it's a lot easier to bury a few artillery shells by the side of the road than it is to mix it up with several million quid's worth of armoured vehicles in a firefight.

I can detect a real tone of resentment from OPTAG when they

tell us this, as if it's somehow all a bit unfair. And the papers are full of it; Our Boys resolutely walking the beat in Basra, while the militias skulk around at night planting bombs and refusing to come out and fight like men. Which is all complete bollocks, of course. Even I know there's no such thing as 'fairness' in war, and you can't get annoyed just because the other side isn't sporting enough to line up in front of your tanks and wait to get mown down. Anyway, if we were in their position we'd be doing exactly the same thing.

The VP drill is simplicity itself. You stop short, dismount, and put two of the boys on either side of the road. Then they walk across the VP while looking at the ground to see if they can spot any enormous bombs. While I wasn't expecting a briefing from Q Branch – if Bond was in the Army he'd be lucky to get a Megabus voucher, let alone a flying Aston Martin – this complete reliance on the Mark 1 Eyeball still comes as a bit of a surprise. There are no metal detectors, divining rods, X-ray glasses or even broom handles to prod the ground with; the game is simply to see the IED before some hidden watcher decides that you'll do, and abruptly sends you to join the fledgling Iraqi space programme. About the best you can say for the drill is that it means fewer people get blown apart than if you had just barrelled gaily through the VP without stopping. But I'd be lying if I said I hadn't rather been hoping for a version where no one got blown apart at all.

By this point, OPTAG tell us, the enemy are getting very inventive in concealing their IEDs. They're wiring them into lampposts at head height, leaving artillery shells in donkey carcasses, and even spraying IEDs with expanding foam and painting them to look like kerbstones. But for all the enemy's fiendish subtlety, it seems the Army has decided that we do need to get some practice at actually 'finding' IEDs. And we haven't got all day. So for these purposes OPTAG are being a bit less fiendish.

By the end of two hours' VP training we have a dozen IED finds under our belt, and should be in excellent shape for the real thing providing the militias have taken to using ACME-style sticks of dynamite, with three feet of bright red wire poking out of the sand.

Wednesday, 22 February 2006 – Tin City

It doesn't look like much, shining dully under the strip lights of the lecture hall. A grey metal tube slightly fatter than a Pringles can, with one flat end and one concave. It is also, says the softly spoken engineer sergeant holding it, about the most dangerous thing in Iraq today. It is called an Explosively Formed Projectile (EFP) and it has killed a dozen British soldiers in six months.

He runs us through the grim mechanics. The tube contains several kilograms of high explosive, which when detonated melts a concave copper disc into the shape of a rod and propels it towards its target at approximately 2,000 metres per second. About Mach 6, give or take. The target is typically the driver's compartment of a Snatch, which the EFP will punch through like it's made out of Andrex. In fact, he tells us, an EFP can take out anything the Army has on the road today. Including – he gives us a meaningful look at this point – Challenger 2.

I glance at our designated Snatch drivers: Schofield, Buxton and Griffiths. If they're worried about the thought of sharing the cab with a molten copper rod going at six times the speed of sound, then they're doing an excellent job of hiding it. All three are wearing the standard glassy-eyed stare that most of B Squadron tend to adopt whenever someone tries to do a lecture at them. I feel oddly proud.

Because they kill you by drilling a hole through your head with 1,200 degree Celsius copper rather than with blast, the EFP has to be aimed a lot more precisely than your common-or-garden IED. According to the engineer sergeant, the most popular method at the moment is to use a Passive Infra-Red (PIR) sensor; basically the same sensor you'd use for a burglar alarm. The PIR sends an invisible beam in a straight line across the road, and the moment that beam is broken by the bonnet of a Snatch, the EFP is activated; offset by exactly the right distance to ensure the copper rod goes straight through the driver's window. Excellent. You can't even catch a break from someone pushing a button half a second too early or too late. In fact, the whole process sounds as baldly functional as a factory assembly line.

The engineer sergeant asks us if there are any questions. There is a long silence. Then someone asks whether it's worth trying to drive faster, so that even if the bonnet breaks the PIR beam, perhaps you'll outrun the EFP itself. Or at least make it miss the driver's compartment and hit something less vital towards the back. The engineer sergeant explains, quite gently, that for this to work your Snatch would itself have to be going several times the speed of sound. Really, he tells us, unless you can somehow spot a small grey plastic sensor about an inch square, buried by the side of the road, there isn't actually a lot you can do.

There are no more questions.

4

Departure

And just like that, training was over. We clambered into some trucks and drove back to camp. Watching the pine trees whip past in metronomic rows, I felt about as content as I'd ever been. Iraq – for now anyway – was in the future, and I hadn't had any more wobbles since the battlegroup riot.

The troop had done well during PDT. More importantly, they looked happy, confident and bonded. You could see it in the cigarettes lit wordlessly for the drivers during endless convoy drills, and the hot brews that appeared as if by magic for the boys on another freezing VCP (*Vehicle Check Point*) in Tin City. And their easy banter in the back of the truck now, as they discussed their plans for the first night back in Sennelager, which was clearly about to have its most traumatic evening since the RAF cleaned out the town centre in 1945.

What's more, they seemed to have accepted me as their troop leader. As far as I could tell, anyway. Say what you like about the Army as an employer, but they know exactly how a 23-year-old feels the first time his soldiers call him 'Boss' rather than 'Sir'. It's probably why they think they can pay you like a *Les Misérables* factory girl.

The squadron was sent on a few weeks' pre-tour leave. I spent the first several days on a Millionaire's Weekend to Copenhagen with Godders and the other troop leaders. When I'd first arrived, they'd been a bit stand-offish, and I could understand why. They'd all been flogged like hoplites through about eighteen months' training before even getting to the regiment, and here I was bowling up with my grand total of four weeks' ambling around Sandhurst to do basically the same job as them.

But PDT had been a great leveller, if only in the sense we'd all got our soldiers massacred at broadly the same rate, and I felt by now that I was in the club. I even had my own nickname, 'STAB'. Which as Godders explained with a broad smile as we drove into Copenhagen, stood for 'Stupid TA Bastard'. Not the 'Ace' I'd been aiming for, but at least it was something.

After a few days of ogling Danish girls, whose lack of interest in the clump of chino-clad subalterns by the side of the dancefloor could only have been clearer if they'd put up a neon sign saying, 'Fuck off, sweaty English perverts', I headed back to the UK to stay with my parents. We all tried to keep it light, but the veneer was millimetres deep. Not least when the news reported yet another Snatch commander killed by an IED the night before I was due to leave. It rattled me – the guy in question had been at Sandhurst with Godders, which felt a bit close to home – but my parents must have been having kittens.

They dropped me off at the airport for the flight back to Germany and we said goodbye at the kerbside. While I wasn't surprised to see Mum in tears, when my dad wished me luck with a catch in his voice, it was all I could do not to fling myself back into their car and beg forgiveness. But it was a bit late for all that. It didn't matter how wretched I felt or how grim the news from Basra; I was committed. Not least because if you didn't turn up now you became an official 'deserter'. Which is probably quite a difficult one to explain on a CV.

I arrived back at camp three days before we were due to leave for Iraq. For an organisation that wanged on endlessly about split-second timing, the Army always seemed to break out in hives at the idea of letting its own workforce put it into practice. It was particularly bad when it came to flights; despite every airline on the planet managing just fine with people turning up two hours before the gate closes, as far as the Army was concerned that was basically the equivalent of sprinting down a retracting airbridge and hurling yourself Indiana Jones-style through the cabin door. So we spent the next three days watching DVDs and popping back and forth to the clerks' office to confirm that yes, we still had our passport, and no, our blood group hadn't changed from whatever it was three weeks ago.

They had already made us pack up our rooms, on the basis that if we were killed it'd be a lot easier to send on our things if they were already in boxes. If I needed any reminder that the Army didn't fuck about when it came to messaging (and by this point, I really didn't), that was probably it. I suppose we should have been grateful they didn't ask us to dig a few deep holes in the rugby pitch while we were at it.

We were also told to choose our 'death shot'. This was the photo which, should you get shot, blown up, or turned into a human polo mint by an EFP, they would show briefly on the News between the *Strictly* results and *Casualty*, accompanied by the words, 'Last night, a British serviceman . . .' You could go a few different ways with it, none perfect. Aim for jut jawed and soldierly, and the world would probably think you were some kind of humourless military automaton. On the other hand, grin too vacuously and it'd give off a slight vibe that you were killed using your penknife to try and find out what they put inside hand grenades. In the end I went for a photo of myself in black tie with what I hoped was a wry, Bond-like half smile playing across my lips. On reflection I looked like a deranged waiter with a gastric issue, so it's just as well they didn't ever have to show it.

Next was the 'death letter'. They weren't obligatory, but were strongly encouraged. After all, some of us might be departing for a new astral plane in the not-too-distant future, and it was felt our loved ones would find the whole thing at least slightly easier if they had a few words on 'why'. It was also made clear that we shouldn't leave them lying around. More than one letter had apparently made its way to someone's next of kin prematurely, leaving them quite confused that their son had apparently 'died doing something I was born to do', when as far as they were aware he was still in Thailand doing tequila slammers and enthusiastically banging backpackers on a pre-tour holiday.

I don't have mine anymore – I burned it quietly in the sink in my room after we got back – but as I wrote it I remember thinking that it was quite strange to be thanking someone for a lifetime of love, in a letter you're having to write precisely because you might be about to throw that same lifetime away. And for reasons that you don't seem particularly able to articulate, as your repeated crossings-out make clear.

The final bit of morbid admin was my Last Will and Testament. Or as the Army would have it, with its usual talent for squeezing even the tiniest morsel of romance out of everything: MOD Form 106. As a final bleak 'fuck you' before you crossed to the other side, the form grudgingly conceded that they'd shout you the funeral, but '*would not* meet any requests that fall outside service entitlements at the time of your death'. And if that isn't enough to make you march off towards your destiny humming 'Rule Britannia', I don't know what is.

In the end I left all my worldly possessions to my mother. Were the worst to happen, she would hopefully find at least some small comfort in £800, a Nissan Almeira without a second gear, and a laptop full of videos that Third Troop had given me on a USB. I put the will in the same envelope as my death letter and marked it, 'To be opened only in the event of my death'. Then I thought for a bit, pulled the will out of the envelope, and scribbled a note saying that on no account should the laptop or USB be allowed to leave Iraq. You really can't be too careful.

The next day was departure day, and after breakfast we all convened in the Mess to watch *Die Hard* and wait for the buses to the airport. After a couple of hours Jonty checked his watch, said, 'Right, then' to no one in particular, and turned off the TV.

We were off to Iraq.

Saturday, 15 April 2006 – Al Udeid, Qatar / Basra, Iraq

The first surprise is the aircraft. I'd always assumed they'd send us to Iraq with the RAF, on something with a red, white and blue roundel. After all, half the battle when you're off to war is looking the part. B Squadron, however, will be starting their journey on a cherry-red chartered 737. It has been rented by the MoD from some outfit called Omni Airways, and is staffed by cabin crew who look as if they began their careers shortly after news of the Wright Brothers broke over the wireless.

They will take us to Qatar, which is as far as civilian charters are able to go (though I wouldn't have bet against Michael O'Leary having a crack at Basra). It seems the same overstretch that has landed me in a troop leader's job extends to the air bridge. The RAF had just about been able to cope when they only had to fly to Iraq, but the whole thing has snapped like a damp Kit Kat now that Afghanistan has kicked off in earnest.

Omni Airways are American, and very much of the good ol' boy variety, so they cannot do enough for us. Trooper Cameron, who turned nineteen three days ago but looks about twelve, appears to have single-handedly fired up a dozen long-dormant ovaries, and is clucked over relentlessly for the entire flight. And when we land in Qatar, the captain appears so overcome by emotion that he can barely get his words out.

We leave the aircraft with his choked-up wishes for our safe return and future happiness ringing in our ears, straight back into the hands of the RAF, who rapidly make it clear they couldn't give the tiniest shit about any of that. They bundle us onto a bus with drawn curtains, then drive us around the airfield like kidnap victims before depositing us in a cheerless, strip-lit tent marked 'Transit Area'.

As is traditional, the RAF have stocked the tent with exactly one-third the number of chairs as there are soldiers. There is a single, dusty PlayStation, which would be quite cool if (a) it had 250 controllers and (b) was not irreparably fucked. A small IKEA bookcase offers a broad selection of three titles; a guide to making furniture for dolls houses, a Haynes Manual for the BMW 3 Series, and a Mills & Boon novel called *Jungle Love: A Tropical Tangle*, which features a black man in a loincloth standing over the inert body of a blonde in a bodice, and which presumably won't be troubling the Booker Prize panel any time soon. The drinking water is bath temperature.

We sit on the floor of the tent along with a mixed bag of other units either on their way to, or coming back from, Iraq. You can fairly easily tell which is which. Some RAF Movements staff sit behind desks at the front, occasionally stirring themselves enough to declare that yet another flight has been delayed by three Venusian months. If anyone asks why, they either vanish immediately like wraiths, or mutter something about 'technical issues' and then vanish. Once in a while someone will approach their desk clutching a little laminated itinerary they were given a thousand lifetimes ago in Germany. The Movements staff just smile pityingly; it ends when they decide.

On this occasion it ends about six hours later; Movements tend to save all their best delays for when you're going home. Shrugging on our body armour, we are bussed out to the airfield where a Hercules[9] awaits. This is more like it. The Hercules' four-propeller engines are already roaring like the Merlins on a 1942 Lancaster about to head sausage-side, and as we stand waiting to climb inside the dim, red-lit interior, we are buffeted with a hot wind that smells like kerosene and adventure. I feel a cold thrill smack me between my shoulder blades.

The loadmaster motions us on board and invites us to 'sit down and don't fucking touch anything'. I'm on a bench-seat opposite

Cameron and Sgt Mason. They are a study in contrasts. Wee Cam is doing his best to look calm and collected, but his head is on a swivel and he's tapping his feet at 180bpm. Sgt Mason, on the other hand, appears to be asleep. His head is tipped back, hands loose in his lap; *sang* so *froid* you could have made ice cubes with it.

We take off and the Herc starts to clamber through the chilly night sky. I am suddenly struck by the thought that this is really it. Alright, we've trained for what feels like a lifetime, and we're about as ready to go as we'll ever be. But for these past few months our days have been so minutely structured, and organised, and timetabled, that it's proving hard to comprehend that life is suddenly all free play again. From here on in there are no more scenarios, or scripts, or OPTAG training programmes.

The next time I take the troop out of the front gate it will be in Iraq, with a living, breathing enemy who haven't read the training programme. And they'll be the ones deciding what does or doesn't happen. There will be no one in a hi-vis vest to blow a whistle and come and reset it all. Or let me regenerate my dead soldiers if everything goes wrong. As realisations go, it is a belter.

Still chewing on the sudden gravity of life, I pop in my iPod headphones. Unfortunately it must have taken a knock somewhere because it won't play anything apart from *Les Misérables*. I had hoped to start my first operational tour with a classic warzone backing track; 'Fortunate Son' or 'Gimme Shelter', or something. Instead it looks like I will probably arrive in Basra to the anguished strains of 'I Dreamed a Dream'. I pray that the engines are loud enough to cover the noise; if anyone in the squadron overhears me listening to showtunes on D-Day then I will have no realistic option except to immediately hurl myself out of the back of the Herc.

We drone on for forty-five minutes. Then without any warning the Herc gives a violent lurch and starts falling like a cartoon anvil. As they should probably have bloody well told us earlier, the RAF don't approach Basra the same way you'd approach Heathrow. Heathrow isn't surrounded by potentially thousands of tooled-up hostile locals (that's Luton). And if there is one thing which keeps the generals up at night, it's the thought of a Hercules with a full manifest of British soldiers on it being blown out of the sky. So instead, the pilot waits until he is more or less directly overhead Arrivals, then shoves everything into a corner.

This produces a series of plummeting corkscrew turns, a bit like the coils on a stretched-out Slinky, which the RAF euphemistically dub a 'tactical landing', but which to the passengers feels a lot like a 'fucking death spiral'. It has two effects; firstly it ensures the aircraft spends as little time as possible exposed to any potential ground fire. And secondly it induces sustained mortal terror in about a hundred squaddies, who all assume that both the wings on their Hercules have just snapped like Ryvita Thins.

By the time I've regained my shattered composure there are runway lights flashing past the windows. A moment later I hear the squeal and feel the *thump* as the Herc's fat tyres smack into the tarmac. 'And I still dream he'll come to me, that we will live the years togethe-e-e-er . . .'

We've arrived in Basra.

Sunday, 16 April 2006 – Basra Air Station / Shaibah Logistics Base

Even though it's after midnight it's still T-shirt weather, and a warm breeze scuds across the tarmac. The terminal building is two storeys of intricate marblework; apparently it was built by some German engineers in the 1980s but was only ever really used by VIPs. In the same spirit, we are marched straight past it and put in a dimly lit shed. The RAF have laid out the hold baggage with all the care that the Libyans laid it out at the Lockerbie crash site, so everyone spends a diverting half an hour trying to pick their Bergen out from ninety-nine other identical candidates, in the dark.

A hugely fat RAF corporal clambers onto a box for our arrival brief. He cracks the usual tired gag about the local time being 0030, 'but-you-will-probably-want-to-set-your-watches-back-three-hundred-years'. Which might get a laugh out of the Foreign Office girls, but earns him nothing but bored stares from B Squadron. He then reminds us that the airfield is being mortared regularly and that if we hear a siren, we are to put on our helmets and take cover. 'Aye, behind *you*,' someone mutters in the gloom, which *does* get a laugh. The corporal briefly machine-guns us with his eyes, then gets off his box and waddles into the night muttering about 'fucking Pongos'.[10]

Then we're shepherded out to the flight line, and after about twenty minutes the *thwack* of rotor blades announces that our ride has arrived. It's an RAF Merlin,[11] and as Buxton puts it breathlessly, it's 'fucking mega'. We clamber aboard, bent double under our kit, then it lifts off and we start thudding low across the moonlit desert. Everything about it feels like being at the tip of the spear, from the loadmaster hunched watchfully over his machine gun, to the circles of night-vision green phosphorescence I can see over the pilots' eyes.

I look around the cabin and see the boys grinning; they feel it too. Leaning back in my seat, I try to imprint it all on my memory; I'll need this when I'm sitting on the Northern Line on a dank Tuesday morning, or walking through B&Q looking for where they keep the topsoil. I could have sat there for hours. But we have only a short hop to do, and before long I feel the Merlin pitch up and prepare to land. Shaibah.

Wednesday, 19 April 2006 – Shaibah

Shaibah Logistics Base is a few miles out in the dirty, greyish desert to the south-west of Basra. It started life in 1920 as RAF Shaibah, home to rickety biplanes mainly used for bombing the locals whenever they did something really beyond the pale, like asking if they might possibly be allowed to run the place themselves.

We had handed it over to the Iraqis in the 1950s, who had replaced the biplanes with Soviet MiGs. These in turn were replaced by smoking holes in the ground during the first Gulf

War. After which Shaibah had been unceremoniously abandoned. It stayed that way until the invasion in 2003, when we had come full circle and hung our names above the door again. It isn't in use as an airfield anymore, but the runway and great oval-shaped taxiway are still there. To the chagrin of most of B Squadron, who know a ready-made running track when they see one.

We are halfway through a week of Reception, Staging and Onward Integration, or RSOI. It sounds fancy, but really it's just the Army's elaborate way of saying 'more lectures'. On arrival we were shown to our accommodation in an enormous tent that the RSOI staff referred to as the 'BFOT', which it has taken me three days to work out stands simply for 'Big Fuck Off Tent'. It contains more or less the entire battlegroup, and judging by the furtive rustling after lights out, is also the venue for a serious bid by the PWRR to create a new Guinness World Record category for Highest Number of Simultaneous Autoerotic Episodes inside a Single Canvas Structure.

The lectures are basically the same ones we had in Tin City, except a bit more up close and personal. So instead of a boxy PowerPoint graphic of where an EFP is aimed at a Snatch, they show us a photo of the real thing – from last week, about three miles from where we're sitting now – a charnel house of shattered windows and blood-soaked seats. One particularly comforting bit of news is that the militia in Basra are actively trying to kidnap a British soldier. Apparently the plan will be to provoke a bit of minor aggro near a patrol, then bundle whoever they can grab into a waiting taxi during the commotion.

We are shown a slide emphasising that we are to take 'all necessary action' to stop this happening. And in case that wasn't clear enough, when the lesson has finished a small, gimlet-eyed Para clicks off the PowerPoint, looks very hard at us, and mutters, 'If youse see your oppo being pulled into the crowd, then youse will take your weapon system, and youse will shoot the men holding him in their fockin' heids. We are no' losing a sodjer to these cunts.'

Roger that.

Saturday, 22 April 2006 – Shaibah

RSOI finishes with ranges. We zeroed our rifles in Sennelager, but since then the RAF will have been lobbing them around like Milanese baggage handlers, so the sights are bound to be off by a mile. It won't make a blind bit of difference for me; I started my sharpshooting career by blowing a range marker to pieces at Sandhurst with the first round I ever fired, and haven't improved since. But it's worth it for the boys. Most of them carry SA80 assault rifles. Luckily these ones have been upgraded since the ones that gave several thousand British soldiers a heart attack during the Gulf War, to a much improved version that doesn't immediately stop working if a solitary grain of sand gets inside it.

We also have three Minimis, fearsome little belt-fed machine guns, which we have entrusted to Greene, Cameron and Womack. I watch them going at it on Shaibah's twenty-five-metre range, and decide to have a quiet word about what to do if they happen to see someone being pulled into the crowd. The way they're shooting they'd slaughter any would-be kidnappers, no doubt about it, but on the other hand I'd also be going down in the history books as the instigator of the Great Minor Aggro Massacre of Op TELIC 8.

With RSOI over, we're moved out of the PWRR's Grand High Masturbatorium and into our permanent accommodation. We will be based in Shaibah for the whole tour; our battlegroup doesn't have a 'patch' in Basra itself, but instead forms something called the Force Reserve. According to our orders, this means being ready to launch at a moment's notice anywhere across southern Iraq to either 'reinforce other units, and/or exploit unexpected success'. And from what we're hearing, by this point in the campaign 'unexpected' would probably be the right word for it.

Our new home is called Tiger Lines, in honour of the PWRR's regimental nickname. It's a small, *M*A*S*H*-style tent village surrounded by high walls of double-stacked Hesco.[12] The tents have seen better days; apparently they only have a notional service life of nine months, which probably tells you all you need to know about the spirit of British Army planning for post-invasion Iraq.

I'm sharing a tent with the other troop leaders; Godders, Brooksie – who is very nice but also the kind of enormous chin whose family has served since Cromwell and stamps 'Army' on the bum of every male child at birth – and Mike, who is very serious and doesn't have a nickname. As well as the accommodation, there is a small gym, a cookhouse, and a tent with a TV and a game of *Risk* with half the pieces missing. This has been optimistically dubbed the 'Recreation Area'.

There is also a small Portakabin with a row of dusty PCs and about half a dozen telephones. Our phone allowance is a lavish twenty minutes per week, which is apparently ten minutes less than we'd get if we were in prison. It's not much for the men with families. But probably about right for me; if my first phone call home is any guide then all I'll be using my minutes for is to prattle on about the weather, while my mother asks whether the other boys are being nice to me, and tries to work out why her idiot child is so determined to end his short life in a warzone.

Finally there is 'ALI SHOP'; a small Portakabin run by the eponymous Ali, who is beaming, squat and would make Del Boy look like Jude the Apostle. It's stocked to the ceiling with soft drinks, DVDs, plastic keyrings with dead scorpions inside them, and presumably an RPG-29 with rockets if you give him twenty-four hours' notice. What Ali lacks in possessive apostrophes he makes up for in an absolute disregard for copyright law; the covers of all of this year's major releases are already lining his shelves (although I'm not totally sure I remember the bit in *Pirates of the Caribbean* where a shirtless Indian Jack Sparrow fires an Uzi into the air).

He is all over us as soon as we arrive; we haven't been there five minutes before he has somehow sold us a TV, a box set of *Glee*, and a lava lamp. I like him a lot. And if half his countrymen showed the same drive, we'd probably be talking about the New Iraqi Century and they'd have headquartered the World Bank in Baghdad.

Just across the taxiway from Tiger Lines sits Shaibah's Welfare Village. The centrepiece is a large café that does hot drinks, snacks, and allegedly, if you quietly ask a particular barista for her 'fifty dollar milkshake', discreet sexual favours as well. This causes great excitement among the boys at first, until it transpires that the barista in question resembles a moody Sir Ian McKellen. The café is flanked by a Pizza Hut and a Subway, the franchisees of which could have taught the US Marine Corps a thing or two about expeditionary warfare. It's starting to become clear why troops in more austere locations call this place Shaibiza.

Indeed, facilities like the Welfare Village cause great tensions deep within the Army's soul. On one hand they offer front-line troops a much-needed slice of normality (if you can call ordering an American Hot from a pair of amped-up Bangladeshi dudes in body armour normal). On the other, you could argue that what we really need out here are austere warrior monks, too focused on the mission to care about trivialities like whether their oat milk's hot or cold. And also that the Welfare Village is mainly used by REMFs[13] anyway.

Watching various clerks and medics with area code BMIs strolling around, shedding Subway meatballs like Zeppelins unloading over Great Yarmouth, I sense I'm in the latter camp. But it's not up to me. The Army has clearly decided that the Welfare Village is a vital prop to morale. And presumably, therefore, that it should be perfectly possible for someone to be sipping a skinny vanilla *macchiato* less than an hour after putting a bullet in another man's head.

5

Reality

Wednesday, 26 April 2006 – Shaibah

We are in the troop leaders' tent, slowly working out that the TV which Ali has sold us (at a price that was at once eyewatering, but somehow also one that he was adamant would leave his wife and infant children literally homeless and begging in the streets), does not, in fact, actually work, when there is a distant *thump*.

'What the fuck was that?' I ask decisively.

'Door,' says Godders.

'Mortar,' says Brooksie, at the same time.

Mike says nothing and frowns. Then comes another bass *thump*.

'Mortar,' all four of us say, simultaneously.

We know the drill, of course; body armour, helmet, take cover on the floor. But that sounded like it was a fairly long way away, and no one wants to look like a massive jessie. Particularly not when it's their first time. So everyone is very careful not to fasten up their body armour any quicker than anyone else, and we hit the deck with all the urgency of guests on a Saga cruise doing a spot of Bikram before sundowners. Then we lie on the floor and giggle a bit.

There are four more *thumps*, none of which seem like they're particularly close. After a couple of minutes someone in Tiger Lines remembers we've got a mortar alarm. It starts to wail, presumably for the benefit of anyone else who thought someone was slamming a lot of doors today.

Five minutes pass. There are no more *thumps* and the mortar alarm stops. We sit up against the sides of the tent, unsure what to do next. Then there is the sound of running feet and the tent zip is peeled upwards. Mr Kite pokes his head inside. Mr Kite is the Squadron Sergeant Major, the most senior soldier in B Squadron, and is responsible to Jonty for the same kind of stuff that Sgt Mason does for Third Troop: discipline, administration and equipment. And now also, it seems, pelting around the place during mortar attacks. He's a big man and is sweating freely.

'Sirs – doing a headcount. Any casualties?'

This is an odd one. Mr Kite lives with the other senior NCOs in the tent next door to ours. You'd have thought that if there were indeed casualties in our tent, his first clue might have been an earth-shattering explosion about fifteen yards away. Perhaps our ruined limbs raining down onto his roof. Or one of our severed heads rolling neatly through his door (the senior NCOs would have liked that; they could have told it to 'get a fucking haircut, sir, you look like a fucking Beatle, har har har.'). Still, the man has a job to do.

'Erm, no, sarn't major, we're all fine, thank you,' says Godders after a brief pause.

He looks at us reproachfully. 'You should be lying down, sirs – set an example to the boys, like.'

Obligingly we all slide as one down the side of the tent until we are prone again, like puppets whose strings have suddenly been cut. Then we look at him, standing fully upright in the doorway.

'I'm doing the headcount, sirs,' he says aggrievedly, by way of explanation. Then disappears. Presumably to check the rest of B Squadron and ensure no one else has been blown apart by a completely silent mortar landing on their tent.

And that's that. Technically we have now been under contact. But as first bloodings go, it's a pretty benign one. Someone has just gone to a lot of effort to blow up half a dozen patches of infidel sand; not one of the rounds ended up within a quarter mile of Tiger Lines, and all but one of them missed Shaibah altogether. Americans often talk about 'seeing the elephant' to describe their first experience of combat; in our case I think we may have caught a fleeting glimpse of a leathery grey arse disappearing into the *veldt*, but nothing more than that.

It is, however, a reminder. That somewhere out there, past ALI SHOP and Pizza Hut, in the orange glow of the city that you can just about see if you clamber on top of the Hesco at night, there are people who want us out of here. Very badly indeed.

Saturday, 29 April 2006 – Shaibah

Today is the day of our first patrol. It's what the Army calls a 'familiarisation patrol'; the experienced outgoing unit takes the brand-new, box-fresh incoming unit out on the ground, to show them the local landmarks and teach them the important dos and don'ts. Their job is to swan around insouciantly looking like hoary old veterans; yours is to write down absolutely everything they tell you in your notebook in case it's important, and try not to throw up all over yourself.

I head down to the operations room with the other troop leaders to get a briefing. We are taking over from the Fusiliers, and they have sent over their intelligence officer, a languid captain called Jeremy. We sit at a map table, which Jeremy tells us he has marked up with different coloured stickers for every incident that has happened to them over the last six months. My immediate takeaway is there are a lot of bloody stickers. In fact, the map wouldn't look out of place on the wall of a specialised crèche for small children who are just completely mad for sticking brightly coloured stickers on maps. Reds are IEDs, Jeremy says, blue is for small arms, purple is IDF (*Indirect Fire*),[14] and green is public order.

'What about yellow?' asks Mike abruptly.

'Yellow?'

'Yes, yellow. Down there, by Shaibah. You've just rubbed it off with your elbow.'

'Oh yes, that,' Jeremy says, picking up the sticker and examining it briefly on his finger, like some tiny exotic insect. He sticks it firmly back on the map, next to Shaibah's front gate. 'Suicide bombings.'

'*Suicide bombings?*' repeat at least 75 per cent of Jeremy's audience incredulously.

Yes, confirms Jeremy. Suicide bombings. Two weeks ago a patrol were leaving Shaibah and had just turned onto the main road when a Toyota Corolla drew up next to them and promptly exploded. No one had been killed, but it had made a mess of a Snatch and four soldiers had been badly hurt.

According to intelligence, who are always full of useful information ten minutes after the car bomb's gone off, the patrol wasn't even the real target. In fact the bomber had been headed north to blow himself up in Baghdad. He'd been detonated via remote control, by his 'second', who was travelling in a chase car behind him.

A back-up triggerman isn't uncommon; according to Jeremy, more people than you'd think start having second thoughts about whether all that stuff about the seventy-two virgins is really true when they're sitting in the car and trying to find a Humvee to blow themselves up next to. But the fact that this was really a martyrdom-by-proxy – and a coincidental one at that – is pretty small comfort. They didn't teach us a drill for suicide bombers in PDT. Basra is Shia, and we'd been confidently assured that Shias don't go in for that kind of thing. Unlike their Sunni cousins further north, who by this point are dishing out noisy hugs to passing Americans on a regular basis.

Feeling a bit suicidal ourselves, we walk over to the tank park and a pair of waiting Warriors. Godders and I get in the nearest one. A couple of Fusilier privates are sitting in the back finishing their fags. They have nut-brown tans, and their combats are bleached nearly white by the sun. Their helmet covers, the true mark of someone who's been around a bit, are in absolute tatters. In short, they look 'ally'.

Looking ally is the lodestar of every soldier who has ever lived. Like any truly defining look, it is a concept rather than a set of rules; an ephemeral, twisting, subtle blend. But you will know it when you see it, because every battered, subtly modified bit of kit will declare, 'This man has *been* places.'

The paras at Arnhem were ally. The marines with drooping Mexican moustaches who yomped from San Carlos Bay to Port Stanley were ally. Even the Wehrmacht lads fighting their way through Stalingrad with MG 42s and stick grenades were ally; providing you look past all the unpleasantness with prisoners and partisans, and just focus on the pure fashion aspect of the whole thing.

Godders and I are not ally. With our immaculate helmet covers and pristine body armour covered in things we thought might come in useful – cyalumes,[15] penknives, lumicolours, and so on – we look like we've been doused in glue and chased through a Mountain Warehouse. We immediately resolve to do something about this when we get back.

The Warrior lurches off and the patrol commander briefs us in Geordie over our PRRs (*Personal Role Radios*). We are going to skirt the edges of Basra but stay clear of the city itself. There is intelligence about a potential ambush and he is understandably not excited about 'getting fookin' whacked wi' two deeys left on the tour showing fookin' Ruperts[16] the area.'

And then, before I've even really processed it all, we are outside the wire.

Psychologists call it 'hypervigilance'; an elevated state in which all your senses are on a constant nerve-jangling 360-degree scan for threats. And if a passing psychologist could have seen Godders and me as our Warrior rolled out of Shaibah's front gate, we wouldn't just have been a case study; you could have put our picture on the front of the textbook. I am scared rigid. After three months of endless, cataclysmic PDT scenarios, it just doesn't seem possible that I won't shortly be wiping Godders' brains off my upper lip while the Warrior goes up in flames around me.

To my Commemorative Royal Wedding Dinner Plate-sized eyes, every pile of sand conceals a daisy-chained[17] EFP array; every roadside shack a snarling RPG gunner. From the way Godders is gesticulating madly at a small boy on a bicycle, whom he clearly believes is mere seconds away from exploding, I sense that he's going through something similar.

It takes a good ten minutes before my pulse drops below the kind of bpm you'd normally associate with a mid-nineties underground speedcore festival. I look at the commander and gunner in the turret above me. They are resting comfortably on their elbows, helmets moving slowly left and right as we trundle down the road. The lads in the back appear to have taken their already considerable allyness up a notch and fallen asleep. It begins to occur to me that I might not die after all.

By this time we've reached the edge of the city. Basra is roughly diamond-shaped; the top right-hand face hugs the slow-flowing, silty Shatt al-Arab river, while the bottom right peters out gently into fields and date plantations. The whole left side is bordered by desert. We are driving along the bottom left aspect. On the other side of a huge and rubbish-strewn wasteland, dotted with stagnant pools of water, I can see the squat, flat-roofed buildings of Al Hayyaniyah.

We've been told about Al Hayyaniyah. It's also known as the Shia Flats and is the poorest – and diciest – part of the whole city. It's a rabbit warren of breeze blocks and corrugated iron, and riddled with militia. Taking potshots at the Brits is one of the few guarantees of a decent payday, the patrol commander tells us, and so any patrol that does go in there is more or less guaranteed to get 'fookin' smashed to fook'.

Grinning, he shows us his map. He'd been stopped round here about a month ago checking his position, he says, when some unseen marksman in the Shia Flats had shot it clean out of his hands. I am fairly sure that if someone had put a 7.62mm hole in a piece of paper that I was holding nine inches away from my face, they'd still be waving the smelling salts under my nose and trying to coax me out of my helmet. But he seems to find the whole thing hilarious.

We head north-east, crossing one of the main highways heading into Basra. Then we park on a bridge overlooking the city and the commander points out some of the salient features; Basra Air Station, where we flew in, and the Technical College ('. . . fook knows what they're teaching, like, but it's got summat to do with fookin' snipers . . .'). In the distance, Basra Palace and the Shatt al-Arab hotel, where the resident battlegroups are currently staging a lengthy, live-action role play of the siege of Lucknow, and getting pasted with mortars three times a day.

Then it's advice time. Don't bother with VP checks within two kilometres of camp; for some reason the militia are convinced we've got optics like the Hubble Space Telescope, so won't try to bury anything that close. It takes them fifteen minutes to set up a small-arms shoot, so make sure you don't stay in the same place more than ten. If you're coming up to anything that looks sketchy, wait for a car to go past it first, then follow him like he owes you money; the militias accidentally atomised some minor tribal celebrity a couple of weeks ago while trying to bag a Warrior, and they're very wary of it happening again.

It goes on and on and Godders and I nod along like novelty dashboard bobbleheads. PDT is all very well, but these guys are living, breathing proof that whatever drills they've been using actually work.

We head back towards Shaibah, and before long we're rattling past the Welfare Village, suddenly disdainful of the RAF Regiment sitting at the picnic tables and drinking the same elaborate coffees we'd been quaffing like Regency aristocrats only a couple of hours ago. The patrol commander drops us off at Tiger Lines, and tells us not to worry, sirs; Basra's a walk in the park, really. Aye, fookin' *Jurassic Park*. Classic.

Still laughing, he drives off and we walk, a very slight strut in our stride now, back to our tent. Peeling off our sweat-soaked body armour, we grin shyly at one another. Our first patrol is in the bag. What's more, the world outside the wire doesn't appear to be the unremitting bloodbath they'd depicted on PDT. Even better, the TV from ALI SHOP has started working, and Brooksie's got the next series of *Glee*. It has been, we agree, a very good day. Then we all go outside to rub our helmet covers in the sand for an hour.

Saturday, 6 May 2006 – Shaibah

The first sign that something has gone wrong is when we see Jonty running past our tent just after lunch. Jonty doesn't run – not unless he's thrashing us up and down the Shaibah runway like Roman auxiliaries anyway – so something is clearly up. Five minutes later he sticks his head through the tent flap and says, 'They've shot down a Lynx[18] in the city. Get your boys ready. Then meet me in the cookhouse. We're on thirty minutes' notice to move.'

For perhaps half a beat we gape at one another. Then there's an explosion of swearing and feet being forced into boots and magazines being stuffed into pouches. I can hear Godders muttering, 'What the fuck?' under his breath as he struggles into his body armour. What the fuck is right; it doesn't make any sense. No one has ever shot down a helicopter in Basra.

Movement by air is supposed to be the safe option; it's how they get the diplomats and police advisors around the city after they started refusing to travel by road. A way of travelling in a few breezy minutes the kind of distances that would take you sweat-soaked hours in a Snatch or Warrior. As far as we know, the other side don't even have anything that could reliably take down a helicopter. And it would have to be a spectacularly fluky shot with an RPG.

Three minutes later, I clatter into Third Troop's tent and give them the news with all the measured gravitas of a Year 9 telling everyone there's a massive fight in the corridor. Within seconds their tent is a whirlwind; Griffiths, Buxton and Schofield sprinting off to start the Snatches, everyone else chucking spare ammunition into daysacks and fixing slings to rifles. Sgt Mason, who of course is already packed, is doing probably the most important job of all – standing quietly by the tent flap, sixteen stone of pure Zen, looking like this kind of thing happens every day.

Except it doesn't. You can tell by the set, grim look on the PWRR CO's face as he stalks past, and by the sound of thirty-five Warriors roaring into life on the tank park. This is as bad as it gets. I find Jonty in the cookhouse, map spread over one of the tables, surrounded by the other troop leaders.

'Guys, I'll tell you what I know, but it's a developing situation. About half an hour ago, a Lynx out of the Air Station crashed smack in the middle of the city. It's about 500 metres from the OSB (*Old State Buildings*).[19] Based on what the guys on guard there are saying, it was shot down, likely by a MANPAD.'

He pauses. MANPADs – man portable surface-to-air missiles – are probably a new one on him as well. The militia aren't supposed to have MANPADs.

'Apparently it's come down partly on a roof, partly in an alleyway, and it's still on fire. No confirmation on casualties yet, but there were five on board. There's already a multiple[20] from OSB at the crash site – they reckon there's zero chance anyone's alive. They're trying to get a cordon in place, but half the city has turned up, so it can't be long before it all goes *Black Hawk Down*.'

I swallow, and look around at the other troop leaders. We've all seen the film, of course; they'd even used clips of it at Sandhurst when it was easier to let Josh Hartnett illustrate some point about small unit tactics than to try to draw it on a whiteboard. But I doubt it's ever occurred to anyone that they might end up in the sequel.

'Guys, everything else in the city has stopped. This is now the Divisional Main Effort – in fact it's the only effort. Even if they are all dead, the General is very clear; we are not leaving without the bodies. Both the battlegroups in the city are inbound to the crash site now, and there is a high chance we'll be going too. Even if the cordon doesn't get breached it's going to take them hours to extract everyone from the wreckage. Any questions?'

There are none – in fact, there's just a stunned silence – so clutching a map marked with the crash site, I run over to the tank park to find the troop. As I arrive, the first company of PWRR Warriors roar past me, heading for the front gate. It has clearly started going techno in Basra.

The boys are standing by our Snatches fitting visors to their helmets. I'm worried about the vehicles; the Fusiliers handed them over a couple of days ago and they look like they've just been dug out of a Norse grave. Then again, maybe they'll all break down before we've even got as far as the Welfare Village and we won't have to go into the city after all. The boys listen quietly as I give them the latest. They don't have any questions either; once I'm finished they simply go back to prepping their kit.

I feel a sudden burst of violent affection. They know as well as I do that the helicopter crew are probably all dead and there will be a crowd of thousands gathering at the crash site, while the militia gunmen slip quietly into position around the cordon. And yet if we were told to go, they'd climb into their battered Snatches without a word and drive straight there without stopping. Not bad for sixteen grand a year.

Back in the cookhouse, Jonty now has a handset tuned into the battlegroup radio net. On the wall-mounted TV above him, Sky's breaking-news ticker is already scrolling across the screen. How they've got the story before the fire's even out is anybody's guess, but there goes any hope of letting the families know before they see pictures of the crash on the lunchtime news. We listen in silence as it all begins to unravel.

The crowd start throwing rocks at the cordon more or less from the start. The first mortars start landing about an hour later. Half an hour after that, the gunmen arrive. What remains of the Lynx is a twisted mess, jammed into a tight alleyway like it's been shoved in there by some giant hand. You can tell from the resigned voices on the net that the boys on the cordon know this won't be quick. They report that they can only see four of the bodies, and there's a horrible, sick-to-the-stomach twenty minutes. Then they put the fire out, and the nightmare everyone has been privately dreading about a British airman strung up on a lamppost is averted when a sharp-eyed infantryman spots the fifth.

By now Sky have got a camera on scene; it must be a local stringer, because I wouldn't give a Westerner five minutes outside that cordon. We watch as the Warriors jockey back and forth to stop the gunmen getting a clear shot, turrets battened down under a hail of paving slabs. Next to them are the boys on foot; trying to strike the delicate balance between fending off the locals – who all seem determined to use the smouldering wreckage as a climbing frame – and making sure they don't get their fucking heads blown off by snipers every time they step out of cover.

Then the casualties start to trickle in. First they're from the mortars, then more and more from the heat. They're mostly T3s (*walking wounded*),[21] but T3s can become T2s in no time when it's 40° in the shade and you're down to half a litre of water per man. The voices on the radio are starting to crack with the strain of it all. Callsign after callsign is getting crashed out to reinforce the cordon; there must be 1,500 troops on the ground by now. The engineers are talking about needing cutting equipment and cranes.

It's an unholy fucking mess, but at the same time, listening to it all in that cookhouse with Jonty and the other troop leaders, I feel a quiet swell of pride. There is never even a hint that maybe we should just cut our losses. Those boys out there are not leaving without the bodies.

By now even the General is on the net. It's not his fault, of course; he'll be feeling as broken by this as anyone else. But I expect it's hard to be balanced when the AK rounds are snapping past your helmet and your soldiers are collapsing all around you with the heat. So when the General starts talking soothingly about the other agencies he needs to co-ordinate, the heavy equipment that needs to be prepped, and how it all needs to be factored carefully into his overall extraction plan, it's no wonder that some anonymous platoon commander finally snaps.

'Mate, I've got four T3s and a T2 who's going to be a T1 before long. I've been getting blast-bombed all afternoon and I ran out of water two hours ago. Factor *that* into your fucking extraction plan.'

Eventually we are stood down, not least because it gets dark and most of the locals pack it in. Getting the bodies out ends up taking all night, but they will all be going home. The next morning the Iraqi Army turn up. Sky News or no Sky News, they take the view that if you throw a rock at them it's the last one you'll ever throw, with that hand at least, meaning our remaining troops can extract in good order. By some minor miracle no one on the cordon has been killed, but there are dozens of heat casualties and six seriously wounded who won't be back this tour.

There are also ten or so from the crowd who have caught something second-hand; stray mortar rounds or ricochets. I'm surprised at my brief, savage happiness when I find out. The militia is one thing, but there is something about the sheer ugliness of that baying crowd, trying to get at aircrew who are already dead, which has stuck in my throat. I think the boys are feeling it too. Between muttered references to fucking *chogis*,[22] and the way Griffiths slams the back doors shut as we unload our Snatch together, you can sense an aggression pulsing off us that I don't think was there before.

Intellectually, of course, I get it. Our post-invasion honeymoon was over in the time it took the electricity to pack up and the locals to work out we didn't have the faintest fucking idea what came next. It's no surprise that they're angry. But that hate-filled mob has still put me on the back foot.

I wonder if it's to do with upbringing. Growing up, you're taught that the 'Other' isn't actually something to fear. At primary school you sit cross-legged on the floor and learn about pilgrims going on *hajj* and draw pictures of Zulus in their *kraal*. The Other is still an unknown, of course – you're eight years old and living in South Buckinghamshire – but the implication is that you should think the best of them. Later on you meet the Other in crowded tourist markets or sharing a taxi bus on your gap year, and it's all very convivial. You're vaguely aware that there are people out there who *aren't* nice; jihadis and terror cells, and traffickers and so on. But in general your worldview is a United Colours of Benetton advert, and the Other are probably just the friends you haven't met yet.

Then you find yourself sitting in a deathly quiet cookhouse, watching on television as a British helicopter burns and what seems like a whole city hurls stones at the wreckage. It's at that point that you realise that you didn't *really* know what the Other was after all.

They're not the friends you haven't met yet. In fact they appear to hate you. And they have their reasons – you've done things to them that you never did to the people in the tourist markets or the taxi bus – but it doesn't make it easier to rationalise when it's happening right in front of you.

And it doesn't lessen the jolt you feel, sitting in that cookhouse, and watching that television, when it suddenly dawns that you might be starting to hate them back.

6

Maysan

The real, enduring sadness is that it probably didn't have to be that way. On the face of it the people of Basra had a lot to gain from Saddam's departure. As Shias under a Sunni dictatorship, they had been getting roundly fucked over for almost thirty years. This wasn't a theological issue; Saddam's own cabinet contained everyone from Sufis to Christians. Indeed his original Ba'ath party mentor was Greek Orthodox of all things (decisive proof, if any were needed, that no one religion has a monopoly on complete tools).

Instead, it was political. With 80 million Iranian co-religionists next door, Saddam never felt as though he could really trust the Baswarians. In all fairness he was probably right; Tehran's influence ran deep, and to the extent he ever faced a meaningful resistance, Basra was one of the focal points.

Ironically, a shared belief system with the Iranians didn't stop Basra getting thoroughly turned over during the Iran–Iraq War. They'd been battered by Scud attacks for eight long years, and the area just north of the city had seen some of the most horrific battles of the whole war; waves of Iranians attacking through chest-deep marshes, while the defending Iraqis tried to electrocute them *en masse* using power lines laid in the water. The population dropped by two-thirds, with whole neighbourhoods reduced to rubble. Operation Desert Storm followed, and while the US Air Force had been more selective than the Iranians, they'd still levelled a good chunk of what was left standing.

After all that it didn't take much to light the blue touchpaper. Enter an Iraqi Army T-72 tank in February 1991, whose shell-shocked crew had driven back home to Basra after Stormin' Norman Schwarzkopf's ceasefire. As they entered the city the gunner suddenly laid his sights on an enormous mural of Saddam, pulled the trigger, and put a 125mm shell straight through the middle of it. This probably qualifies as the single most cathartic act in human history, and certainly puts writing a letter to your MP into perspective. It was also all the nudge the Baswarians needed.

Alongside Shias and Kurds all over Iraq, they rose up. Government ministries were overrun and many members of the *al-Amn (Internal State Security)* found themselves in the kind of sticky situations which secret policemen often encounter when their boss looks like he's about to get toppled. Unfortunately, after about a week of rallying their former oppressors up and down the desert tied to the tow hooks of their own cars, the rebels were faced with a flood of Republican Guard reinforcements from Baghdad. A week later the regime was back in control. The customary payback followed; 400 shot dead in the central square, fifty tied to rocks and thrown into the Shatt al-Arab, and God knows how many other smaller reprisals.

Saddam wasn't one to let bygones be bygones, so by the time of our invasion in 2003 Basra was on its knees. Most of whatever international trade Iraq still did was deliberately channelled through Umm Qasr instead of Basra's own port. Jobs in the nearby Rumaylah oil field went only to the Sunnis of Az Zubayr, a few miles to the south. Birth defects, caused by depleted uranium ammunition, mustard gas, and any number of other nasties from two major wars, were through the roof. Between all that and a vicious UN sanctions regime, the city's reputation as the 'Venice of the East' (which had always been a *bit* of a stretch; I suspect most gondolas would have dissolved if you'd dropped one in a Baswarian canal) looked like a bad joke.

So it was no wonder that when the first British soldiers arrived in Basra it was like Carnival in Rio; they were cheered, garlanded with flowers, and – according to some of the QRH lads who'd been there – enthusiastically French-kissed by beaming eighty-year-old dudes with no teeth. The fighting itself had been straight-forward; most of the Iraqi Army had booked it for home, mean-ing the enemy were mostly Saddam's own *fedayeen*, as well as a few foreign jihadis keen for a crack at the Great Satan. These lads hadn't exactly been a pushover; at one point our tanks had to 'clean' off *fedayeen* climbing on their turrets by hosing each other down with machine guns, until the blood ran so thick over their gunsights that they needed to use the little wipers to see. But there hadn't been many of them. So despite a bit of damage, we'd successfully avoided turning Basra into Stalingrad.

It was only then that things started to go wrong. Military plan-ning is typically divided into four phases; phase I is the prepar-ation, phase II the logistics, phase III the battle, and phase IV the post-conflict operations. Generals love phase III planning; they can point at big wall maps and use their hands like Maverick in *Top Gun* to show you how they're going to flank someone. Phase IV planning, on the other hand, is very boring; you can't flank anyone, and have to spend the whole time worrying about trivial admin like whether civilians will have enough to eat, and what the plan is to restore power after you flanked straight through that major substation during phase III.

But don't take my word for it; here's General Sir Anthony Pigott, Deputy Chief of the Defence Staff and a key figure in the pre-war planning, for his cogent take:

I hate the term 'Phase IV' and I hate the term 'aftermath'. And I wouldn't have invented or used either of them myself. And the phasing [*sic*] of phase IV implies a phase V or phase VI and it has got this sort of nature of going into the future and I think it is concurrent shaping all the time that was required, not phase IV planning, let's now plan for phase IV.

Well, quite. Anyway, Anthony and his pals had 'concurrently shaped' their ideas for post-war Basra so thoroughly that you could have got the whole plan onto the back of a fucking postage stamp. What's more, they'd signed up to do the whole thing with slightly fewer troops than you'd want to marshal a Wigan Athletic away game.

Tony Blair comes in for a lot of flak – and rightly so – but presumably at some point he did actually ask the generals for their professional opinion. And if someone asks you whether you can restore good governance and basic necessities to a city of 1.5 million that has been ravaged by war and neglect for the thick end of thirty years, using a few thousand squaddies, the correct response is to stare at them briefly to confirm they are not, in fact, taking the piss. And then tell them very firmly that no, of course you fucking can't.

But the generals didn't say that. Instead they probably steepled their fingers, frowned thoughtfully, and said they'd 'just crack on with it'. This despite the fact that 'just cracking on with it' has got more British soldiers killed than the Luftwaffe; they 'just cracked on with it' at the Charge of the Light Brigade too. And thus in one fell swoop, those same generals established a decent claim to have fucked the British Army harder than Rommel, King Cetswayo and the Sangin Taliban combined.

Immediately after Basra was liberated, there was an orgy of looting which made the sack of Rome look like an angsty teenage shoplifting phase. The Army didn't have the numbers to do much more than stand back and watch, like a timid supply teacher, as thousands of Baswarians redecorated their homes with swivel chairs and air-conditioning units they'd lifted from schools, hospitals and government ministries. They even took the floorboards out of the university. And while all this was going on, someone quietly emptied every police and Iraqi Army armoury in the city. Winning a war and then just watching as your enemy immediately rearms with two divisions' worth of heavy weaponry always struck me as an odd tactic. But then again, I never went to Staff College.

Once the looting was over, Basra settled down. For a while. It's often said that generals always fight the last war. Well, in our generals' case the last war was Northern Ireland. It didn't matter that Belfast had dick all in common with Basra; it was off with the helmets and on with the berets. The MoD Media Ops team gurgled happily about hearts and minds, and the *Sun* ran photos of 'Our Boys' patrolling on pushbikes.

All seemed well, particularly when you compared Basra to the increasingly high tempo shitshow the Americans were experiencing in Baghdad. Whether it was thirty years of soldiering in the Province, some kind of collective colonial memory of what really makes Johnny Arab tick, or just the fact that we were bloody nice blokes who took our sunglasses off to talk to people, it was pretty clear that we just 'got' counterinsurgency.

Except we really didn't. In the absence of anything resembling a government, there were more than fifty political parties operating in Basra within a month of the invasion, practically all of them Shia. A dozen had their own full-blown militias. Some of these groups were moderate; quite a few had manifestos based on decapitating anyone who didn't agree with them and then wearing their head as a hat. Several reported directly to Tehran.

We didn't notice this at the start; the militias had their hands full trying to annihilate one another and so didn't really turn their attention to the Brits. Besides, we were too busy looking for mythical Saddam loyalist death squads under the bed. We also didn't really know what 'normal' was for Basra; perhaps they'd always had a big kidnapping problem, and wire-bound corpses strung up by the roadside were just a local tradition, like piñatas or something. But mainly we were spread so thin that we couldn't really have a clue what was happening anywhere.

Basra has roughly the same population as Merseyside, and yet in the aftermath of the invasion we were trying to garrison it with less than 4,000 troops. By comparison, Merseyside police employs nearly twice that. And they're not trying to contain endemic violence and serious crime in a city where the law has long since ceased to have any meaning (at least, not every day). To top it all off, at about the same time someone in the Coalition Provisional Authority in Baghdad seems to have done a shot from every single one of the optics in the embassy bar, then staggered back to the office and issued an order to sack all the Ba'athists from the police (i.e., pretty much everyone). In short, there wasn't much to stop the militias taking over. And within a year of the invasion, they had.

You can only imagine what the locals thought. It must have been a trip reading smug little reports in the world press about how the Brits had that whole counterinsurgency gig nailed down, while just up the road female students at Basra University were being beaten by militiamen who'd decided that wearing jeans made you an apostate whore.

We were eventually apprised of what was actually going on via a quite exceptionally violent summer of street-fighting in 2004. Having blown away their major rivals, the surviving militias now had the time and energy to take us on. They had also correctly worked out that there is nothing like sticking the nut on an occupying power to prove your credentials as their successor, and win support among a city full of people who are seriously starting to wonder if the electricity will ever come back on.

The head start which we'd given the militias meant that putting a lid on them would be all but impossible. Not least because the interim government in Baghdad were by now heavily reliant on many of their leaders for political support; I say 'sectarian death squad commander', you say 'key parliamentary ally in the task of building a better (and incidentally much more Shia) Iraq'. They took a dim view of the 'wrong' people being arrested. It also turned out that quite a few of the people we'd hastily issued with police hats and truncheons a year ago after de-Ba'athification were themselves members of some of Basra's most head-bangingly extreme militias. And all the while, the living standards of ordinary Baswarians continued to plummet.

By the time we arrived they'd had a daily diet of kidnappings, murders and power cuts for more than three years. And if there was a plan for turning that around, no one had told us; they certainly weren't sending any more soldiers to help. But it probably explains why the locals were throwing stones at our helicopter.

Friday, 12 May 2006 – Shaibah / Camp Abu Naji

We're being sent north to al Amarah. I find out in the usual way; one of the boys mentions it casually while we're queuing for a Snapple in the Welfare Village, then I wait twenty-four hours for Jonty to confirm it at OC (*Officer Commanding*)'s orders. The operation is called Op BLAST, which is an interesting choice and quite possibly an omen; al Amarah is the capital of Maysan province and has quite the spicy reputation. Apparently we'll be doing something called 'Security Sector Reconstruction'.

Jonty tells us it'll mostly be inspecting police stations and border posts, but we'll get a much more detailed briefing when we get to al Amarah. We won't, of course, but it's something the Army likes to say – see also: 'Don't worry about that, we'll issue that in theatre' or 'We're sorting out your accommodation as we speak.' From the sounds of it, Hollywood aren't going to option the screenplay any time soon, but it probably beats sitting around in Shaibah watching *Glee* and drinking *frappuccinos*.

B Squadron will be tagging along with one of the gigantic, ponderous RLC (*Royal Logistics Corps*) convoys that resupplies the small British garrison in al Amarah every couple of weeks. Two years ago you could have got to al Amarah from Basra in a couple of Land Rovers; an easy drive of two hours on the wide tarmac road known as Route Six, which runs north alongside the Tigris and links the two. But since then Route Six has become a byword for mile-long ambushes and horrific daisy-chained IEDs. So now the convoys take anything from eight to twelve hours and the best part of a thousand soldiers. Unsurprisingly, no one enjoys them very much.

We link up with the convoy, which must have a hundred vehicles in it; a constellation of HGVs, escort Snatches, and a whole fleet of recovery vehicles to sweep up the breakdowns, which will inevitably start littering the route like something out of the Retreat from Moscow about five minutes after we leave Shaibah. We are put smack in the middle.

This suits me just fine; we won't have to do any map-reading and we're very unlikely to get IED'd. I can see a dozen way more tempting targets just from where I'm sitting, including a brand new fuel tanker that may as well have a big sign on the side saying, 'BLOW ME UP FIRST'. No one's going to pick a B Squadron Snatch for their IED when there's a *Con Air*-style explosion on offer. It sounds callous, but it's basic convoy maths and everyone does it.

We roll out of the gate and settle into a numbing 25mph convoy pace. The route takes us past the Air Station, and then through the Qarmat Ali district of northern Basra. This is home to two of Basra's most pugnacious tribes – the Halaf and the Garamshas – and is regularly lit up like a *son et lumière* show that you can see from Shaibah. Several British patrols have recently found themselves in the middle of quite spectacular firefights while passing through here, only to find out later that it was nothing at all to do with them, it was simply the Halaf and the Garamshas trying to sort out an argument about parking or Leylandii trees or something.

Today, though, it all seems reasonably quiet. I peer out of the Snatch's thick windows as we chunter past the main market. It's not the Shia Flats, but it's not South Ken either, and there are enough hard stares to suggest that the militias have a following here too. A minute or so later, stones start thumping into the Snatch. It's mainly teenagers, and from the grins on their faces there's no real malice in it; I doubt Qarmat Ali has much in the way of youth centres, so it's probably just something to do. But they've clearly got their eye in, and I can hear Cameron and Womack on top cover swearing as bits of kerb start bouncing off their helmets.

In truth, there isn't much we can do about this kind of thing; they're only stones, and we're supposed to be here to help these people, not to hurt them. Unless you're Womack, who eventually snaps, and nails one of the stone throwers directly in the crotch with an ice-cold bottle of Lemon Tea Snapple he'd been saving for later, thereby rather neatly doing both.

We continue north, out of Qarmat Ali and into the countryside proper. By now we've been joined by a pair of Apache attack helicopters, patrolling in protective figures of eight above the convoy as it trundles slowly along Route Six. They are squat, black and so ugly that it's often said they can't actually fly, it's just that the Earth rejects them, but they look beautiful to us. Even the most unhinged militiaman is going to think twice about taking us on with £50m of violent airborne payback clattering around the skies above them.

It takes us another eight stultifying hours to get up to al Amarah; no one blows us up, but two of the Snatches break down and have to be towed. The sun is merciless and our uniforms are black with sweat. But as I gaze at the palm trees and irrigated fields either side of Route Six, with the glinting Tigris on my shoulder, I think back to Enfield in December and smile. And I realise that I am enjoying myself very much indeed.

Saturday, 13 May 2006 – Camp Abu Naji

Camp Abu Naji – CAN – sits in a patch of desert about six miles to the south of al Amarah and about half a mile off Route Six. It's named after the locals' own historic nickname for the British, dating back to when we ran Mandatory Iraq.

The origins of the nickname are disputed. One version is that it means 'Father (Abu) of things left behind (Naji)', by which the locals mean things like roads and hospitals (although presumably not the oil, which we'd specifically tried to take with us). The other version is that we're named after an Abu Naji who was chauffeur to an Iraqi king, Ghazi bin Faisal, and who allegedly killed him – on British orders – in a fake car accident in Baghdad in 1939. My money's on the second one; it sounds like exactly the kind of thing we *would* do. Either way, the most important thing is probably not to enquire too closely as to what the locals are calling us now.

One look at the place when we arrived the day before, and it was clear that we were in for a *frappuccino*-free week. CAN is a kilometre square and enclosed on all sides by a great berm of reddish sand twenty feet high. In each corner are sangars; fortified sentry posts constructed from sandbags and plywood. The sentries can either monitor the southern edge of al Amarah and the bustling traffic of Route Six, or slowly die of boredom from staring at a thousand miles of completely flat desert, depending on which side of camp they're on.

Al Amarah is a good ten degrees hotter than Basra and CAN is basically a deep-sided baking tray. Everyone lives in small, air-conditioned boxes called Corrimecs and doesn't leave them if they can help it. I could see them as we drove in, darting from box to box like sweaty geckoes. I could not see a Pizza Hut. Most of B Squadron are accommodated in a large Corrimec with a single, tiny air-conditioning unit. This Corrimec, when it's not rammed with eighty-odd soldiers lying naked on cot beds trying not to die from heat exhaustion, apparently constitutes CAN's welfare facilities. It's like the Black Hole of Calcutta, if those lads had also been allowed a ping-pong table with one bat.

The regimental sergeant major of the CAN battlegroup briefs us first thing in the morning. Despite the thick layer of reddish dust that covers everything here, he is six foot two of immaculate combats and razor-sharp creases; most of B Squadron, by contrast, already look like the Sand People of Tattooine. Like most RSMs, he is also about as subtle as a house brick. This is not 'fucking Shaibiza', he informs us in his opening sentence; this is the Wild West. Every patrol entering al Amarah for the last month has come under some kind of contact, and there have already been a number of epic, company-level firefights. As a result there is a ban on Snatches even entering the city and all movement is now by Warrior or Challenger 2 only.

He sounds slightly apologetic at this point, as if we'll be disappointed that we won't get the chance to commit suicide by driving into al Amarah to mix it up with the militias in cardboard Land Rovers. But personally speaking, it works for me.

Just in case anyone's still feeling a bit too chipper, the RSM then turns to the IDF threat. From his description it sounds like CAN is being pasted like something out of Third Ypres. The militias haven't hit anything important yet, he tells us, but they're getting better with practice and it's only a matter of time. We are to keep our helmets and body armour within arm's reach at all times.

Irrespective of the fact that CAN appears to be rapidly turning into the Iraqi Alamo, the RSM finishes with a dour reminder that he still expects the usual high standards of dress and deportment; shirts tucked in, trousers bloused into boots, and so on. Death-lasering us with his eyes, he vows that if he finds anyone 'bimbling around the place like they're on a fucking Club 18 to 30', he will 'fucking thrash them until they fucking melt'. Switching tack somewhat abruptly, he finishes by saying he hopes we enjoy our stay in CAN. Then he walks off, presumably to find someone who hasn't done up all their buttons so he can do at least one crucifixion before breakfast.

This kind of briefing, covering everything from the local tactical situation to what the rules are for your trousers, but not mentioning – even in passing – what the fuck it is we're supposed to be doing here, is absolutely vintage Army. I'm almost impressed. But eventually someone decides we've been in the dark for long enough and we troop over to the ops room for an O Group. We are here, it transpires, to make sure that Maysan finally hits its PIC deadline.

PIC stands for Provincial Iraqi Control. This is the process by which Iraq is going to be handed back, province by province, to whichever coalition of sheikhs, imams and criminal strongmen the locals in each territory have been told they should vote for if they'd like to live past the end of the week. Two provinces in the British area of operations, Muthanna and Dhi Qar, have been deemed broadly under control and have achieved PIC. Both are notable for their tiny populations, and vast, trackless expanses of uninhabited desert. Maysan is a different kettle of fish.

There are some places in the world that are just plain trouble; places where they rustle cattle, raid their neighbours, and given half a chance, kidnap local administrators and butcher them inventively in the town square. Maysan is one of those places. Al Amarah itself started life as a fort built by the Ottomans to try to reduce the number of revenue collectors being slaughtered by the local tribes, who had very clear views on whether they should be paying taxes or not. (Not.)

It had been restive under Saddam too; he'd had to keep an entire armoured division permanently parked outside the city just to keep a lid on things. These lads had been pretty good at rounding up dissidents and digging mass graves, but shortly after the 2003 invasion, they had promptly disbanded themselves and fled to Baghdad. Unfortunately this gave rise to a popular myth that Maysan had liberated itself, and didn't actually need Westerners interfering in its affairs. This feeling has only intensified since, particularly once the Maysanis worked out that we didn't have much of a plan for their province other than digging the occasional well, and sending Sebastian and Jocasta from DFID to lecture them about gender equality.

As a result the British Army has been getting a thorough kicking here for over three years now. Indeed al Amarah is where the PWRR went in like Terminator T-800s on their apocalyptic first tour. Memories of this are apparently still quite fresh among the locals, which probably explains why the PWRR haven't been sent back there again. There are also several other towns that are effectively 'no-go' zones. Like Majar al-Kabir, where six RMP (*Royal Military Police*) lads were overrun by a mob and slaughtered with their own weapons two years ago. This is about the fourth deadline for PIC that Maysan has missed.

PIC is based on four conditions: (1) the threat level, (2) the local governor's ability to deal with it, (3) British forces' ability to intervene if it all goes sideways, and (4) the preparedness of local security forces. The answers to the first three are pretty clear: (1) Maysan is absolutely riven with vicious militias, (2) probably quite good; his last job before becoming governor was running the single most vicious one, and (3) we'd claim to be able to intervene in the Alpha Centauri star system if it meant getting out of Maysan.

Getting an answer to (4) will be our job during Op BLAST.

7

Michael Owen

Tuesday, 16 May 2006 – Al Musharrah

Jonty appears at the door of the Welfare Sauna the morning after a sweat-soaked night. I'm taking Third Troop to visit a police station. It's in a town called al Musharrah twenty-five kilometres away. I'm to ask them some questions – he drops a ream of paper into my hands – and have a 'general look round' to 'see how they're getting on'. The detailed briefing over, Jonty disappears back to his accommodation in the CAN HQ building, where the air-conditioning is like the Harvey Nicks in Dubai Mall.

In fairness, there isn't much more he can tell me: it's left out of CAN, right off Route Six, then drive for an hour until you hit a police station. But it's our first proper outing as a troop, and there won't be any Apaches for a three Snatch patrol. The RSM's dire warning about the beach scene from *Saving Private Ryan* which apparently starts just outside the front gate seems to hang over us as I brief the boys on the plan. They're unusually attentive; perhaps they're feeling it too.

Sgt Mason heads to the interpreters' accommodation and returns with Ali, who wears a knock-off Man United shirt and a thunderous scowl. He doesn't know our destination, and we won't tell him until we're nearly there. Most of the terps are trustworthy, but the militias will have infiltrated them like they have everything else, so there's always a small chance you'll be met by a reception committee in balaclavas if you tell too many people where you're going. It's not the textbook approach to people management. But then again not many of those textbooks have a chapter on what to do when a small but sizeable minority of your colleagues would quite like to see you blown into tiny pieces. I introduce myself; Ali sighs, then climbs into the back of my Snatch like an early Christian martyr dragging himself to the cross.

It takes us an age to get to al Musharrah. It's a bit like the familiarisation patrol all over again, except this time there's no one who's done it all before to show us the ropes. So we crawl along the road like pensioners negotiating the baking aisle on their mobility scooter, our eyes on stalks. And we stop. A lot. We stop at junctions, at culverts, by patches of rubbish, and just about anywhere else that looks even a tiny bit unusual. We even stop for a Coke can by the side of the road; it looks suspiciously new and is for some reason standing on its end and not its side.

We assess it for so long that eventually even Ali is moved to pop his head out of the Snatch and say, 'It's just a Coke can.' By now we all privately agree, but you can't look like you're letting the interpreter make important tactical decisions, so we stare at it for another five minutes before Sgt Mason settles the matter by volleying it into the desert.

The order of march is Corporal Robbins – the troop corporal, and third in command – then me, then Sgt Mason. The theory is that we'll miss Cpl Robbins least should he be unexpectedly turned into pink mist (because he's the most junior commander, not because we don't get on). So he travels at the front to prove the route and absorb any surprises; his own views on this arrangement, as a 33-year-old with a wife and two children, are fairly forthright. The troop sergeant's world is resupply and casualty evacuation, so Sgt Mason stays at the back and comes forward when needed. This leaves the troop leader, ensconced happily in the middle, and a clearly identifiable target for the militia IED teams, who worked all this out ages ago.

Eventually we motor into town and find the police station on what passes for al Musharrah's high street. It's a fort-like compound with high walls, a sentry post at each corner (deserted), and a large, rusting main gate (wide open). The only sign of life is an ancient dog licking its balls on the front steps. We park up and Sgt Mason takes out a clearance patrol in case anyone is thinking about dropping in unexpectedly. I set off with Ali to find whoever's in charge.

It takes a while. The morning has slipped away while we've been conferring endlessly about Coke cans, so we're now well into siesta time. And these lads would make the Spanish look second-rate. Eventually we find a few men in police uniforms snoring gently on some mattresses in a darkened side room.

They look so peaceful that it seems a shame to wake them, but well, there's a war on. I clear my throat loudly and one of them cracks an eyelid open. He smiles uncertainly.

'Tell him, hello,' I say to Ali.

'You don't need to say, "Tell him",' replies Ali, who has been very grumpy ever since we left CAN. He translates. The owner of the uncertain smile sits up and replies slowly, in the manner of a man trying very hard to get his story straight. I can hear quiet footsteps in the corridor behind me.

'He says welcome to the police station of al Musharrah. He wants to know what do you want.'

'Tell him we are on an inspection visit to look around the station and ask some questions. Where is the commander?'

'You don't need to say, "Tell him". He says there is no need for an inspection, they had one last week and it was very good.'

'I don't think that's actually true, is it? No one has been to this police station in at least six months. Where is the commander?'

'He is called Majed. He asks what is your name?'

'That's not really relevant, but it's Lieutenant Owain Mulligan. Where is the commander?'

'Like Michael Owen?'

'Well, yes, but not spelled the same. Where is the command—'

'Michael Owen!'

A small chorus line of police officers has now formed in the corridor outside. They loudly express their delight that I am – in their eyes at least – intimately related to England's premier centre-forward.

'Listen, Ali, tell him we need to speak to the commander and conduct an inspection of this police station. Where is he?'

'Manchester United! Arsenal! Yes, yes, Liverpool! Welly good!'

And so on. After about five minutes – and presumably after they've hidden everything they're not supposed to have – Majed mournfully informs me that the commander is 'at a ceremony'. Next time we should let them know we're coming. Fat chance; if we'd told them that I'd be sitting two miles outside al Musharrah looking at a burning Snatch and picking pieces of Womack out of my hair.

In the meantime we can talk to Captain Abdullah, the second-in-command. We find Captain Abdullah in his office next door; an effervescent little rubber ball of a man in a crumpled shirt with elaborate epaulettes. He is thrilled to see us. On the wall behind his head hangs an enormous portrait of Moqtada al-Sadr, who leads the single biggest Shia militia in southern Iraq.

Captain Abdullah pours the tea himself, and Ali and I sit down on a sofa opposite his desk. I pull out the sheaf of paper that Jonty gave me and start scanning the list of questions I'm supposed to ask. By conservative estimate there are about 350,000 of them.

I flip the sheaf open at a random page:

Q67a: Does the station have Internet access? Yes/No/Unclear

Q67b: Does the station have an Internet use policy? Yes – written/Yes – but not written/No

Q67c: Does the station have a designated Internet officer? Yes – primary duty/Yes – secondary duty/No

I look up from the page and through a broken window into the courtyard outside. The dog we saw earlier is curling one out next to a generator that looks like it's been salvaged from the wreck of the *Titanic*. Briefly I wonder if I've been given the wrong set of questions, and these are the ones for a police station somewhere else. Like Surrey, for example. I find another random page – uniform policies; health and safety in the workplace; school outreach. I close the sheaf.

'Right, Captain Abdullah. Let's start with how many arrests you have made this month.'

It's not in the script, I know that. But I also know that we've got about an hour in al Musharrah at the outside. Any more than that and we'll be pushing our luck, because we're a long way from CAN and we're going to have to go out the same way we came in. Our major issue with the Iraqi police at the moment is their vexing habit of deliberately sending British patrols down roads with enormous IEDs on them; perhaps once we've got that cracked, we can come back and ask them questions about how fast their broadband is.

With one eye on my watch, I rattle through some of the less lunatic questions on the list. Captain Abdullah answers an emphatic 'Yes' to every single one. Yes, he has made many arrests. They have been very good arrests actually. Yes, he has a properly secured armoury. Yes, he has an operations room, manned twenty-four hours a day. Can I see the operations room? Yes, I can see the operations room. But not now, it's locked and Hassan has the only key, and he has gone to see his uncle in al Maymounah. The rest of the questions, I decide, will get filled in during the drive home.

We tour the station next. Walking down the corridors, Captain Abdullah alternately flings doors open or slams them shut and makes apologetic noises about Hassan and his uncle (I hope he's had a lift to al Maymounah, because he must be carrying his bodyweight in keys). Sgt Mason, back from the clearance patrol, manages to get his foot in a couple before they close, and we catch the occasional glimpse of piles of VCRs and hi-fis.

It's clear Abdullah and his colleagues are taking their cut from the rampant cross-border smuggling with Iran. This isn't ideal, but it's also not worth dying in a ditch over (or dying in a remote police station in Maysan over, shot dead by rogue policemen who are annoyed you want to stop them taking their cut from the rampant cross-border smuggling with Iran). In certain police stations down in Basra they're opening similar doors and finding people hanging from the ceiling by meat hooks, so a few knock-off Hitachis are not that big a deal.

We stop briefly at the armoury. It's filled with enough heavy weaponry to take Berlin, but apparently this is pretty par for the course for a police station in rural Maysan. Beaming, Abdullah reaches into one rack and pulls out a gold-plated AK-47 complete with faux-ivory pistol grip. He tells us it previously belonged to an ex-member of *al-Amn* – ex because the last time he'd seen him he was being dragged screaming through al Musharrah tied to the back of a Toyota Corolla – but that now it's his. Quite right too; it looks fabulous on him.

It's nearly time to leave so we return to Abdullah's office to wrap things up. Perhaps sensing that we're the last Brits he'll see for another six months, he starts asking whether we might see our way to buying a few small items for him. Like a satellite dish. Or a flat screen TV. He's particularly keen on a new generator. He can hardly be expected to run an efficient policing operation, he says with a sad shake of his head, if their generator can't even power the charger for the walkie-talkies they use on patrol. I look at the dust-covered walkie-talkie charger behind him, then at the small television set next to it, which is showing what appears to be a very lively football match. Abdullah follows my gaze and grins. Najaf–Erbil, he explains. Semi-final. There isn't anyone on patrol anyway.

And on that note it's time to go. On the drive back to CAN, Sgt Mason and I take half the questions each to fill in on our knees.

Not best practice, but we could have spent a Bank Holiday weekend getting told soothing lies in that police station by Abdullah and it still wouldn't have given us the slightest clue as to whether they were ready for PIC.

The answers we'd need for that aren't the kind you can get by dropping in for an hour every six months. They're the answers to questions like: 'How many of your officers – truly how many – wouldn't just turn round and shoot you in the head the minute they were ordered to by the right cleric?' Or, 'What are you turning a blind eye to? Who can get away with murder? Come to that, who has actually got away with a murder?' Or even, 'When we do eventually leave Maysan, will you actually recognise the legitimate Iraqi government? Or have we just spent several billion dollars putting a militia into police uniform?'

But in all honesty, I doubt we'll get the answers to those questions until after we've left.

Wednesday, 17 May 2006 – Maysan

Another patrol to visit a police station. This time it's my turn to collect the interpreter. I head to their accommodation, which Sgt Mason tells me is down by the front gate of CAN. As I approach the door, a curtain in one of the windows is pulled aside. A bleary face appears at the glass, registers me, then disappears again with impressive speed.

I knock on the door. No reply. I knock again. Nothing. Sweat trickles into my eyes. Fuck everything about this. I give the door a shove and walk into a dim room; three men sit up on cot beds, rubbing their faces and stretching.

'*As-salaam aleikum*,' I say, torturously. The men stare at me. 'Who is the duty interpreter?'

Silence.

'We are going on patrol. I need an interpreter. Who is on duty?' I say, a bit testily this time.

The men gesture vaguely at one another and make unhappy little noises in Arabic.

'Look, one of you must be the duty interpreter. So tell me who, so we can go on this patrol, and you can do your jobs.' I am uncomfortably aware that I am starting to sound a little bit shrill.

The men stare at me again. Suddenly I feel very hot.

'For fuck's *sake*, guys! Which one of you is actually on duty? We are going on patrol, and one of you is fucking well coming with us. I can stand here all day if I need to – we're paying you good money to do a job – and that doesn't mean just sitting around on your fucking beds, having fucking naps!'

I trail off, staring somewhat wildly at the three men. They in turn stare back at me, wide-eyed. Then Sgt Mason pops his head inside the door.

'Interpreters are next door, boss. These lads work in the laundry,' he says. Then, grinning, adds, 'You fucking tube.'

Friday, 19 May 2006 – Camp Abu Naji

We don't go on patrol every day; some days it's someone else's turn to drive out to police stations in the middle of fucking nowhere and ask them about the last time they changed the batteries in their smoke alarm. On those days we do guard duty. For Sgt Mason and me it technically means a day off; officers and senior NCOs don't really do guard. But it's considered bad form to kick back drinking Cokes and playing *Monopoly* while the boys are slow-cooked in the sangars. So we spend most of our time bringing them cold drinks and commiserations, trying to share in at least a bit of the misery.

Just after lunch I'm in a sangar with Buxton, digging around in my daysack for a Peach Tea; for a man who regularly scrapes other people's plates onto his at mealtimes, he is surprisingly fastidious about Snapples. Then he nudges me with his leg.

'Er, boss,' he says, pointing into the middle distance. 'What do you reckon they're up to?'

I stand up and stare in the direction he's pointing. We're in one of the eastern sangars, facing towards Route Six, about 600 metres away.

'There, by that fuel tanker. Quarter left.'

Then I see it. A white pickup – it is always a white pickup – parked on the verge, with three tiny figures at its rear. Two of them are dragging a large object off the tailgate; the third stands behind them like he's waiting for something.

'Fuck knows,' I say expertly. 'Pass me the binos.'

Buxton is ten seconds ahead of me, already propped on his elbows on a sandbag and fiddling with the magnification.

'That's a mortar,' he says, in quiet wonder. Even before he's finished the sentence, I hear a muted *pop*.

We stare at one another. Despite the RSM's doom-laden briefing, we've actually only been mortared a couple of times since getting here. The impacts were as haphazard as they are in Shaibah; most of the squadron hadn't even got out of their cot beds. And it had been in the middle of the night, when mortar attacks are *supposed* to happen. This – calmly parking up by the side of the road in broad daylight and pulling out a mortar like you or I would pull out a hamper and a picnic rug – is something new. There is another muted *pop*.

I grab the binoculars from Buxton and focus on the pickup. Two of the figures are already climbing back into the truck's bed. I can't see the third man at first, then I spot him in the driver's seat, presumably gunning the engine like Roger in *The Italian Job*. Despite everything I can't help feeling a small burst of admiration; we've just witnessed as neat a bit of guerilla warfare as you're ever likely to see.

Whoever these hoods are, they've got two rounds off against a well-defended British Army camp in a little under fifteen seconds, in the middle of the day, next to a busy main road. I suppose it helps that they don't need to worry about the authorities. In fact if the police had seen them, they'd probably have given them a hand to pack up the mortar. But still, it's quite impressive.

I am jolted out of these reflections by Buxton, who reminds me that, as interesting as he agrees the tactical aspects of the whole thing are, we're still getting fucking mortared. I join him on the sangar floor. There's no point shooting at the mortar crew; our rifles only have an effective range of about 300 metres, and with my luck I'd inevitably drop either a passing imam or the local MP.

A few seconds later we hear the rounds land in the desert the other side of camp; they have overshot by a country mile. Even so it's still a win for the opposition; something like a thousand soldiers will have to stop what they were doing for at least half an hour, while the mortar crew will be halfway back to al Amarah and a celebratory *chai* by the time the IDF alarm stops wailing.

I congratulate Buxton; he did bloody well to even spot the pickup in the first place. We share his Peach Tea Snapple until the all-clear's given. Then I walk back to the Welfare Sauna to tell the rest of the squadron about what I've just seen. The other troop leaders struggle to capture in mere words my stunning ineptitude in not at least attempting to shoot this supposed 'mortar team' dead, and conclude sadly that it must be because I am a STAB. I reply evenly that it was 600 fucking metres away you twats, and that I'm pretty sure you aren't supposed to open up on major roads like fucking Rambo, when there's fuck all chance of hitting what you're actually fucking aiming at.

But in amongst all the friendly banter I sense that we're all thinking the same thing; the RSM wasn't kidding when he said that it was like the Wild West up here.

8

Mortars

Sunday, 21 May 2006 – Camp Abu Naji

It starts like it always does; a distant *whump*. There's a general stirring in the Welfare Sauna. My watch says a quarter past four; I can't
see much, but I can make out the vague outlines of a few people sitting
up. I hear the tearing of Velcro tabs as body armour is shrugged on,
and the clunk of helmets being picked up and then dropped by sleepy
fingers. The person next to me rolls over and mutters, 'For *fuck's* sake.'

The explosion, when it comes, is less a sound and more a whole
body experience. We find out later that the round – probably a
120mm mortar – hit the corner of the Corrimec next to ours,
turning it into a shattered mess and sending shrapnel thudding
into the Hesco all around. All I know is that my cot bed feels like
it has leapt a foot off the floor, and if I do not get my helmet and
body armour on this instant, I will surely die.

I fling myself sideways, completely forgetting about the
mosquito net I've erected around my cot bed, which wraps itself

around me as I crash to the floor. Trussed up like a hysterical burrito, I scrabble for the zip. From the thrashing noises all around me, it sounds like half the squadron are having the same problem. Another thumping explosion punches me in the sternum. I hear a distant scream that sounds like it's coming from outside. Someone bawls at us to take cover and get our fucking body armour on. No one in the Welfare Sauna needs telling; if a 120mm comes through the roof they'll be taking us out of here in sandbags.

I find the zip and squirm out of the mosquito net. Then I fumble blindly under my cot bed for my body armour and drag it towards me, not daring to raise my head. Still lying on the floor I shuffle along until I'm lying on the back plate, and pull the front plate over my chest. Then I clamp my helmet to my skull with one hand, roll onto my front, and try to become as one with the linoleum floor.

Another round slams in nearby, rocking the whole Corrimec. From the corner of the room, where some of the female RLC drivers have put up their cot beds, I hear someone start to cry.

I'm not far from tears myself. This is utterly horrific. It doesn't seem possible that nothing's landed on us yet. The detonations – rolling, deafening crashes – aren't even the worst of it. It's the waiting. In the hideous silence between explosions, I wonder whether they'll even be able to tell us apart if one of those vicious rounds lands in here. Will it detonate when it hits the roof, and drive the red hot shrapnel down into our backs? Or wait until it goes through the Corrimec and hits the bare earth underneath, flinging our shattered bodies into the ceiling?

I start to bargain, and hate myself. Please, God, let them not hit us. But if they do hit us, please let it not be Third Troop. If it has to be someone, let it be one of the other troops. But if it has to be someone in Third, please let it not be me.

There are another half a dozen shattering explosions in quick succession, and I feel the bile rising in my throat. I am close to panic. Then – thank you God, thank you for this – the barrage seems to start moving on. For the first time we can hear the descending whistle-roar of the incoming rounds; when they are landing right on top of you, the first you know of it is the explosion.

I look up and see the massive outline of Sgt Mason crouched next to me. He tells me he's been counting the impacts. Of course he has – he is Sgt Mason. There have been thirty-eight so far, he reckons; a mix of 82mm and 120mm mortars, and 107mm Chinese rockets. I haven't the faintest idea how he knows this – I couldn't have told you that if you'd given me a seismograph and a research grant – but I'll take his word for it.

There are more explosions, but they're definitely further away this time. It doesn't mean we're in the clear; these guys aren't professionals, deliberately 'walking' their rounds to somewhere else in camp. They'll be firing rockets they leant up against piles of sand, aiming roughly towards where they think they last saw CAN before it got dark. So the fact the rounds have moved on might just be because a pebble has shifted under a loose mortar baseplate somewhere; another shift and we'll be right back in the middle of it.

I wonder how long they can keep it up. As long as they want, I expect. CAN does have a counter-battery radar, which will tell the ops room exactly where the rounds are coming from, but we won't be firing our own mortars back. The militia aren't stupid. They deliberately choose firing points inside the city, close to civilians. And the war is already unpopular enough at home without us levelling an infants' school trying to nail an enemy mortar team in the playground.

More explosions. Then, miraculously, there is thirty seconds of silence. Then a minute. Then two. That has to be it, surely? Someone turns the lights on; they've been off this whole time, which is just as well given I've probably spent the last ten minutes looking like Munch's *The Scream*. The Welfare Sauna is a mess; half the cot beds are on their sides and I'm clearly not the only one to have struggled with their mosquito net. But it doesn't seem like there's any actual damage. A few of the boys look very pale.

Presently, Mr Kite intimates that we should all shut the fuck up and listen in; the RSM is on the radio. There are casualties in the female accommodation, two Corrimecs over. I shudder; this must have been the screaming I heard earlier. They need medics, says Mr Kite, and they need them now.

As taskings go, this is an absolute peach; head out into the pitch-black, with Christ knows how many unexploded rounds fizzing away in the darkness, to deal with what might well be a slaughterhouse that you'll never recover from even seeing. It's not even like it's definitely over; it wouldn't be the first time the enemy had dropped a couple of late rounds to try to catch the medics in the open. But our medics, Buxton and Womack, don't so much as hesitate.

Dumb with pride, I watch as they simply nod, heft their medical packs and run out into the night. Then and there I decide that it doesn't matter what they do next – they can burn down ALI SHOP and flog our Minimis in Basra market for all I care – they'll be getting a bye from me.

The rest of us sit around for a bit waiting for the soak period[23] to finish. The banter has started again, if a bit less quickly than usual; I can hear Cameron accusing Greene of having blubbed, to which the accused responds that he fucking well hadn't, and anyway how the fuck would Cameron know, he'd been too busy trying to build himself a bunker out of fucking daysacks. But for all the back and forth, I notice that no one is taking off their body armour.

Then Mr Kite details a few of the boys to search the area around the Welfare Sauna. They come back in less than a minute; there is a still warm 120mm mortar lying less than ten yards from the back door. Time to go. By now there is a faint glimmer of light, and I can make out the back of Godders' helmet in front of me as we file out in search of somewhere with a bit more cover, and ideally fewer enormous unexploded mortar rounds. We sit down next to some Hesco and Godders lights a cigarette. I didn't know he smoked.

We sit there in silence for a couple of minutes. Then Sgt Porter appears and squats down next to us. He asks us how we're doing. We're doing existential angst, as he well knows, but that's not really officer-like behaviour, so we make all the right positive noises instead. Sgt Porter isn't fazed. Sgt Porter is *never* fazed. He is ginger, wiry, and the First Troop sergeant. He's been everywhere the regiment has been for the last twenty years, normally towards the front, trying to kill as many people as possible before he has to go back to his wife, whom he hates.

He chuckles; he can see straight through us. Then he stares back towards the Welfare Sauna.

'Make sure you talk to your boys, sirs,' he says, gravely. 'Promise me. That was fucking horrific. And some of them will need to talk. They'll tell you they don't – they'll want to just crack on. But that doesn't do anyone any good. Believe me.'

We stare at him. Of all the people in B Squadron, Sgt Porter is the last one you'd expect to break out the digestives and talk it all out. He'd once told me a story about the first Gulf War, when the tank next to him fired its main armament lengthwise down an Iraqi trench. Grinning, he described how the round hadn't actually hit anyone, but the pressure wave as it streaked above the occupants' heads had been enough to pulverise every last man in the trench. It had looked like the inside of a jam jar, he said. Then again, perhaps that explained it after all.

He looks at us pointedly. Hurriedly, we mumble agreement. He nods, then stands up.

'Mr Goddington,' he says over his shoulder as he walks away, 'you might want to be careful with that cigarette, sir. That's the camp fuel bladder you're leaning up against.'

He's right; what we'd taken in the dark to be just another row of Hesco is in fact the side of an enormous rubber bag containing 80,000 litres of aviation fuel. As a piece of cover, it's a bit sub-optimal. Godders swears violently and stubs out his cigarette. Then we cut our losses and go for an early breakfast.

Monday, 22 May 2006 – Camp Abu Naji

During our O Group, Jonty gives us the latest on yesterday's attack. In all there were sixty-seven rounds in eight minutes – a mix of 82mm and 120mm mortars, and 107mm rockets, exactly as Sgt Mason had guessed from the floor of the Welfare Sauna. They came from no less than eight different firing points, all within the city; apparently the militias are now offering $300 a pop to anyone who lets them borrow their back garden to set up a mortar baseplate. This makes it, by some distance, the most sustained barrage the coalition has yet experienced anywhere in Iraq. It even ends up on the BBC.

This is a bit of a double-edged sword; on the one hand we're all secretly delighted that we've been in an attack so gnarly that it's made national news. On the other, my parents know we're in CAN, and will probably be quite upset to find out it's not exactly the Kuwaiti Rest & Recuperation Camp that I might have told them it was. Even the provincial governor has got involved; he called the CO in CAN to express his deep shock, and to say he'll make sure it doesn't happen again. Given he was in charge of the same people who probably did this until literally a month ago, this is a bit like Herod saying, 'No, leave the kids with me, they'll be fine'. But I suppose it's the thought that counts.

Clearly something this big means that the local militias had help. According to the CAN intelligence cell there is no shortage of candidates. There are rumours of mysterious convoys of cars from Najaf, out to the west, as well as up from Basra. Alternatively, given the Iranians are themselves supplying the rockets, it's not inconceivable that they've sent a few lads to help fire them too. Theories abound, and the most important thing for the intelligence cell is to keep generating such a steady stream of them that nobody thinks to ask any awkward questions about how it is that they've been utterly blindsided by the biggest IDF attack of the war. They're not called Green Slime[24] for nothing.

Astonishingly no one has actually been killed, but a Royal Engineer has lost his leg. The females in the Corrimec near ours have some bad cuts from shrapnel, but haven't been seriously hurt. Physically, at least. Mentally they're still in battle shock; according to Buxton, trying to get a field dressing on them had been like trying to bath a stray cat. He and Womack don't seem any the worse for the experience, but with Sgt Porter's advice still ringing in my ears, I tell them I'm here to talk if they want.

Fat lot of good it'd do them; I feel a bit like breaking out a feelings wheel myself, and I didn't even see any blood. But it's the first time anyone has made a very concerted effort to kill me. And while I know that whoever was firing those mortars doesn't have the first clue about me – to them, I'm just a small cog in an idolatrous horde which shouldn't be here – for some weird reason it feels intensely personal. And even more weirdly, somehow as if they've made a mistake.

It's probably to do with upbringing. I've spent twenty years being told what a special little flower I am; winning prizes at school and sitting in candlelit halls at Oxford while white-haired old men chunter on about how much I'm going to go on to achieve. So the idea that someone would want to just erase all that in an eyeblink – casually rub me out like that subaltern in the Kipling poem – just doesn't seem to make sense.

Perhaps if I'd been less sheltered I'd be better able to take it in. Perhaps, in fact, if I'd had a childhood like Griffiths or Buxton, who I know grew up seeing things at home that no child should, it would seem more reasonable that someone was trying to hurt me. But I hadn't, and it doesn't. It doesn't feel like this is supposed to happen to someone like me.

Friday, 26 May 2006 – Maysan

Op BLAST finishes tomorrow and I can almost taste the butterscotch *lattes* in the Welfare Village. More to the point, CAN is getting old, fast; we were IDF'd twice last night. I'd been listening in on the radio net after the second one when a very quiet voice came up to report that there was a 107mm Chinese rocket in his bedspace. It was one of the engineers, who'd been on the loo when the attack took place.

It's a good job it was number twos, because after returning to his Corrimec, he'd been very surprised to see his room much less tidy than he'd left it, and a three-foot warhead fizzing gently in the floor where his mattress used to be. It's said that he carefully put a duvet over the top before running like hell. Quite why you'd want to tuck in a live 107mm rocket is beyond me, but it's probably more constructive than fainting on the spot, which is what I suspect I might have done.

I have one last patrol to do before we leave; Godders and I are to visit a local power station. We're taking a camera crew from BBC West Midlands with us. They're doing some feel-good 'local boy' stories – about half the QRH is from Birmingham – and want to get some action shots to mix in with vox pops of senior officers lying through their teeth about all the great progress we're making out here.

If it had been me, I'd have just filmed it inside camp; one patch of dirty sand looks very much like another, after all. But it's their funeral. We pick them up by the front gate. There's a reporter and a cameraman, both wearing navy-blue body armour emblazoned with 'PRESS' in English, or 'KILL THIS ONE FIRST, HE LOOKS IMPORTANT' in Maysani Arabic. They explain that they want footage from a typical patrol, and ideally a few interesting quotes from the 'ordinary soldiers'.

Godders smiles warmly, says we'll do our best, and that they should feel free to ask the boys whatever they want. Twenty yards away on the other side of the Snatches, his troop sergeant quietly reminds everyone that if they deviate so much as an inch from our Media Ops-approved 'Lines To Take',[25] he will rip off their arms and fuck them to death with the soggy end.

The drive out to the power station is uneventful except for a very deliberate VP check at a brickworks about halfway there.

There are piles of rubble on both sides of the road and on the previous tour a patrol from the Staffordshire Regiment had hit a massive EFP hidden inside one of them. It had killed the driver, commander, and one of the top cover gunners. I explain all this to the BBC, who are in the back of my Snatch, and they get some shots of Godders leading the VP check. He takes his time. I can understand why.

When we arrive at the power station, Godders disappears with his interpreter to find whoever is claiming to be in charge today. Everyone else lounges around outside; there's nothing but desert for miles, so we're unlikely to get caught on the hop. Ten minutes later Godders comes out again, red-faced and muttering. He might have gone to the right accommodation to get his interpreter, he informs me through gritted teeth, but he may as well have brought one of the fucking laundry workers.

Capabilities do vary a bit, but apparently this one would have struggled to accurately render the dialogue from an episode of *Postman Pat*. Faced with sentences like 'What is this station's load factor, defined as average load in kilowatt hours over maximum load?', he'd apparently had some kind of mild stroke and just covered his face with his hands. Either way, concludes Godders, it has all been a gigantic fucking waste of time and we may as well go home.

We set off and make good time as far as the brickworks. Godders carries out another careful VP check and we have just emerged onto the open road when I feel an urgent tapping on my shoulder. It's the BBC. They tell me they would like to 'go back'. I look questioningly at Griffiths, who's driving. He shrugs and suggests that maybe they've left their packed lunches behind or something.

'What do you mean, "Go back"?' I shout over the engine noise.

'We need to go back to that bit just there,' replies the reporter from behind me.

I twist in my seat and stare at him.

'What, you mean the brickworks?'

'Yeah, that. Alan,' he gestures towards his glum cameraman, 'hasn't got any shots of your cars going past.'

I stare at him some more. I'm not sure I'm getting this. Maybe it's the heat.

'You want to go back to the brickworks, and film the Snatches, going past?' I ask, slowly.

'Yes. It's atmospheric – you've got the smoke from the chimneys, and the rubble and all that. We'll just put the camera on the ground, then you drive slowly past it. Called a low angle shot.'

'Yes, but . . . it's David, isn't it? David . . . it's a known IED site, mate. I mean . . . I told you that. Three people were killed there last year,' I say, slightly testily now.

David sighs. 'Yeah, I get that, but we've already been through it twice today, haven't we? It won't take five minutes. Just send a couple of the cars if it's such a big deal.'

I look at David. He is middle-aged, with thin, wispy hair and a big nose. I have a sudden urge to slam it repeatedly in the back door of the Snatch. I can't imagine this is his dream gig either; presumably at journalism school you rather hope you'll end up handing back to Trevor McDonald from the White House, rather than filming red-faced Brummies on an abortive visit to a small power station in Shitkicker, Maysan. But my tolerance for his particular brand of lunacy is wafer thin.

'No,' I say, through gritted teeth. 'We're on a patrol, not a bloody film set. It doesn't matter if we've already been through – for all we know there was someone trying to set off an IED the whole time. We are not fucking well going back.'

David scowls but slumps back in his seat. I turn round too, shaking my head at Griffiths at the sheer brass neck of it all. We motor on. Then, just as we're about to turn back onto Route Six, Godders' lead Snatch encounters a small flock of goats being driven by a tiny, wizened Bedouin. Surprisingly for a man who appears to be at least 150 years old, he is also clutching a Chinese-made AK-47.

This is tricky. Iraqi law is very clear on the inalienable right of every citizen to keep one powerful military-grade automatic weapon, per adult, in the home. Carrying one around outside is different, though. It's as much for the Iraqis' own protection as anything; US Army patrols frequently get confused and shoot up other, identical US Army patrols, let alone a bunch of locals who've been allowed to run around the place like *Universal Soldier*. Godders radios the ops room for advice. They are unequivocal; Old Man Maysan is not supposed to be carrying a fucking AK, so take it off him and write him a receipt. If he wants it back, he can go to a local police station and claim it there.

As soon as he realises what's up, the Bedouin comprehensively loses his shit. I'm not surprised; AKs go for about $300 each in the bazaar and it's probably the most valuable thing he owns. Gently Godders' troop sergeant prises it out of his hands. As he clears it so he can put it safely in his Snatch, the bottom of the magazine falls off and about a dozen rounds clatter onto the tarmac. I watch, feeling a bit sick as the Bedouin scrabbles in the dust, trying to keep hold of his bullets at least.

We drive away slowly; running over a goat at this stage really would be the icing on the fucking cake. The Bedouin watches us leave, practically airborne with rage. I'm fairly sure that whatever he's saying won't be in our cultural *aide-mémoire*. The spitting is pretty unambiguous anyway.

I'm not a counterinsurgency expert, by any means, but I'm also not sure what we've just done is going to help much. Sure, we're up one rusty AK-47, but I expect the militia are up one seismically pissed-off volunteer. I remember what Jonty told us about them offering $300 to anyone who helps them fire a rocket or mortar at CAN. I wouldn't blame the Bedouin. In fact there would be a certain Zen-like neatness to it. We get back to camp shortly afterwards, and the BBC do a couple of interviews with the boys. Then we bid David and Alan goodbye. For the rest of recorded time, with any luck.

That evening Jonty asks me and Godders if we've watched BBC West Midlands today. We haven't, of course – Jonty appears to have missed the fact we don't actually have a TV – but it's OK because he offers to fill us in. It's a good piece, he says; lots of lingering shots of the desert vista, and soldiers doing professional-looking VP checks. Then at the end there's a bit where they ask the boys what they think. They've stuck to the script immaculately, says Jonty.

He's particularly taken by the bit where Cameron talks about the warmth of the local population and how pleased they all seem with what we're doing here. This is immediately followed by a lengthy shot of a tiny Bedouin spitting at a Snatch and going, in Jonty's words, 'absolutely fucking banzai'. Touché, David.

We are rocketed that same night and I cower on the floor of the Welfare Sauna along with everyone else. But I hope it was him, and that he gets his $300 for a new AK.

9

Fun Runs

**Monday, 29 May 2006 – Camp Abu Naji /
Camp Sparrowhawk / Basra Air Station / Shaibah**

We've been expecting to drive back to Shaibah and everyone has steeled themselves for another marathon convoy. But if it's either that or stay in CAN, then I'll take eight hours staring at the Snatch in front of me and sweating like a glassblower's arse any day of the week. We were rocketed again last night, and from the way half the squadron have mild conniptions every time someone accidentally slams a door, I can sense it's starting to weigh on people.

But as it turns out we won't be driving after all. Instead, Jonty tells us, we'll be flying down, while the vehicles go back on HGVs. Apparently they're trying to keep Snatch movement to a minimum; while we've been away another four soldiers have been killed by IEDs. One of the incidents happened only yesterday; a troop leader and his driver from another cavalry unit, who copped an EFP into their cab on some nondescript side road in the north of Basra. But it's the other incident, in Qarmat Ali, where we'd been stoned on the way up here, which has got Jonty particularly exercised.

A patrol from the Royal Anglians had been approaching a bridge, he says tightly, aiming to cross on the left-hand side. They'd been redirected to the other carriageway by a cluster of Iraqi police flashing their lights and waving. The charitable interpretation is that they'd been warning the patrol not to cross the bridge against the flow of traffic. The less charitable – and only realistic – interpretation is that the police knew exactly what was waiting on the right-hand carriageway.

They were certainly nowhere to be seen ten seconds after an EFP went off and killed both top cover gunners in the lead Snatch. Which was probably very wise given the close proximity of a platoon of Royal Anglians, who'd happily have cut out their hearts with a bayonet. Jonty reminds us that if he catches any of his troop leaders following instructions from the Iraqi police, then we might as well put in an application to join them, because we'll be out of his squadron so fast our fucking feet won't touch.

We wander over to the tank park to help the HGV drivers strap on our Snatches. Most are civilian contractors from India, on track to make in a couple of months what it would take ten years to earn back home. I'm not sure if it's the money, or their certain conviction that whatever happens on Route Six it will all be part of the great circle of rebirth, but they are also quite the happiest people I've met in Iraq.

After the vehicles have been secured, they wave cheerfully and we leave them to it. It feels a bit incongruous that B Squadron, cocooned in body armour and bristling with guns, are being flown home because the drive is considered too dangerous, while these lads will have to do the whole thing with nothing to preserve them but a jaunty dashboard statue of a four-armed elephant god. But they seem to be fine with it.

According to Sgt Porter, on the last tour one of them had been blown clean out of his cab by an IED (ending up sprawled on the tarmac a bit like a four-armed elephant god himself, apparently). His first question upon regaining consciousness in the CAN medical centre was whether the casts would be off in time for him to do the drive back. Frankly it's a wonder we held on to India for as long as we did.

CAN itself has no runway, so we are decanted into half a dozen Saxons and driven a couple of miles to a desert airstrip called Camp Sparrowhawk. Saxons are apparently armoured personnel carriers, in the same way that I am apparently the greatest footballer on the planet. They are even older than Snatch, and have been such a roaring success that this infrequent taxi run is now their sole function in Iraq. They are also hot enough to slow cook anyone who is forced to sit inside one for three hours waiting for the RAF to turn up – like us, now – and the entire squadron hate everything about them.

The RAF for their part hate Camp Sparrowhawk; it's really just a patch of open desert where the Army occasionally insists they land a very expensive aircraft, and they worry endlessly about someone putting an IED on it when no one's looking. The Army can't see what those blue-job wets are fucking complaining about. They sweep the airstrip every time it's used, don't they?[26] But when the Hercules eventually does turn up, the loadmaster pulls us on board like he's got a stick of ginger up his arse, and the pilot takes off more or less vertically. Within a few minutes Maysan is nothing but a brownish-red haze.

Soon enough we're approaching Basra Air Station. The engine note changes and I tighten my grip on my bench seat for the 'tactical landing' I know is coming. Sat opposite me is a stout little man wearing a polo-shirt that says 'Ecolog', and underneath, 'Brian'. Brian is one of the small team of civilian contractors who're being paid an absolute fortune to run the creaking plumbing system in CAN.

Full credit to him for wearing the company polo – I've noticed that quite a few of his peers have taken to wearing plain safari shirts and cargo pants, and what they appear to think are steely, thousand-yard stares. Presumably they're hoping that some impressionable barista in the Welfare Village might take them for CIA or MI6, rather than a middle manager in charge of keeping the shitters going. But not Brian, who is still fast asleep as the aircraft gives its familiar, sickening lurch.

He doesn't stay asleep for long. As the Herc plummets, his eyelids snap open like roller blinds, and his mouth forms a gaping 'O' of terror, so wide he looks like a horrified Pez dispenser. No one can hear you scream in a Herc at full power, which is just as well because Brian looks like he's singing the song of a thousand kettles. Eyes bulging like a Mr Potato Head, he flings his hands out in a desperate grab for purchase. I have never seen a face quite like it and very nearly piss my combat trousers laughing.

The lads either side of him, who are clearly much nicer than me, grab his shoulders and mime landing motions. Gradually he seems to get it, and his great heaving breaths subside. I feel suddenly ashamed. The poor man; he clearly thought it was curtains. That was me a couple of weeks ago.

We land about five minutes later and I watch as Brian staggers weakly off the tailgate and into a waiting minibus. Presumably to go and look at pictures of his kids and ring Mrs Brian to discuss whether paying off the mortgage early is really worth it after all. B Squadron, conversely, go back to our familiar arrivals shed and lie on the floor for seven hours until someone eventually lets us have a helicopter. Then we fly back to Shaibah. Home.

Saturday, 5 June 2006 – Shaibah

In retrospect, it was a mistake leaving the PWRR's RSM down in Shaibah for Op BLAST; it means he's had time to come up with a 'training programme'. They say that nature abhors a vacuum, but I bet it doesn't abhor it nearly as much as the Army abhors an empty calendar. Particularly sergeant majors.

Normal people might look at a clear diary and see freedom, or a chance to indulge their hobbies; sergeant majors look at those empty little boxes and see *Battleship Potemkin* and the Kiel mutiny. So they fill the boxes, typing away ritualistically with two fingers, until they're full of cross-hatching and timings and different shades for different activities and packed-lunches-will-be-provided. And we've given the PWRR's RSM a clear two-week head start.

So life in Tiger Lines now comprises the kind of mind-numbing routine that even a closed order of hardcore Cistercians would find a bit much. We clean our weapons until you could do keyhole surgery with the longer bits. We clean the Snatches until pieces start coming off in our hands. We take all the rounds out of our magazines, count them, clean them individually, and then put them all back in again.

In between we do 'Military Skills' competitions. Quite why doing a hundred sit-ups while someone holds onto your legs qualifies as a 'Military Skill' beats me; on the other hand, I can see the 500m Snatch push coming in handy at some point. We also do endless 'Fun Runs', which is really only fifty-per-cent accurate. Then we start cleaning weapons again. In short, we do a level of pointless make-work that would have made the Reich Labour Service proud. All of a sudden even CAN doesn't seem that bad.

It's not all one-way traffic, though. B Squadron is full of independent thinkers and the boys are making their feelings known. In the beginning it was just graffiti in the loos; minor gems like, 'Why doesn't the RSM get tea breaks? Because it takes too long to retrain him,' or 'Why doesn't the RSM eat pickled onions? He can't get his head in the jar.' The stakes were raised a notch when someone took standing orders for Tiger Lines off the main notice-board and replaced them with a similar version for 'Stalag Luft PWRR': *Appel vill take place at zero sechs hundert hours; all personnel are reminded zat if zey continue to use ze vooden horse vizout cleaning it aftervards, zey vill be shot: by order of ze Camp Commandant.*

There have been a few escape attempts too. One of B Squadron's most successful wheezes involved the big air-conditioned coaches that constitute Shaibah's internal bus service. If the boys moved fast, they found they could dash out of Tiger Lines without anyone noticing, then ensconce themselves happily on the back seats with berets over their eyes, doing endless lazy circuits of camp in the cool. I even joined them once or twice, both sides discreetly pretending they hadn't seen the other.

Sadly, even the RSM eventually clocked that B Squadron's accommodation was practically empty, while the Shaibah bus service looked like the Mumbai Railway. They started stopping the coaches after that, ejecting protesting B Squadron soldiers like stowaways being flushed out of a lorry at Calais.

It all came to a head with PT uniforms though. The PWRR have an approved dress state for PT, just like they've probably got an approved dress state for going for a shit; black shorts, black socks, regimental T-shirt. We have squadron T-shirts of our own, but due to some balls-up with numbers not everyone got one before we left Germany. So they decided that B Squadron would be allowed a bit of latitude, as long as everyone kept it sensible. But the boys are resentful, and it wasn't long before they started pushing the envelope.

It began innocently enough, with minor flair like white socks or colourful trainers. Enough to make the RSM spasm slightly, but not enough to get in serious trouble. In due course the boys started mixing up their shorts; either hideously shiny three-quarter-length Nikes, or the kind of vanishingly tiny scrap of material Seb Coe might have worn at the 1984 Olympics. The denouement came with T-shirts. Muscle singlets were bad, football tops were worse, but when Womack jogged past the front gate of Tiger Lines this morning wearing a hot-pink crop-top with the word 'PIMP' written in gold sequins across his chest, the RSM blew a fucking ventricle. From now on, it's brown issue T-shirts only.

Wednesday, 14 June 2006 – Shaibah

Jonty wants some maps laminating. As the most junior troop leader by miles (and the only STAB, at that), it was only ever going to be my job. I am standing in the Squadron HQ tent surrounded by screwed-up sheets of laminate and muttering darkly, when Sgt Mason walks in. I inform him at length of the crashing unfairness of my life. He considers this, then asks if I've heard what happened to the honeysucker driver.

The honeysucker is the small tanker that goes round and round Shaibah emptying all the portaloos with a big rubber hose. Given it's June, this is southern Iraq, and there are 2,000 squaddies living here, it's a strong contender for Worst Job in the World, and the turnover in drivers is understandably high.

About three days ago, says Sgt Mason, a new one – let's call him Hashmat – was undergoing a bit of on-the-job training from a more experienced colleague. There isn't much to it, he's told; you put the hose inside the portaloo, set it to 'SUCK', turn it on, then wait until it's hoovered up all the turds before turning it off and moving onto the next one. The only real watch-out, Hashmat, is that the hose does have another setting: 'BLOW'. Whatever you do, Hashmat, make sure you haven't set the hose to 'BLOW'.

Inevitably, on his very first solo mission Hashmat immediately sets the hose to 'BLOW'. He is subsequently rescued, shrieking and covered head to toe in human shit, by some RAF firefighters, who strip him naked and hose him down on the taxiway.

Astonishingly, the very next day Hashmat is back at work, bright as a button and ready to put the past behind him. Perhaps even more astonishingly, on his very first portaloo of the day he sets the hose to 'BLOW' again. Once more resembling a human 99 Flake, Hashmat has to be rescued yet again by the RAF, who by now presumably think that maybe he's got some kind of very niche fetish going on. His second naked jet washing of the week complete, Hashmat completes the rest of his round without incident.

Perhaps this gives him false confidence, or perhaps it's just that the traffic out of Basra was bad that morning, because the next day Hashmat doesn't turn up for work at the appointed time of nine o'clock. But from the sounds of it he's a diligent employee, who doesn't want to lose a job he's only had for two days, and who probably suspects he might be on thin ice after that whole SUCK/BLOW thing.

Which would certainly explain why at a quarter past nine the two sentries on the Shaibah front gate are met with the alarming sight of a speeding honeysucker truck slaloming on two wheels through a queue of waiting vehicles, then pinballing off the sides of the anti-car bomb chicane straight towards them.

Without much choice in the matter – a flustered Hashmat hunched over his steering wheel and glancing at his watch muttering, 'come on, come oooon', probably *does* look a lot like a suicide bomber – they hit the sangar alarm and fire a burst of three rounds into the engine block. One of which goes straight through and hits Hashmat in the foot. He falls out of the cab screaming – and still fifteen minutes late for work – and is currently recovering in Shaibah's field hospital.

I immediately resolve never to complain about my job ever again.

Saturday, 24 June 2006 – Basra province

We've been in Iraq a couple of months now and haven't used the tanks once. So Jonty organises a range day in the desert, for us to check how many of them are still actually working. This is very wise; Challenger 2 is generally about as reliable as a Parisian baggage handler. Its supporters like to claim it's because it's a complex, sophisticated war machine; a thoroughbred, like Red Rum. Which is fair, providing you're talking about Red Rum as of now (i.e., ten years after they put him to sleep and turned him into glue).

We load the tanks onto some tank transporters and make for an abandoned Iraqi airbase a few dozen miles to the west. The PWRR intelligence cell thinks there's a handy six-laned motorway which goes almost all the way there. Presumably they also think we can levitate tank transporters, because it turns out that all the slip roads onto it were blown to smithereens during the invasion.

We drive bad-temperedly up and down looking for one that the US Air Force might have missed, and repeatedly confirming that no, you definitely can't drive an 80-ton tank transporter straight up a 45-degree slope. After the dozenth attempt, some anonymous joker starts whistling the *Benny Hill* theme tune over the squadron net and Jonty blows a gasket. Eventually we arrive at the airbase, three hours late and in a foul mood, and unload the tanks.

Mr Kite talks us through the rules of the 'range'. It doesn't take long; from where we're standing on the edge of the runway there is nothing in front of us apart from 150 miles of desert and the Saudi border.

In the UK, range days are miserable; dull, wet, and endlessly interrupted by elderly dog walkers doddering happily past, somehow unaware that the air ten feet above Patch's head is being ripped apart by a machine gun firing 800 rounds per minute. This range is nothing like that, and for the next hour our little patch of sand rings to the sound of cyclic fire and whooping as we pour out weeks' worth of Tiger Lines frustration into the desert.

We fire machine guns from the hip like Arnie in *Commando*, and our pistols on their sides like Tupac. We fire until our rifle barrels are red hot and the ground around our feet is piled with empty cases. We even fire our baton guns[27] straight up in the air and then play chicken, seeing who can stand still the longest as the heavy plastic rounds *thunk* into the tarmac around our feet. In short, we dick about with deadly firearms in ways I didn't know were possible. It's like a Kentucky wedding.

Finally it's time for the main event: firing the tanks. As the other troop leaders never get bored of reminding me, filthy military casuals like me aren't allowed on tanks, so I sit on my Snatch and watch as they roar up and down pretending they're at El

Alamein. In fairness it's quite impressive; ten Challenger 2s all firing their main gun simultaneously sounds like the End of Days.

Then out of the corner of my eye I notice a small figure pelting across the runway, waving his hands above his head. It's Sgt Porter. He sprints past me and grabs the handset of a radio in the next Snatch over.

'All callsigns, STOP, STOP, STOP!' he bellows. 'There's fucking Bedouins on the range. I . . . say again, STOP, STOP, STOP!'

I look down the range and nearly swallow my tongue. There, in the shimmering far distance, I can just make out a pickup full of people moving slowly left to right. In front of me, heads start popping out of tank hatches, looking confused.

It's the brass they're after, pants Sgt Porter, bending over with his hands on his knees. Apparently they're mad keen for empty cases to melt down and sell for scrap. It makes sense; we've just gone through about a year's ammunition allowance in two hours and there's probably several thousand pounds' worth of metal lying on the floor. It's also fucking suicidal, and a minor miracle that the Bedouins' pickup isn't a smoking crater with a bit of hair stuck to the edges by now. Jonty calls me on the radio and tells me to go and get the Wombles of Western Basra off our range.

I head down in a Snatch with Sgt Porter to find a few small boys plucking away industriously at the ground picking up shell cases, and half a dozen men trying to lift one of the huge metal tank targets into their pickup. We haven't brought any interpreters so this will be a mime job. I'm not sure what the International Sign Language is for, 'This range is utterly deserted 364 days a year, lads; why the ever-loving fuck would you try to collect scrap metal on the one day it's like Passchendaele?', but I give it a go. Next to me I see Sgt Porter gesticulating madly in support.

The Bedouin stare at us blankly. Then one of them detaches himself from the group and puts his arm around me, murmuring reassuringly. Clearly they've concluded I'm having some sort of mental episode. Another one disappears into the pickup and comes back with two glasses of tea.

It's a complete waste of time, of course; they want their brass, and if getting hosed down by ten Challenger 2s didn't stop them, then Sgt Porter and I bebopping away in front of them like Bez from the Happy Mondays definitely won't. So we give in and help them pick it up. The matter of the tank targets is more vigorously debated; eventually we settle on an unspoken agreement whereby Sgt Porter and I are allowed to retrieve them from the back of the pickup and replace them carefully on their stands, and the Bedouin are allowed to come back thirty seconds after we've left for Shaibah and nick them anyway.

We shake hands. The Bedouin look very pleased, and obviously consider their brief head-to-head with 750 tons of British armour to have been well worth it. I'm fairly gratified myself; the kids' ragged clothes and bare feet tell their own story about how poor these people are. Anything we can do to make their lives even slightly easier is A-OK by me.

While no one ever pretended we'd spend this tour building donkey sanctuaries or fingerpainting with orphans, it also hasn't escaped anyone's notice that we've been in Iraq two months now and have yet to really help anyone. Directly, anyway. I know why, of course; it's tricky to Angelina Jolie your way around the country when half the population are actively trying to vaporise you. But it doesn't stop me wondering why it is that letting some Bedouin have our empty shell cases is probably the most useful thing we've done since we got here.

10

2 BLAST 2 BLURIOUS

Just towards the back of Shaibah, a five-minute walk from Tiger Lines, lay the old RAF station. It was gutted by the time we arrived of course, but the buildings were still up, and it didn't take much imagination to put yourself there in 1925; rickety biplanes trundling over the uneven sand on take-off, and pilots in their tan tropical uniforms drinking pink gin on the terrace after the heat had died down. It was also a salient reminder that this wasn't our first rodeo in Iraq.

It had all started – like lots of other things in what would turn out to be quite a busy year – in 1914. Ironically our first invasion really *was* about the oil. With the Ottoman regime having declared for the Kaiser, the Royal Navy was now a bit too reliant on Persia for fuel. As far as the British government was concerned, they didn't have a choice *but* to invade. Basra fell within a week of our landings, but Baghdad was a tougher nut altogether. At the first attempt to take it in 1916, 13,000 British soldiers went into the bag.

Later on it transpired that they'd only been sent north in the first place (by Kitchener, no less) to seize Baghdad for the prestige, with the plan then to immediately abandon it again as tactically useless. This was the first recorded CORGI (*Commanding Officer's Really Good Idea*) in the history of the British Army in Iraq, and at least serves to put into perspective some of the more mental stuff they were asking us to do ninety years later.

In those days getting a hiding from Johnny Turk was enough to cause a serious outbreak of apoplexy on Horseguards, so they took another run-up at Baghdad in 1917. This one worked, and the city fell to a General Maude, who presumably enjoyed it very much for the nine months he had left before dying abruptly of cholera. Interestingly he also issued something called the Baghdad Proclamation, containing the line, 'our armies do not come into your cities and lands as conquerors or enemies, but as liberators'. Which just goes to show, you're never as original as you think you're being.

That was more or less it for our first excursion to Iraq, and the Armistice followed shortly afterwards. The real question was what came next. To the Arabs living in Baghdad, Mosul and Basra provinces (who had recently woken up one morning to find that they were no longer Ottomans but 'Mesopotamians') the answer was clear: independence. After all, hadn't T.E. Lawrence been running around the wider region for months now, blowing up Ottoman railways and promising the Arabs exactly that?

The League of Nations pointed out that most Mesopotamians had completely swerved *that* particular call to arms, so couldn't very well start crying freedom now. Instead Mesopotamia was designated a 'Class A Mandate', under British control. Class A status meant the Mesopotamians had 'reached a stage of development where their existence as an independent nation can be provisionally recognised', but were still not seen as 'able to stand by themselves under the strenuous conditions of the modern world'.

Less than pleased at being patted on the head and told to run along in case their brains overheated, the Mesopotamians revolted in May 1920. They did so *en masse*, the differences between Sunni and Shia temporarily put aside, thus proving that just like the World Cup, you can bring even the most disparate communities together as long as it means giving the English a shoeing.

In response Churchill sent in the RAF, giving rise to two myths still peddled to this day; firstly that they dropped poison gas on the rebels (they didn't, though to be fair Churchill did confess to being mystified at the War Office's 'squeamishness' about doing so), and secondly, that Iraq's (surprisingly many) ginger-haired citizens are all direct descendants of RAF pilots shot down during raids and co-opted into marriage by local tribes. Given that the RAF lost only nine men during the course of the entire campaign, this is either untrue, or suggests pilots of such epic horniness that it's no wonder they crashed given the amount of testosterone that must have been sloshing round the cockpit.

By October it was all over. We'd technically won, but the rebels did succeed in killing the mandate. It was replaced by an Anglo-Iraqi treaty (Iraq being derived from Uruk, the much older Arab name for the region) which allowed for self-government, while still ensuring we could keep a paternal eye on minor matters like all foreign relations and the military. In choosing a king to run the whole thing, we dispensed with the tired old tradition of picking someone who the locals had ever heard of, and appointed one Faisal ibn Hasayn, who'd been born in Mecca and whose CV boasted a whole six months as King of Syria before his violent deposition.

In all fairness Faisal didn't make a total hash of it, and ended up negotiating the kingdom's notional independence in 1932. It wasn't the real deal – we reserved the right to 'advise' on government affairs, keep our military bases, and so on – but it was a start. Faisal died the following year in Switzerland during his annual check-up, of an apparent heart attack. Which came as a surprise to everyone, not least the team of Swiss doctors who had just pronounced him fit as a fiddle.

He was succeeded by his son, Prince Ghazi, whose ardent Iraqi nationalism was matched only by his love of spanking around Baghdad's pleasant avenues in sports cars. He died in one of the latter in 1939 after a crash about as convincing as his old man's heart attack (and which, as CAN's name implied, the locals still thought we'd arranged). Faisal II, his asthmatic infant son, duly succeeded him, with his uncle acting as Regent until such time as his handwriting improved.

Then came the Second World War. At first everything went smoothly; Iraq broke off relations with Germany and made all the right noises about guaranteeing oil supplies. This lasted two years before the Iraqi Army launched a coup d'état, kicked out the Regent, and installed a pro-Nazi cabinet. Frankly, in 1941, with London taking a beating and Rommel running riot in the desert, this was something we could have done without. The response was roughly along the same lines as in 1914; land near Basra, head north, and it's Baghdad or bust, boys.

After a sticky start at RAF Habbaniya – where the Iraqi Army caught our garrison so short-handed that they had to reactivate the decorative artillery pieces in front of the Officers' Mess just to have something to shoot back with – it all went like a charm. The Regent was re-installed by June, and we ended up staying in force for another six years to prevent any more dicking about. Which pleased the growing ranks of Iraqi nationalists no end.

After our occupation came to an end, Faisal II's government tried to keep a lid on things, but it was never going to last; between Nasser flying the flag for Arab independence in Egypt and a struggling economy at home, some sort of convulsion was inevitable. It ended up arriving in 1958 in the form of another military coup. Faisal was killed on the steps of his palace in Baghdad and his Hashemite dynasty died with him. Iraq was declared a republic, and those British forces remaining in the country were kicked out shortly afterwards. This time for good. We wouldn't be back for another thirty years.

Monday, 10 July 2006 – Maysan

One of the Army's absolute favourite sayings – up there with classics like, 'You're in your own time now,' and 'I don't mind if it takes all fucking night, fellas; my tea's a salad' – goes something like, 'Time spent in reconnaissance is seldom wasted.'

I'd learned what it meant at Sandhurst, when I didn't bother with a recce before the final attack, led a platoon assault on the wrong hill, then got chased up the correct one by a colour sergeant offering to rip out my ribcage and 'play it like a fucking xylophone'. The PWRR battlegroup engineer learned what it meant fifteen minutes ago, when the first HGV in the convoy drove straight into a low-hanging power line.

To no one's great surprise, Maysan has missed yet another deadline for PIC. If it was the Wild West before, then by now it's *A Fistful of Dollars* meets *Terminator 2*. The last time the CAN battlegroup ventured into al Amarah in force, they'd had to fire more than 7,000 rounds to get themselves out again, and very nearly lost a Warrior.

So we are on the way back up to CAN for another go at Op BLAST (they're calling it Op BLAST II, which is a bit disappointing; 2 BLAST 2 BLURIOUS was *right* there). No one is exactly thrilled about this, but at least it's two weeks away from the RSM and his ongoing crusade to turn Tiger Lines into a Soviet Young Pioneer camp.

By now driving up Route Six in a Snatch is like flying up the Death Star trench in an X-Wing, so we're trying something new. Instead of following the Tigris straight up to Maysan we'll head forty miles west into the desert from Shaibah, then make a sharp right, up through the Rumaylah oil fields and the Central Marshes, flummoxing the militias and arriving dusty and triumphant in CAN like pioneers of the Old West. Ours is a smallish, experimental convoy, mainly Snatches, with three HGVs to prove the going for heavier vehicles. But if it works, this could be a whole new supply route for much larger convoys to al Amarah in future, avoiding Route Six entirely.

That was the plan anyway. And to be fair, it was going quite well. Right up until the HGV hit that messy tangle of power lines at the edge of the village in front of us. Route selection and reconnaissance, including a thorough check for obstacles – like, for example, electricity pylons three feet shorter than the tallest vehicle in your convoy – is the battlegroup engineer's job. Which explains why he's now standing on the verge staring blankly at an HGV wrapped in wiring, and presumably wondering whether the Deloitte grad scheme has any spaces left.

The first the HGV driver knew of it was a choked 'blaaaaargh' sound from his top cover as he was abruptly clotheslined, Stone Cold Steve Austin-style. Luckily it seems that this village is in the middle of a power cut, which means he's at least avoided becoming a human earthing wire for the Iraqi national grid. Even more luckily we'd been going quite slowly, and several of the lines had snapped; a faster convoy, or newer power lines, and his head might well have ended up in the driver's lap. I expect the RSM would still have made him do the next Shaibah Fun Run though.

The convoy commander – a red-faced PWRR major whose current vibe would make Ivan the Terrible look like Dipsy the Tellytubby – gives the battlegroup engineer some concise thoughts on how he feels today has gone so far. Then he stamps up and down the convoy, apparently working through all seven major stages of grief. Everyone else, me included, fixes their gaze on some imaginary point in the middle distance and tries not to catch his eye.

I can see why he's grieving; up ahead there are at least another dozen power and telephone lines just like the one the HGV is tangled in. And the road we're on is a single lane on top of a levee, with a fifteen-foot drop to marshes either side. There's certainly nowhere obvious to turn the trucks around; the last main road was twenty miles ago. The ops room has already been on the net twice, enquiring with acid politeness about whether the valuable supplies in the HGVs couldn't be put to better use in CAN, rather than on the outskirts of a small Iraqi village in the middle of fucking nowhere. And it will be dark in less than two hours.

Possibly somewhere between 'denial' and 'bargaining', the convoy commander stops stamping and bellows for all the officers to gather round the bonnet of his Snatch.

'Right – fuck this,' he announces. 'If we don't get a move on we're going to be out here all night. Get back to your vehicles, and we'll just fucking drive through.'

I glance at Godders, who raises an eyebrow. This village isn't a known trouble spot; not least because we're probably the first British soldiers they've ever seen. But drag racing down their high street and ripping out all their power lines is a good way of making it one. It's a shame we don't have Jonty here – he's been on R&R and will join us in CAN – because the convoy commander outranks us all and I don't like the look of the slightly mad gleam in his eye.

Like most of the PWRR, he seems very 'Infantry'. That is to say he hasn't yet encountered a problem in life which he doesn't think can be solved with a knife-hand chop and a confident, 'Right – fuck this.' The battlegroup engineer is no use; he's retired dazedly to his Snatch and is sitting in the front, staring through the windscreen like Whistler's Mother. In my mind's eye I can already see the locals pulling their AKs out from under their beds and ringing their boss to let them know they'll be ten minutes late for work.

Mike is the senior troop leader and we all eye-fuck him relentlessly until he quietly clears his throat.

'Er, sir . . . do you think we might instead want to think about . . .'

'What the fuck is that guy doing?' says Sgt Mason abruptly, from behind me.

I look up, and see an Iraqi standing on top of the HGV.

This isn't unusual, of course; by this point in the campaign the locals are clambering on our vehicles on a regular basis. But those vehicles tend to be either upside down or on fire (or both), while the Iraqis hit them with their shoes and chant 'Death to the British'. This Iraqi, by contrast, seems to want to help. He is brandishing a long wooden pole and gibbering animatedly to himself while he lifts up the power lines draped over the HGV's cab.

He's also only wearing one shoe and has a haircut like Stig of the Dump. In fact he's clearly, God love him, what my grandmother would have called a 'head-the-ball'.[28] But he's also the only man in this convoy with a plan. And it's a good one, too. We drive the HGVs forward slowly, one by one, while the Wild Man of the Marshes leaps nimbly around on top of them holding the wires up with his stick so they can pass underneath. Every time he does, I steel myself for a blue flash and a breakdancing Iraqi to fall off our lorry, but it never happens. He must know something we don't.

After about forty-five minutes we're through. Our lovely assistant jumps to the ground and we pile water and rations at his feet in tribute, while he coos and chuckles in delight. From the way the other locals gently lead him away by the arm as we leave, it does seem like he is some kind of ward of the village. I just hope there's someone to look after him, and that he's happy.

One thing's for sure; we owe him. He might not be playing with quite the full deck, but he's just saved us from a nasty detour, and potentially his own village from an abrupt return to the Stone Age. Perhaps most importantly, he's gifted B Squadron a really excellent dig at the PWRR. After all, it's not every day you see someone out-planned by a literal village idiot.

Tuesday, 11 July 2006 – Camp Abu Naji

We've been back in CAN all of twenty minutes before we're reminded that – the RSM's All Units Egg and Spoon Race Invitationals notwithstanding – Shaibah isn't such a bad place after all. I'm cleaning out the Snatches with the troop when a roar like an Intercity 125 sends all of us sprawling in the dust. No one says anything; it is pure feral instinct. And I swear I actually see the fucker – a long black tube flashing past the top of the Hesco next to us – before there is a shattering explosion and the shrapnel whines overhead.

The rocket has landed just the other side of the wall; ten feet lower and Jonty would have been scrubbing a whole troop off the ration return. Brooksie is even luckier; he'd *been* on the other side of the wall, coming back from the loo. He'd stopped to tie a shoelace, he tells us later, and was about to stand up again when the rocket slammed into the sand forty yards ahead of him. He is untouched, but looks about one ill-timed party popper from bursting into tears.

This kind of thing is now par for the course in CAN, and people have started sleeping in their body armour. In response, we've dug in some mortars of our own. Not to fire back – the ban on lobbing high explosives into al Amarah still stands – but instead to put up illumination rounds. These burst at a height of about a thousand feet, ejecting a brilliant white flare that hangs under a parachute and floats to earth, lighting up the desert for hundreds of metres in every direction.

The theory seems to be that we'll light up the militia mortar crews like rabbits being lamped, and that they'll somehow stand frozen in shock for long enough for a Warrior full of hairy-arsed PWRR to turn up and kick their heads in. It feels like a long shot. Even better, CAN is now getting hit so much that in order to save ammunition, our own mortars only fire illum when something actually lands inside camp. I'm not an expert in counter-battery tactics, but it doesn't feel like sending up an 80,000-candlepower 'BULLSEYE!' every time your enemy hits something important is the most sensible idea we've had this week.

11

Mines

Wednesday, 12 July 2006 – Maysan

After three IDF attacks last night – two of which were good enough to qualify for a luminescent thumbs-up from our own mortars – it's almost a relief to be told we're heading out on patrol. According to Jonty our objective is the Iranian border, which lies about eighty miles north. We are to take two days' rations, a Psychological Operations team, and a satellite phone; eighty miles is about seventy-five miles further than our radios can manage, even on a good day. We'll be visiting remote police and border posts, flying the flag to the locals, and reminding everyone that – despite the fact they probably haven't seen a British soldier in two years – we are actually still here.

We ditch the Snatches for open-top Land Rovers; according to CAN's intelligence cell (Motto: '*We* Bet *Your* Life'), the IED threat further north is 'minimal' and if we stick to backroads we'll be 'golden'. Sgt Mason stares bleakly at the pigeon-chested corporal who tells us this and growls that if we do get IED'd, he should make sure he brings a 'gumshield', but we decide to take their word for it.

As the boys line the Land Rovers up in the morning sun, all roll bars and camouflage netting, it's hard not to let your imagination wander. This is the Long Range Desert Group, the SAS, Paddy Mayne crouched behind a Vickers gun ready to give the Luftwaffe the Good News. This is adventure.

We stop by the front gate and pick up an interpreter. Musad looks like he's in his mid-fifties, unusually old for a terp. From the way he trudges along the well-worn path from the accommodation block, carved out by the dragging feet of dozens like him, I guess that a two-day patrol to the Iranian border is not exactly top of his bucket list.

After a mile or so on Route Six, we plunge off it and onto the back roads north. They're rutted single tracks, but our Land Rovers eat up every jolt. We only stop once, for a VP check on a dead cow next to the road. Carcasses are a popular spot for IEDs, the militias having rightly concluded that no one wants to root through Buttercup's bloated corpse looking for a command wire. This time it's Womack who loses the coin toss, and comes back five minutes later, gagging and threatening to wipe his hands all over Greene's fucking face if he doesn't stop laughing.

Then we're away again; on our left the scrubby green fields of the Tigris flood plain, on our right a billiard flat desert. The miles slip away, every passing minute another sixty seconds away from CAN, and its mortars and rockets and rules about trousers. The troop is on cloud nine; my headset is filled with happy banter and even Womack sounds like he's recovered.

It must have been catching, because a couple of hours later I hear myself suggesting we stop for a swim in a small stream coming off the Tigris. The OPTAG staff would have had an aneurism at the very thought of it, but we haven't seen a soul in an hour and the sun is sparkling off the water in a way that tells me it'd be a crime to miss this chance.

Musad just shakes his head when we ask if he's joining, and we leave Womack with his Minimi on the bank, but the rest of the troop are soon buck naked and frolicking like water nymphs. They all look very young. It's easy to forget that under the layers of uniform and Robocop body armour there are such gawky adolescent bodies. Except for Sgt Mason, of course, who looks like a silverback at a swimming gala. God knows what their mothers think.

We arrive at our first stop – a small village called Ali al Gharbi – in such good spirits that even a two-hour inspection of the police station can't wipe the grins off our faces. It's the usual story. Half the workforce are at their cousins' funeral in Baghdad, the keys to the evidence locker are with Mahmoud, who's visiting the outermost ice-water rings of Saturn, and the station itself would make the *Marie Celeste* look lively. But it's hard to get annoyed on a day like this.

We don't even miss a beat when the station commander looks us straight in the eye and tells us he doesn't think there's any smuggling here. This is a spectacular fib, even for the Iraqi police – we're five miles from the Iranian border and this bit sees more illicit trading than the Barbary Coast – but we just nod and smile anyway.

While Sgt Mason finishes up, I wander outside to see how the PsyOps team are getting on. It's a grand title for a couple of chubby reservists who've been rushed through a brief course on the myriad complexities of the human mind (which should take, as far as the Army's concerned, just shy of two weeks) and poured into a set of desert combats. Then again, you don't exactly need to be Derren Brown to hand out a few leaflets and play pre-recorded Arabic messages on a loudspeaker. And the local press is streets ahead of us in the propaganda game anyway.

One of the most popular headlines at the moment is about how we're losing a hundred soldiers killed per week, but then loading the corpses into a Hercules and pushing them all out over the Persian Gulf so no one finds out. Another is that we have released a scourge of man-eating honey badgers into Basra to terrorise the local population. You have to take your hat off to the journalists responsible; they make the *Sunday Sport* look like the *FT Market Report*. They have also so convinced the locals that the Army recently had to put out a press release saying: 'We can categorically state that we have not released man-eating honey badgers into Basra.'

I find the PsyOps team surrounded by a smallish crowd and ask them what they've gleaned about the locals' feelings. Dick all, is the refreshingly honest answer. They don't speak a lick of Arabic between them and we've got the only interpreter on the patrol inside the police station. Still, no one's stoning us, so they'd give it a solid 8/10 for atmospherics.

I pick up one of the leaflets they're handing out. It's a two-panel cartoon; the right one shows a darkened alleyway filled with demonic eyes, and three children clutching at one another in terror. The other one shows a pair of terrorists locked in a cage, with the same children gleefully playing football next to it. On the back is a phone number for CAN. Underneath is some Arabic script, which presumably tells the reader that if they're tired of life, they can always commit suicide by ringing it up and reporting local militia activity to the British Army. I don't expect we get many takers; CAN is seventy miles away, but it may as well be on the moon as far as the people of Ali al Gharbi are concerned.

Time is ticking on, so we leave our new friends with their leaflets and tell them that we hope they find them helpful (or at least absorbent). Then we head out into the desert. We will lie up somewhere remote overnight before dropping in on a couple of border forts tomorrow.

This area was one of the most bitterly contested fronts in the Iran–Iraq war, and all around us is a warren of trench systems, revetments, and vast defensive earthworks which must have held battalions of tanks back in the day. It's also seeded with about 25 million landmines, so we stick to marked tracks for our sightseeing. We stop for a quick VP check and I spot a helmet lying on the verge. I pick it up; it's made of some kind of compressed canvas and has 'Product of Korea' stamped on the inside. I wonder which one. The poor bastards.

An hour or so after leaving Ali al Gharbi, we find a good spot and leaguer up the vehicles. While the boys sort themselves out for the night Sgt Mason and I chat to Musad, the interpreter. It soon becomes clear why he's been in such a funk all day; this is the exact sector he'd fought in during the Iran–Iraq war.

No wonder he's been low; while we've been Gumball-rallying through the desert and going wild swimming, he's been curled up in the back of my Land Rover reliving the worst years of his life to the soundtrack of some foreign knucklehead prattling on about the awesome blown-up tank he's just seen. He had spent three years up here, he tells us. I stare at the battered moonscape around me; it certainly puts our bitching about the Welfare Sauna into perspective. Apparently the Iranians had had regiments of artillery in the mountains on their side of the border, so you could only move at night. Once, he'd moved during the day. And they'd caught him in the open.

At this Musad pulls up his shirt and shows us a colossal, jagged scar running diagonally across practically his entire torso. We gape. He must have been gutted like a fish. He'd been taking ammunition to a forward machine-gun post, he explains, when an Iranian shell had exploded a few yards away, ripping open his chest and stomach and bowling him into a slight dip in the ground. He'd called for help but knew it was useless; any kind of rescue attempt would only have prompted more shells. He could either wait for nightfall, if he even lived that long, or make his own way back. So he'd made his own way back.

Too afraid to roll onto his front in case his intestines fell out, he had used his heels to push himself, inch by inch, the hundred yards back to his own trench. By some miracle he'd survived long enough to reach a field surgeon, who had sewn him up with 400 stitches and packed him off home to Basra. He hadn't been back here since. Until the British Army had stuck him in the back of a

Land Rover and taken him on a Magical Mystery Tour through a twenty-year back catalogue of psychological anguish.

Well, there's not much you can say to that – 'sorry' doesn't really cut it when you've just accidentally press-ganged someone onto the Good Ship PTSD and pushed them firmly down the slipway. So we leave Musad with his thoughts, and some ration pack Biscuits (Fruit) by way of a gesture. The poor man.

The sun in the desert sets fast, but the moon's so bright you could have read a newspaper article about the British Army's latest model of hunter-killer honey badger by it. With the boys bedded down, I wander slowly away from our leaguer into the greyscale desert. In the distance I can just make out the gas flares from oil wells further south, painting the horizon a dull orange. Otherwise there is not a trace of human life to be seen.

I squat for a moment in the sand and stare back at the dark outlines of the vehicles. The air is utterly still. Even a small cough from one of the cot beds a hundred yards away sounds like a gunshot, and I wonder how Musad is doing in this blanketing silence, surrounded by his ghosts. I don't think I have ever been anywhere so remote, and it is awesome – in the original meaning of the word. Not to mention the most serene poo I've ever had.

Thursday, 13 July 2006 – Iran–Iraq border

We're up at dawn and after a quick breakfast we start driving towards the border fort we're due to visit. I keep a close eye on my GPS; despite the fact that the countryside round here looks like the Maginot Line, there's no actual fence showing where Iraq finishes and Iran starts. Even if there were, the Iranians don't give a tinker's toss about trivial shit like internationally recognised borders and will happily light up anyone they consider is getting too close. Either way, I don't fancy accidentally leading the first British invasion of Persia since 1941, so I tell Sgt Mason to keep checking his GPS too.

After about an hour we arrive at the fort. It's been built for the

Iraqis by American engineers. They've clearly been watching a lot of *Beau Geste*; it has whitewashed walls, a guard tower in each corner, and crenellations cut into the wall at the top. About a kilometre away, on the other side of the border, is another fort almost exactly like it. As we climb out of the Land Rovers I can see some small figures milling about on its roof. They pull a tarpaulin off something that looks a lot like a heavy machine gun. It's all willy-waving, of course – they're almost certainly not going to use it – but they do appear to have quite a big and dangerous-looking willy, so we don't hang about getting inside the fort and out of sight.

The guys who garrison this place are from the Department of Border Enforcement. It's a new outfit but the basic border-guard job description is as old as time; sit in your fort, stare at your opposite number sitting in *his* fort, and try not to put a bullet in your brain with the sheer unrelenting tedium of it all.

The DBE boys have two main jobs. The first is to keep an eye on the Iranians and make sure they don't invade, in which they seem to do a decent job; we certainly haven't seen a single Ayatollah the whole time we've been here. The second is to stem the endless tide of smuggled goods across the border, in which they seem to make King Canute look like a fucking effective operator. It's not entirely their fault: each fort has to cover a shade over thirty kilometres of border, and the smugglers have been at it for generations. But that doesn't stop this area being a major crossing point for everything from consumer electronics to the same 107mm Chinese rockets that are scaring the shit out of everyone in CAN three times a night.

The DBE seem delighted that we're here. And it's not the usual feigned pleasure, stalling you at the front door with pistachio nuts and tea while someone else hides all the smuggled VCRs. This feels genuine. Once they've got over the fact of their real-life human visitors, they even insist on laying on breakfast. I get the distinct sense that no one comes to see these lads much.

If we thought the police live in austere conditions, the DBE is something else. The shift pattern is supposed to be three weeks on and one week off, explains Musad, but such are the vagaries of transport and resupply that some of them end up doing months at a time. There is a generator and a well, but that's about it for creature comforts.

We sit down for breakfast and a chat. They've provided some bread and tea, while we contribute a few ration packs, which as far as the DBE are concerned is the tasting menu at The Fat Duck. As they tuck into British Army corned beef hash with broad smiles – there is a first time for everything – I ask Musad what the DBE do for fun. He doesn't translate the question. He just stares at me briefly then answers out of the side of his mouth.

'These men are here for a long time,' he murmurs.

'Well, yeah. But what do they do for fun? Do they have a television?'

'It is a very long time,' repeats Musad gravely. 'Sometimes for months they do not see their families, or their wives.'

'Yes, but what do they *do* all day? You know, when they're not doing patrols or on sentry. Sports? You know, football?'

Musad looks me straight in the eye, and sighs.

'There is no room for football. The guards have nothing, the Ministry sends them nothing. They are here for a . . . very . . . long . . . time,' he says, very deliberately. 'They must find . . . other things to do.'

I stare back at him for a moment. Then my eyes must have widened, for Musad nods his head almost imperceptibly.

'*Other . . . things?*' I whisper.

'Other things,' he confirms solemnly.

I look back at the convivial little group around the breakfast plates. They do seem very close. I'd taken it for the natural cama-raderie of men who spend all their time together, but on reflection there is *quite* a lot of arm touching. I think back to when they came out to say hello. Had one of those guards been riding another one piggy-back, or was I misremembering things?

Then I catch the eye of the DBE guard sitting opposite me. He is wearing eyeliner. And not the light touch of kohl you sometimes see on the older Iraqis; this lad looks ready to be the face of Elizabeth Arden's Spring collection. He smiles coquettishly then bats his eyelids and looks away. Holy shit.

It shouldn't be a surprise, of course. Firstly, these men are soldiers, and it's a well-documented fact that we've all been fiddling with one another since the Sacred Band of Thebes. Secondly, they live in a country where even the suggestion of premarital sex is a pretty reliable precursor to a bout of epic interfamilial bloodletting. Finally, they're in the DBE, who can probably add 'living in the middle of fucking nowhere' to a long list of reasons they won't be pinging a bra strap any time soon.

That's not to say, of course, that some of these guys wouldn't still be gay in any other circumstances; I'm sure the DBE are as spread all over the wondrous scatterplot of human sexuality as the rest of us. But it's quite likely that lots of them are batting for the same team mainly because most of the other side have been forced into a *niqab* and locked in the changing rooms by their mothers until some poor bastard can scrape together a year's wages for a dowry. Maybe it's Maybelline, maybe it's just because Mahmoud looks fine as hell when it's been three months since you so much as saw a woman. I doubt they'd even consider themselves gay; like Musad said, they probably just see it as, 'other things to do'.

More power to them as far as I'm concerned. They can put 'I Will Survive' on loop and run their border post like the Stonewall Inn if they want, as long as they at least try to stop the Iranians shipping high explosives over the border.

Fortunately it seems that unlike for the police, no one up in HQ has yet had time to draw up 45,000 questions on recycling policies or who the mental health first aider is for the DBE. So after a quick wander round and the usual empty promises to look into getting them a Smeg fridge and an espresso machine, we make our excuses.

It's probably not a moment too soon; a couple of the guards seem to have conceived a violent affection for Cameron and keep trying to wrestle him. You can tell from Cameron's face that he's started to wonder whether all this horseplay is quite normal. The last thing I need is to explain to Jonty that one of my soldiers is now working as an indentured sex slave in a remote DBE fort, so after what briefly becomes some kind of erotically charged tickle fight, we prise Cameron out of their arms then head back to the Land Rovers.

We need to go south next; there's a tarmac road but it looks like it goes the long way round. Before we leave, I ask one of the guards what they reckon about using the various tracks I can see marked on my map instead. It's probably not best practice to ask the locals for advice like this, but these guys are DBE not police, and they all seem pretty on side. My new pal beams, nods vigorously, and via Musad, pronounces the tracks 'totally fine'.

Ten minutes later, it becomes evident that the DBE have a very different take on the meaning of 'totally fine' than the rest of the world. Either that or Musad missed the second half of a sentence that concluded with the words, '. . . as long as you're OK with landmines, that is.'

Head down reading my map, the first I know of the problem is when Griffiths slams on the brakes and my face abruptly pancakes into the dashboard. Before the squawk of outrage has even died on my lips, he points at the Land Rover in front. We have almost gone into the back of it. Then I hear Cpl Robbins clear his throat on the PRR.

'Er, boss, I think this might be a fucking minefield. I can see pressure plates. There's some behind us, too.'

Oh, brilliant. *Brilliant.*

I feel a surge of panic rising in my chest and suppress it with difficulty. We're on a marked track; how in fuck's name have we ended up in a *minefield*? Then I feel a nudge on my arm.

'Look,' says Griffiths, pointing. I follow his finger. The track here is sunken, with the ground either side at about waist height. Just outside Griffiths's window sits a squat green canister about the size of a baked bean can, with prongs sticking out of the top. It's connected via wire to a second canister just like it ten yards behind us. Ten yards behind *that* there is another one, also wired up. I feel my heart start trying to rabbit punch its way out of my chest. I know what those canisters are. They are Valmara-69s.

We had a couple of briefs on mines on PDT, and these have stuck in my memory, largely because I couldn't conceive of what kind of sick fuck would invent them in the first place. Valmara-69s are bounding mines, so called because when one is triggered, a small charge in the base of the mine explodes and propels it up to waist height. A tether wire, attached to the ground, then tugs on a spring-loaded firing pin which in turn detonates the main charge, sending about a thousand pre-cut steel fragments whirring out viciously in all directions. It has a lethal range of 25 metres. The one outside Griffiths's window is ten feet away.

I dig my fingers hard into my palms, fighting the waves of adrenaline. We're in real trouble here. The rulebook for minefields is clear; you freeze, you warn everyone around you, then you request engineer support and wait for them to get you out. If engineers aren't available then you self-extract using your personal mine kit. This sounds more technical than it is; in essence it just means lying on your belly and prodding hopefully into the topsoil with a metal stick.

The idea is that your prodder will plink harmlessly against the side of a buried mine, thereby allowing you to mark and avoid it (as opposed to crawling over the top of it and abruptly salmoning 200 feet into the air), before going on your way. It's exacting, dangerous, and more importantly, it takes *hours*. Literally – the rule of thumb is an hour for every ten yards. If we try it here, we'll be out for a month.

The engineer option doesn't sound great either. It's the best part of a day to CAN by road from here; even if our rescuers came by helicopter, it'll be the afternoon before they get to us. The threat level this far north might be low, but spending several hours sat in exactly the same spot, like some kind of military diorama entitled, *Utterly Fucked: Why They Shouldn't Have Listened to the DBE*, is asking for trouble. Self-extracting is painful at the best of times; trying to do it while getting battered by 7.62mm from the boys of the Ali al Gharbi militia doesn't even bear thinking about. And if I request engineer support, it'll mean telling the ops room what I've done.

This shouldn't be a consideration really, but I can't help it. Things have been going pretty well on the tour so far, but announcing to the world that I've put an entire troop in the middle of a minefield – and on the say-so of a DBE officer at that – is not a *great* look.

Fu-u-u-uck.

I open my door and scan the ground by the Land Rover. I can't *see* anything. I look back up the track. There are a few bits of metal lying on the road but nothing that looks much like a pressure plate. Maybe the fuses, or the triggers, or whatever it is that makes mines explode, have eroded or rusted away or something. Anything here had to be a minimum of twenty years old after all. Or perhaps, I wonder with a sudden jolt of hope, we're only on the edge of the minefield.

In fact, the more I think about it, the more improbable it seems that we'd have got this far if we were truly all the way inside one. Third Troop's drivers are very competent, but they're more *Days of Thunder* than *Driving Miss Daisy*, and I very much doubt they've all been following neatly in one another's tyre tracks. If we haven't set anything off while skidding through the countryside like the Subaru Rally Team, we might get away with it yet.

I make my mind up.

'We're reversing out,' I announce over the PRR, in a voice like Aled Jones finding out the Snowman has melted. Then I tell Sgt Mason and Cpl Robbins to dismount and guide their drivers back on foot.

There is a brief pause. Then they both ask for clarification, in much the same tone as I imagine the Israelites asked Moses, 'You want us to walk across the *what* now?' I repeat the order. Then I take a deep breath and hop gingerly out of the Land Rover.

Nothing explodes. Eyes screwed nearly shut, I practically tiptoe round to the back of the vehicle. I can feel the stares of the troop, and do my best to look like I've got it all in hand. But frankly I'm surprised I'm not hyperventilating; hopscotching through a minefield would give Rambo pause for thought. I examine the track behind us. It looks clear enough. The metal I'd seen before seems to be bits of shell casing; not that encouraging, but probably not lethal either. I see Sgt Mason climb carefully from his Land Rover. He too skips to the back of it like Darcey Bussell, but at least he's out.

I tell Griffiths to go slow as all fuck and then start guiding him back using hand signals. From the stricken look on his face I'm not the only one whose adrenal glands are squirting out cortisol like a multi-barrelled Supersoaker. Between the tiny adjustments required to keep us in our own tyre tracks and his tendency to overcorrect, I'm flinging my arms about the place like I'm dancing the Charleston. But it's working, and we gradually roll backwards up the track.

I start to breathe again. Another fifteen minutes or so and we'll be well away. I tell Griffiths that he can ease off the clutch a bit. I continue to put one foot carefully behind the other, but faster now. Then I see it, six inches from my left heel; a perfect circle in the dust.

I feel my legs turn to rubber. There are no perfect circles in nature; that is the metal pressure plate on a landmine. I croak to Griffiths to stop. Then I let Cpl Robbins and Sgt Mason know what I've found, and listen to their bleak acknowledgement. Then, back to the glacial pace of before, we start to creak backwards again. I watch as the evil little disc disappears between the back wheels of the Land Rover. Then I resume scanning the ground behind us again, mentally sorting each pebble and bump until the picture blurs and the sweat stings my eyes. All the while I brace myself for the sharp crack and shocked cries of pain that will mean that I have really, truly fucked up.

It takes another half-hour before we feel confident enough to turn the vehicles around. Even that's a nightmare; no one wants to go so much as an inch onto the verge, so it's like playing a hideous game of Land Rover Tetris. But eventually we're all facing the right way. As I climb back into my vehicle, more spent than I think I've ever been, I can sense the boys' eyes boring into me. Quite right, too. Fucking stupid fucking shortcuts get your fucking soldiers fucking killed. I've been told that often enough.

We drive back up the track and past the DBE fort again. The guards spill out of the front gate laughing and waving, no doubt hoping we've returned with more corned beef hash, or perhaps to let them have a go on Cameron after all. In high dudgeon, I don't wave back.

I don't suppose I'll ever know for sure whether my pal from the DBE had meant to send us into a minefield, but on reflection I suspect not. More likely most of the tracks were safe and we'd just been unlucky. That or he simply couldn't read a map, but the culture of face-saving in Iraq being what it is, he'd rather we were all fucking vaporised than admit it.

Anyway, it turns out that the man with all the answers was sitting right behind me the whole time. As we rejoin the tarmacked road, Musad leans forward and starts to wax lyrical about how some tracks round here were built with the express purpose of deceiving the Iranians. If they ever crossed the border, he explains, they would see these tracks and follow them, assuming that they were the best routes between the Iraqis' forward positions. Right up until the point that they drove straight into the tripwire of a Valmara-69.

I twist in my seat and stare at him. With forced politeness, I suggest that this might have been useful information earlier. Say, a couple of hours ago, before I took the whole troop down precisely one of those tracks. Musad looks back at me, and for the first time on this entire patrol I see him smile. The way I'd been carrying on, he replies, it had looked like I knew what I was doing.

And anyway, I hadn't asked.

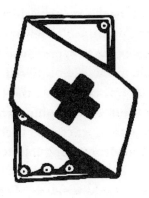

12

Mortality

Monday, 17 July 2006 – Camp Abu Naji

Back in CAN I've picked up three extra orderly officer duties. My crime is to have used the wrong radio codes during our patrol to the border. As a result I'd spent two days sending in position reports which put Third Troop variously in the middle of the Euphrates, on the outskirts of an Iranian national park, and smack bang in the centre of al Amarah city. Hopefully, said the ops officer as he handed over the orderly officer walkie-talkie with a sardonic grin, we'd been able to find an acceptable hotel.

Orderly officer duties themselves aren't hard; it's mainly checking that things are still there. Like armouries, or vehicles, or the same number of sentries as the number you started with, and so on. The hard bit is Ben.

Ben is a goat, and CAN's longest-serving inhabitant. He was originally bought by the Welsh Guards – presumably on the basis that buying a sheep would create too many love triangles in the battalion – to trim the scrubby grass in front of the ops room. Quite how people in the midst of a raging insurgency found the mental energy to worry about the state of the lawns beats me, but that's the Household Division for you; rumour has it that the Coldstreamers even tried to organise a litter pick at their base in Basra during the same tour. On the *outside* of the perimeter wall.

Ben stayed when the Taffs left, and has been inherited by every CAN battlegroup since. The press love it, and Ben has had more features done on him than Kate Moss. They're normally head-lined something like, 'Don't Kid About!', and claim that Ben enjoys 'playfully butting soldiers to ensure they stroke him'. This is complete bollocks; Ben is 150lb of pure caprine malevolence, who abhors stroking and isn't happy unless he's rupturing people's spleens with his head. There's never any warning; one minute you're strolling pleasantly past the ops room; the next, sprawled mewling in the dust, feeling like you've just been punched in the kidneys by Floyd Mayweather.

Privately, most of the battlegroup prays that one day we'll wake up and find that Ben's been splattered all over the Hesco by a mortar. But every morning, there he is, chewing the grass and eyeing up the passing trade for his next victim. There's a reason goats have a reputation for being hard as fuck; Ben has probably survived more incoming than the Wehrmacht.

He's particularly bad at night. It's pitch-black in CAN, and by the time you've clocked the glint of his freaky little goat eyes in the darkness, he's right on top of you. I've gradually learned that swearing loudly, and waving my headtorch in front of me like some kind of magical amulet, can put him off his stride a bit. It doesn't always work – often he'll just erupt out of the night and mow me down anyway – but sometimes it gives him pause, and me enough time to work out whether I should stand my ground or run for my life.

In any case, that's how I'm going to explain it to Jonty tomor-row when he asks why I suddenly leapt out from behind some

Hesco tonight and shouted, 'OH JUST FUCK OFF, WILL YOU!' at the Commanding Officer.

Tuesday, 18 July 2006 – Camp Abu Naji

It's the last evening of my orderly officer stint and I'm on the way to the ops room, mentally steeling myself for Ben to Jonah Lomu me into another dimension, when my walkie-talkie crackles to life. I'm wanted at the guardroom.

I arrive to a lively scene; five or six Iraqis gathered round the guard commander's desk, all waving their arms animatedly and shouting. Ali, the interpreter from our patrol to al Musharrah, is standing off to one side, looking like he's given up even trying to get a word in edgeways. The guard commander, a huge, red-faced Ulsterman from one of the other B Squadron troops, looks up despairingly as I enter.

'Ah, sor, they're all at it all at once, so they are! Fellas, shot the fock op, will ye . . . Fellas . . . Fellas . . . FELLAS, SHOT THE FOCK OP!'

The din dies away in an instant. I'm not surprised; you could have heard the last bit in Baghdad. The guard commander sighs heavily and gestures to Ali.

'About fockin' toime. Now, Ali son, tell the officer what it was they're after saying.' He turns his enormous Easter Island head to face the other Iraqis. 'And youse can all keep your fockin' mouths shut. Or I will fockin' shut them for you, so I will.'

Ali doesn't bother interpreting this bit; from the look on their faces the Iraqis don't need a Duolingo subscription to work out the gist.

'These men, they are the LECs for the camp,' Ali begins. 'They say they have been getting threats. The militias – they say these men should not work with the British. They know where they live.' Ali indicates a mournful older man with a prodigious squint. 'This one says they came to his home last night. They said if he comes back to Abu Naji then they will kill him. Then they will burn down his house.'

I nod. It isn't, sadly, that unusual a story. LECs are Locally Employed Civilians. Every camp here has them, doing the kinds of work no one really wants to do: laundry, pot-washing and so on. But in a country where the official unemployment rate is north of 40 per cent, even those kinds of jobs have a lot of takers.

No one tends to pay them much attention; they're part of the furniture, working their mops back and forth with glacial slowness, or simply sprawled under a tree having a big 'fuck you, RSM' nap in the shade. Now and again one of them will turn out to be a wrong 'un; CAN recently lost its barber when it turned out he was pacing out the distance between Corrimecs, and passing the results to his brother in a militia mortar crew. But generally they're seen as pretty harmless.

It's no surprise that LECs – or at least, those ones who aren't moonlighting as mortar fire controllers – need to be very careful about anyone finding out what they do for a living. While the militias aren't at all keen on the Little Satan, they reserve a special brand of hatred for Iraqis who empty His bins and wash His skiddies. And unlike the interpreters, who always work away from their home province to stop them being recognised, the LECs are all locals.

Their other disadvantage is that we probably just care a bit more about the terps. I'm not saying it's right, it's just the way it is. After all, the terps speak English, and they come on patrol with us, and understandably that creates something of a bond. Like the kind of bond I might have had with Musad had he not just sat there like Silent Bob while I drove into a fucking minefield last week. But these men, standing in the guardroom in their grubby work shirts, looking back and forth at Ali and the guard commander as they try to follow the conversation; well, if one of them doesn't turn up for work one day, they'll probably just scrub whatever name he's given us off the roster and forget all about him.

I ask Ali what it is that they want. He pauses, then says that they want to know if they can stay in CAN. At this there is a kind of supplicatory murmur from the LECs, who must have caught the Abu Naji bit. They don't want to stay permanently, says Ali; just for tonight, and perhaps a couple of nights after. Just until things in al Amarah settle down a bit.

I look at the guard commander. He raises an eyebrow. I grimace in return. If it was up to me – and him, by the looks of it – the LECs could bunk up with us in the Welfare Sauna if they wanted. Anything but send them back to homes where the militia are going door to door. But he's a corporal and I'm a second lieutenant, and the Army doesn't really give a shit what we think. I can imagine the hierarchy's reaction if they discovered half a dozen LECs having an illicit sleepover in CAN. We'd be on guard commander and orderly officer duty until the universe died a heat death.

With a sinking heart I radio the ops room. I've barely taken my finger off the pressel switch before they say no. I ask again; there's only a few of them, and it's just for a day or two. No, and more forcefully this time; CAN is not a fucking Travelodge. The LECs have homes to go to and that's all there is to it.

Come down here and tell them that yourself then, you heartless cunt, I don't say. I glance at Ali, who turns to the LECs and shakes his head. This sets off another brief cacophony, until the guard commander bangs his fist on the table and repeats his earlier trick.

'You'll have to go, I'm afraid,' I say, quietly. The LECs just look at me. I feel like throwing up. If they don't go, I'm not sure I can say it again. Then God bless him for doing what I cannot, because the guard commander slowly stands up, his great arms spread wide, and speaks in a soft voice.

'Come on now, fellas. Youse heard the man. We'll see youse again in the morning, so we will,' he says soothingly, gently ushering the LECs towards the door.

They go without a struggle – of course they do, he's built like Andre the Giant and there isn't a man among them more than ten stone dripping wet. They mill around for a moment outside the guardroom, speaking quietly to one another. It is quite dark by now. Then they make for the front gate. But they walk straight past the battered Toyotas they've parked outside, and instead turn right, out into the open desert.

The guard commander swears softly and we follow them. As we walk out through the front gate, we see the LECs spread themselves into a line. Then they start trotting over the lumpy desert, towards a distant sodium orange glow.

'Ah, Jaysus. They're only fockin' hard targetin'[29] all the way home,' murmurs the guard commander.

I feel abject.

We watch them for as long as we can see them. When they have disappeared over a ridge a few hundred metres away, we climb into a sangar and scan the desert with our night vision until we pick them up again; little black figures scurrying along against a greenish background. Now and again one of them pauses and looks carefully around them before carrying on.

In truth, I find myself almost wishing they *would* bump into the militia. I could crash out the QRF (*Quick Reaction Force*)[30] then, and they could fuck up some people who think a man trying to bring home a hundred dollars a month for his family deserves to be killed on his way home from work. I think the guard commander feels it too; I can sense the tension on him as he stands next to me in the sangar. He is silent, but for the occasional, 'Go on boys. You're stickin' out, so y'are.' We keep on watching until the LECs are out of sight.

I go to the ops room and hand in my report. The usual characters are all in there, bustling about doing their Planning, and Shaping the Battlefield for whatever lunatic endeavour HQ would like us to try next. I doubt they even remember being asked if the LECs could stay the night. But it's all I can do not to grab them by their shirt collars and drag them down to that sangar with me, to see if we can still pick out the figure of that old man with the squint.

Then we can watch him together, stumbling across the desert in the pitch-black, back to a home that might well be ashes by the time he gets there. All because he empties our wheelie bins to feed his children, but we won't even let him sleep on our floor.

Wednesday, 19 July 2006 – Maysan / Dhi Qar

Today B Squadron are escorting a convoy of RLC trucks to Dhi Qar, the province just to the south-west of Maysan. We are doing this because the trucks are needed for a resupply mission in Basra. This mission is the brainchild of some genius in Divisional HQ, no doubt destined for a glittering career as a staff officer, who has planned the whole thing without realising that the requisite lorries are still 120 miles away in CAN.

We haven't finished Op BLAST II yet, so we can't escort them all the way ourselves. Instead we will take them as far as the Dhi Qar–Maysan border. Then we will hand them over to some Italians, who are in charge of running Dhi Qar, and they will in turn hand them over to some Brits at the Dhi Qar–Basra border for the last stretch. It's easily twice as long, three times as complicated, and ten times as annoying as a normal convoy run. And with planning like that, it's a wonder that Dunkirk isn't still full of snowy-haired old men, sitting in lines on the promenade and asking when the fucking boats are going to get there.

Our stretch is uneventful. Going from Maysan to Basra via Dhi Qar is like going from London to Brighton via Bristol; it's very unlikely the militia will be expecting us to leave CAN and head in more or less the opposite direction to our only other major base in Iraq. They probably think we're playing some kind of devious, infidel game of 4D-chess; I suspect they'd die laughing if they knew the truth. It's a dull four hours, enlivened only by listening to the RLC convoy commander, a taciturn Scottish major, reading out the report lines on the map as we go.[31]

Some comedian in the CAN ops room has named each of these lines after a different champagne house. This kind of thing is an absolute scream to cavalry officers. They'll tell the story at dinner parties in Balham, very often before wondering aloud – with genuine puzzlement – why it is that the rest of the Army thinks they're such insufferable wankers. In the event, the convoy commander gets on reasonably well with Bollinger, pronounces Krug to rhyme with 'rug', wobbles severely on Veuve Cliquot, and then completely falls apart at Report Line Burtin Besserat de Bellefon.

The airwaves are silent for a moment, before an unknown voice, so cut-glass you could have served sherry in it, sighs, 'I mean, the heat is bad enough, but good grief, the *people* . . .' Even Sgt Mason, who doesn't usually have much time for what he considers (with some accuracy, in fairness) to be 'crap officer gags about cricket and who bummed who at fucking Eton', has to admit it's quite a good one.

We arrive at the handover at dusk. The Italians turn up a full forty-five minutes late. You'd hang for that in the British Army, but they clearly don't give a fuck and are not in the least bit apologetic. I like them immediately. The convoy commander – who, from the way he stares *very* hard at Brooksie when we dismount, looks like he's got a strong suspicion about the identity of B Squadron's answer to Noël Coward (and he'd have been right) – stalks off to find whoever's in charge. The rest of us take the opportunity for a leg stretch, ambling down the line of Italian vehicles and exchanging hellos like we're on a post-dinner stroll in Puglia.

They might struggle a bit with their timings, but it's immediately clear that the Italians know how to go to war in style. For a start, every man jack of them looks like a *GQ* cover model; there are more sculpted torsos in this small patch of Iraqi desert than at Milan fashion week, and they make B Squadron look like a tribe of bog-dwelling Cro-Magnon men by comparison. Secondly, their rations come with red wine included, which I discover when someone hands me a very acceptable glass of Chianti over a tailgate.

Shortly afterwards – in the middle of this vast expanse of nothing but sand and gravel, mind you – I am passed a hot *cappuccino* and a *biscotti*. This is followed by a small glass of something that is never identified, but must be at least 75% ABV; it immediately blows the top of my head off. No wonder they were late; if they've been drinking this stuff on the way it's a wonder they even found the handover in the first place.

Gasping, I thank my hosts for the wine, coffee, and my newly stripped oesophagus. Then I walk down to the next vehicle, where I can hear laughter, and what sounds like pidgin Italian delivered in an accent veering erratically between *Super Mario* and Solihull. It's Greene and Womack. They're standing at the tailgate, leaning over it so far that they're practically on tiptoes, and talking to someone in the back. I walk up behind them.

'Fellas . . . ,' I start. Then the words catch in my throat and I just stare.

Sitting in the back of the truck, smiling broadly at the boys, is a woman. And not just any woman – this is a young Sophia Loren. Cat-like eyes, waves of glossy auburn hair, sitting on a bench seat with her long legs tucked demurely under her. She is fully made up, I notice; she's even painted her fingernails, in a deep cherry red. I spot a white armband with a red cross; she must be the medic.

'You must be the medic,' I say, automatically. She nods and turns her megawatt smile on me. Then Womack sniggers and it breaks the spell. In the distance I hear someone shouting for us to mount up; it's time to go anyway.

I walk with Greene and Womack back to our Snatches, Greene flinging a heartfelt '*Adios!*' [*sic*] into the night. Then we watch as the Italians' tail lights disappear into the distance with the convoy. As we start the drive back to CAN, Womack and Greene speculate at length about whether I have any other hot tips for speaking to women. Have I had much success walking up and saying, 'You must be a woman.'? Or perhaps it's the 'staring at them like a fucking sex-pest' that wins them over? I smile to myself in the darkness. This will be enough to keep them going for weeks. Then the radio crackles. It's the CAN ops room.

'All callsigns, be advised; the Italians you handed over to got hit, about thirty minutes ago. Contact IED. One dead, two T2, multiple T3s. Out.'

I put down the handset slowly. Then I tell the rest of the crew. No one says a word. I sit and stare straight ahead, and think about cherry red fingernails scrabbling to open a first field dressing in the dark. With a sudden horror, I feel tears prickling at the back of my eyes, and rub at them until I can see stars. Of all the rotten fucking luck. We drive the rest of the way in silence.

13

Mr Sandman

Friday, 22 July 2006 – Maysan

We've been tasked to escort the Commanding Officer to a meeting at an Iraqi Army camp near CAN. It's not the road move he's worried about; it's more what happens when he gets there. And with good reason. Only a couple of weeks earlier, a Danish liaison officer visiting the same camp had been quite surprised to find a chloroform-soaked rag being pressed against his mouth while he zipped up after a visit to the gents. I've actually met him since, and wonder what the fuck his would-be kidnappers were even thinking; the man is built like Harald Hardrada.

He hadn't come quietly – in fact he went at it like he was in the shield wall at Hastings – and sixty seconds later his three assailants were lying on the floor of a bathroom that resembled the opening scene of *Casino Royale*, covered in bits of mashed-up urinal cake and mumbling incoherently.

The theory was that it had something to do with cartoons of Muhammad that had recently been published in a Danish newspaper. Equally, it might have been that the camp in question has just been thoroughly infiltrated by the militias, and cartoons were neither here nor there. But no one is taking any chances now, so we spend a long hot day on the camp's front gate, checking every vehicle that leaves to confirm it's not carrying a rolled-up carpet with a commanding officer stuffed inside it.

Eight hours standing next to a gate leaves ample time for reflection. Today I am mainly reflecting on how the fuck B Squadron keep getting away with it. We're going through our nine lives at a rate of knots and it can't last. We won't always be the boys who hand over the convoy half an hour before it gets whacked. The boys who're sleeping in the Corrimec next to the one that takes a mortar through the roof. Or the ones who miss the pressure plate on an anti-tank mine by all of six inches.

Forget a sense of mortality; that kicked in the first night we'd been properly malleted in the Welfare Sauna. This is a sense of inevitability. We are well overdue.

Sunday, 23 July 2006 – Maysan / Shaibah

Op BLAST II finished today. Maysan isn't so much as a picometre closer to PIC, but the coloured-in boxes on a calendar somewhere in HQ have evidently run out, so B Squadron travel back down to Shaibah using the same roads that we came up. The enemy don't seem to have clocked that we've got a new route to and from CAN. Which is just as well, because between border patrols, thrice-nightly mortar barrages, and endless guard duties, the whole squadron is completely ball-bagged,[32] and I doubt we'd be able to fight off a moderately determined pack of Girl Guides, let alone a militia ambush. And it's definitely the excuse I'm sticking to if Jonty ever asks me why exactly it was that I fell asleep during a halt and woke up to find the rest of the convoy had left without me.

It's late afternoon when it happens, and the golden sunlight slanting through the Snatch's thick windows is making the dust motes in the cab look almost as if they're dancing. We're sat idling, the last vehicle in the convoy, while someone up ahead carries out a VP check.

I lean back in my seat and stretch out my legs as far as I can manage in the cramped footwell. The gentle throb of the V8 is soporific. When I look up, which surely can have been only a couple of seconds later – five at most – the road ahead of me is completely empty. Someone raps on the window; I turn and look. It's an Iraqi. He's smiling and holding up a watermelon.

Oh *fuck*.

Momentarily stunned, I turn to look at Griffiths in the driver's seat; he's slumped forward with his helmet resting on the steering wheel, a thin ribbon of dribble on his chin. I can't see Womack and Greene, who are on top cover, but if I had to guess from the contented snuffling noises coming from the back of the Snatch, I'd venture that they're also completely fucking sparko. The Iraqi raps on the window again and lifts the watermelon to head height. He raises an enquiring eyebrow. He appears to think I have stopped to buy fruit.

I snap out of my torpor and immediately set about resolving the situation; letting out a panicked squawk and heaving Griffiths back and forth in his seat like I'm trying to shake him off my sister.

'Griff! *Griff*! Fucking wake *up*, Griff! The fucking *convoy's* gone! *Griff*!'

Griffiths's eyes flicker, then open, then bulge halfway out of his head. Then he slams the Snatch into gear like a getaway driver. I have just enough time to register the look of surprise on the watermelon salesman's face before he disappears in a cloud of blue exhaust; I imagine he thinks this is somehow part of the haggling process. Behind me I can hear a yelp as Greene and Womack tumble backwards with the sudden acceleration. Good, I think savagely. And unfairly; a British soldier can fall asleep in

141

six inches of freezing rainwater on a Welsh hillside, so the late afternoon sun and a warm Snatch is like a Dreams memory foam mattress by comparison. Besides, I'd passed out too.

After five minutes and still no convoy, I am having a severe 5p–50p moment.[33] No one's quite sure how long we were all asleep, but it was long enough for Maysan's answer to HelloFresh to find us, and we hadn't been anywhere near a village at the time. And I can't get anyone on the radio either.

Although that's not necessarily a reliable guide to how far away they are; it might just be that the water table's low round here. Or the ionospheric density's too high. Or Mercury's in retrograde and all our chakras are out of alignment. Or any one of a million different reasons that the Signals Platoon keep giving us for why our fucking radios never seem to let us talk to anyone further than shouting distance away. But if we're anything more than a few minutes from the rest of B Squadron, then we could be in real trouble here.

It's happened before; just before leaving Shaibah we'd heard about a convoy that some artillery boys were escorting from Kuwait. The rear Snatch in that convoy had also been left behind – although that crew at least had the excuse that they'd broken down, rather than just passing out *en masse* like milk-drunk infants. They had the same problem as us though; they were completely alone in a very unfriendly part of the world.

At first they made as if this was all part of the plan, the top cover gunners scanning their arcs[34] calmly, while inside the Snatch the corporal in charge tried frantically to raise someone on the radio. Nothing doing. Still, they reasoned, it couldn't be long before someone in the convoy cottoned on, and sent a patrol back for them. Then one of the top cover said that they were pretty sure that black Mercedes had driven past at least twice now. The driver and his passengers had looked about as friendly as a gallows. There was the suggestion of a rifle in the footwell.

Clearly something was up. And the next time that Mercedes came back, it was going to have company. The corporal knew it too, and made a very brave decision. Striding out into the middle of the road, he stopped the next car he saw, which happened to be a taxi. Then he told his men to grab the radios and the ammunition and put it all in the taxi's boot. As soon as they'd finished he walked back to the Snatch, emptied a full magazine into the back, then tossed in a phosphorous grenade for good measure. No one would be getting their hands on his vehicle intact.

Then he climbed into the taxi with his crew, and told the open-mouthed driver – who presumably didn't get too many fares methodically blowing up their own vehicle – to make for Shaibah. Less than thirty seconds later, they met the patrol of three Snatches that had been detached from the convoy to go back and pick them up. Still, when they got back to Shaibah a few hours later, it was the convoy commander who got crucified. The corporal had his hand shaken by the General.

We'd taken two lessons from this story; firstly, if you want to blow up your own vehicle (and by this point there isn't the Snatch crew in Iraq who wouldn't dearly like to) then do it quickly, before they send a rescue party and you miss your chance. Secondly, a vehicle crew by itself is considered easy meat by the opposition. It's this that is playing on my mind as Griffiths flogs our Snatch at its deeply disappointing 43mph top speed down the still empty road.

From the way he keeps glancing worriedly in his wing mirrors, it seems like I'm not the only one. The sun looks a lot lower in the sky than it did even a couple of minutes ago. Christ, alone in Maysan, and at *night*. If the militias do want to kidnap a British soldier then they don't need to bother pulling someone out of a baseline; I've just put four of them into a shiny box, chucked in a few decorative cinnamon sticks, and tied an enormous bow around it.

Whatever happens, I tell the boys, we don't stop. Even if there's a roadblock, we'll just blitz through it with Womack giving it big licks on the Minimi. If they disable the vehicle, then it's pairs fire and manoeuvre to the nearest bit of cover, and hope that the rest of the squadron at least manage to spot our smoke signal when the Snatch explodes. It's not much of a plan. But then again I'm not much of a troop leader, otherwise presumably we wouldn't be here.

I check the magazine on my rifle then feel for my fragmentation grenade nestled in its little pouch. If there is a roadblock and we do manage to run it, then I'll crack the door open and drop it as we go past. It might buy us a minute.

There is a frantic hammering on the roof above my head. Simultaneously Griffiths lunges forward, his nose practically touching the windscreen.

'*Boss*! It's the convoy, boss! They're still fucking there!'

I look up, and feel like sobbing with relief. There, on the shimmering horizon, is the most beautiful sight I've ever seen; the squat, boxy rear of a B Squadron Snatch. I hear Womack and Greene yell in triumph behind me. It can't have been much more than a quarter of an hour since we all jerked awake, but this feels like being born again. The images of a burning Snatch and matching orange jumpsuits fade in my mind's eye; we've got away with it.

As we approach the squadron, I start to mentally rehearse the case for the defence. In reality it's going to be more of a plea for mitigation. Even if Jonty is somehow inclined to mercy (and I've got precisely zero reason to believe he will be), the Army is going to slaughter me. Falling asleep on duty is one of a select group of offences, like telling your boss to go fuck themselves, or having a cheeky duvet day, which might get you a meeting with HR in civilian life, but which as far as the Army is concerned is their cue to dig out the black cap and start finding volunteers for a firing squad. Literally. Well, in the First World War at least. They haven't actually shot anyone for it since then, but it's still a Very Big Deal; I'll be lucky to get away with losing a month's pay.

In the event, I don't even get a mild ticking off. When we catch it up, the convoy is still ploughing on at a steady 25mph, and it's immediately clear that no one has the faintest idea we were even missing. We tuck ourselves sheepishly in at the back, and try to look like we've been there the whole time. Which, as Griffiths, Greene, Womack and I agree in a hurried conference at the back of our Snatch once we're back in Shaibah, we definitely were.

Thursday, 3 August 2006 – Shaibah

All has not been well in Basra while we've been away. In fact it's gone completely off the deep end. The Iraqis held their first proper general election last December, but it has taken nearly eight months of negotiation for a government to be formed. In Basra this has been quite the process; indeed, in the last two months alone 200 people have negotiated so robustly that they are now dead. And the violence doesn't show any sign of letting up.

The militias haven't restricted themselves to knocking lumps out of each other either, so the two battlegroups in the city are now more or less under siege. The militia mortar teams are getting horribly good with all the practice, and people have started to die. Two days ago it was a Warrior commander in Basra Palace, who had the rotten luck to be standing upright in the turret when a 120mm shell landed directly on the back of his vehicle.

The biggest gang in town is the Jaish al-Mahdi. Or more simply, JAM. We'd previously referred to them as the 'Mahdi Army', until someone realised it made them sound less like a vicious sectarian militia and more like a group of likely lads who enjoy drinking twelve pints of Carlsberg on match day then winding up a police horse. JAM is named for the twelfth of the Twelve Imams, who Shias believe will appear to save mankind at the 'end times'. Given the state of Basra at the moment, you have to wonder what he's waiting for.

JAM started life as a small group of seminary students in Baghdad protecting local Shias in the security vacuum after the invasion, but had quickly spread south. They answer to Moqtada al Sadr, whose beaming photo we've seen on the wall of the police station in al Musharrah, and quite a few other places since. Al Sadr is a cleric whose father was Iraq's Grand Ayatollah before his assassination by Saddam goons in the late nineties. He's rumoured to be a few pitas short of a mezza, but the power he wields has always been abundantly clear. Clear to everyone, that is, except the British Army.

For the first six months or so the Army was in Basra, we had called a series of 'engagement meetings', in order that anyone who considered themselves a player in the city could turn up and introduce themselves. We'd then been able to write their names down, ask – in a roundabout kind of way – where exactly it was that they lived, and colour in our maps accordingly.

The wily Al Sadr, with incredible fox-like cunning, simply decided not to come to any of these meetings. So when his black-clad JAM militiamen started parading around Basra's streets a few months later, it had taken our intelligence people a little while to thumb through their Rolodexes and realise they did not know who the fuck he was. Anyway, we know now; JAM are responsible for most of the EFP attacks in the city, and are lobbing so many mortars at us that it's a wonder the bastards haven't all gone down with tennis elbow.

The Iraqi government, having realised that the two British battlegroups in Basra now have their work cut out protecting themselves, let alone the 1.5 million people living here, have sent down a couple of battalions of reinforcements. They are in Shaibah now, tearing around the place in their khaki-coloured Nissan pickups and trying to feel up the baristas from the Welfare Village. They are much less enthused about getting felt up themselves by JAM. And anyway, there aren't nearly enough of them. The city needs more bodies, and those bodies need training.

So tomorrow, less than two weeks after we got back to Shaibah, B Squadron are heading north again. We're going to a town called Kumayt, about thirty miles from al Amarah. There to find 3/4/10 – the 3rd Battalion, 4th Brigade, 10th Division of the Iraqi Army – and to teach them everything they need to know.

Friday, 4 August 2006 – Shaibah / Kumayt

We head up north on the back roads again. As the Snatches crawl along, I wonder what 3/4/10 will be like. No one in the squadron has ever had much to do with the Iraqi Army – with the exception of Sgt Porter, who spent a blissful couple of days machine-gunning them in 1991 – but I've done a bit of reading.

They've certainly been to war a lot. Although they don't appear to be great at actually winning them; beaten by the Israelis in 1967 and again in 1973, a score draw against the Iranians in the 1980s (with both sides ending the match with half a million fewer names on the team sheet than they'd started with) and capitulation in less than a hundred hours in the First Gulf War. So not exactly the Spartans, then. In fairness though – and as so often seems to be the case with armies run by swivel-eyed, megalomaniacal socio-paths – it wasn't really their fault.

Given Saddam's own path to power was considerably smoothed by a number of rivals leaping unexpectedly out of windows or accidentally shooting themselves eleven times in the chest, it was no wonder that he worried quite a lot about coups. He was particularly worried about the Army; they'd been responsible for a succession of spectacularly blood-drenched takeovers that made the October Revolution look like an afternoon at the bowls. Right from the off, Saddam was convinced that if he didn't keep the officer corps firmly under his thumb, then there was every chance he'd be the next one standing in his PJs on the front lawn of the Presidential Palace, firing an ornamental flintlock at a tank.

This paranoia only worsened over time; by the late nineties, maps of Baghdad were being deliberately withheld from his generals (including the ones who were supposed to defend it), and he'd banned joint exercises between different units lest their commanders form a conspiracy during a fag break. In the mean-time he was issuing a stream of instructions so bizarre that they made Hitler's madder edicts from the Führerbunker look like *The Art of War*: 'Train all units' members in swimming', 'Train your soldiers to climb palm trees so that they may use these places for navigation and sniper shooting', and the undeniably sensible – if somewhat lacking in detail – 'Train in a way that allows you to defeat your enemy'.

And here we are complaining that the RSM's Military Skills competitions are a waste of time. Anyway the upshot was that he'd turned an army that had once managed to stop the Israelis in their tracks on the Golan Heights, to a politicised, unhappy shambles which had been routed in less than three weeks during the most recent invasion.

We arrive at 3/4/10's camp in the late afternoon; a desolate collection of low concrete buildings just off the main road, surrounded by a high wall with sangars at each corner. Per the local tradition, every one of the sangars is utterly deserted. The welcoming committee is non-traditional, in the sense that there actually is one. It is led by 3/4/10's Commanding Officer; a squat, pock-marked colonel sporting enough gold braid to have made Idi Amin blush. He welcomes us into camp with the rictus grin of a man who knows very well he has precisely zero choice in the matter, and invites us to make ourselves at home in the unit garages.

The garages are half-finished, but seem to be doubling up as the unit toilet in the meantime; the concrete floor is literally covered in hundreds of desiccated Mr Whippys. We spend a couple of hours sweeping out the worst of it then hump sandbags onto the roof to build ourselves a sangar. If it all goes completely tits up, then we'll fight from here.

There are probably more glamorous places to make your last stand than on top of 3/4/10's regimental crapper, but it's good and high and we can see for miles up and down the road. The sangar is nearly finished when Jonty climbs up and tells us to move it so that we've got arcs back into camp as well as over the perimeter wall.

Better safe than sorry.

14

3/4/10

Saturday, 5 August 2006 – Kumayt

We've arranged to meet 3/4/10 at seven sharp to kick off, so we're up with the larks. Jonty has already given us his orders; he wants the troop leaders to inspect various bits of the battalion – personnel, stores, finance, and so on – while the NCOs run the training. Everyone else is in charge of keeping their wits about them to make sure we're not all abruptly slaughtered in the middle of the night by some combination of the local militia and/or rogue elements of 3/4/10.

We're on the parade ground at five to seven, in a lunatic triumph of hope over experience. It's completely deserted. Ten minutes pass. Then twenty. Then Jonty sees a solitary *jundi (Iraqi soldier)* strolling unhurriedly past the front gate a hundred metres away. He calls out to him. The *jundi* freezes, like someone caught on the landing without a towel by the window cleaner. Then he turns on his heel and scurries round the corner out of sight.

'Right,' says Mr Kite meaningfully, and starts striding towards one of the accommodation buildings, flanked by half a dozen senior NCOs like the colour men in *Reservoir Dogs*. There is some shouting, and the faint sounds of sleepy, aggrieved protest. But turning people violently out of bed is what sergeant majors live for – if they're not allowed to do it at least every couple of months they start going off their food and moulting – so it's not long before 3/4/10 start drifting unhappily towards the parade ground.

Eventually there are about a hundred of them standing in a ragged square. They stare at us. We stare back. They don't look much like soldiers. B Squadron might not be the Grenadier Guards – one look at Buxton absently scratching his nuts on parade is enough to remind me of that – but at least we're all wearing the same clothes. 3/4/10 look like plane-crash survivors who've dressed themselves in the contents of whichever suitcases they could drag out of the wreckage.

Someone seems to have issued them with US BDUs (*battle dress uniforms*) at some point, but the fashionistas of Kumayt have clearly deemed that wearing a matching set is an egregious *faux pas*. Berets are worn either *chignon*-style on the back of an immaculately coiffured head, or pulled so far down the wearer's face that they look like an Iraqi Andy Capp. The footwear varies from normal boots to the kind of two-tone patent leather winklepickers that wouldn't have disgraced Fred Astaire. I can feel the heat coming off our senior NCOs from ten yards away.

Jonty gives a fairly florid introductory speech, telling 3/4/10 how thrilled we are to be here and that we're now 'brothers in arms', which seems to me to be testing the bounds of credibility just a little bit. Suleiman, one of the interpreters we've brought with us, appears to be giving them the abridged version, and says about one word for every ten of Jonty's. So either hackneyed rhetoric is shorter in Arabic, or Jonty's speech has been a complete waste of time because all 3/4/10 have heard is: 'These English are weirdly happy and they think you're related.'

To be fair, I can't imagine it's easy for 3/4/10. After all, the invasion is still fairly recent, and there's a good chance that some of these men fought in it against us – even if only for a very brief period between seeing their first ever Challenger 2 and commandeering a passing taxibus back to Baghdad. Being trained by the same people responsible for wiping out several thousand of your colleagues not that long ago must be quite the headfuck. A bit like the Greeks sacking Troy, then offering woodworking classes to the survivors the morning after.

I'm also not completely sure how credible we are as trainers. 3/4/10 have certainly got their share of downy-haired youths, but I can see enough grizzled chins and steady gazes to suggest that some of these lads have been around the block a few times. Alright, the QRH has done some hard service in Belfast, and Bosnia wasn't exactly a picnic, but that's a different ballgame from the kind of fighting an old-timer in 3/4/10 might conceivably have seen. And if good training is about learning what to do when you're down to your last ten rounds and half the platoon's been obliterated by artillery, then it's not totally clear where that experience is going to come from. Not from our half of the parade ground, that's for sure.

I wonder how 3/4/10 feel about it all. Bored to the point of brain death, if the blank expressions on their faces are anything to go by. Jonty finishes with a flourish, telling the assembled *jundis* that we'll defeat JAM together, 'hand in hand and shoulder to shoulder'. But it doesn't elicit so much as a slow clap. For all the energy 3/4/10 are showing, he may as well have read them the shipping forecast. Or maybe they've heard this one before.

Looking a bit deflated – he's not a showman by any stretch, but he has just died on his arse out there – Jonty dispatches the troop leaders on our inspection visits. I've got the quartermaster's department, presumably because in some previous life I ran over a priest or molested someone's family pet or something. That or Jonty does actually hate me. Already feeling tired, I ask Suleiman to come with me and we head off to 3/4/10's stores.

It doesn't take long to locate their quartermaster; the stores building is ringing to the sound of a violent argument, so I just follow the noise. We find the QM in his office, shouting at a cringing *jundi* and smacking him lustily around the head with a clipboard. Suleiman whispers that it has something to do with twenty missing rifles. This sounds intriguing, but I don't get a chance to ask any questions because the next moment the QM has dropped his clipboard and is roaring a welcome. The *jundi* sees his chance and scarpers, and I am steered forcefully towards a pair of low sofas where glasses of tea and bowls of pistachios have appeared as if by magic.

I sit down and watch as the QM thumps into the sofa opposite me. He is incredibly fat, even by quartermaster standards, and has an impressive sweat on for eight o'clock in the morning. He has apparently been looking forward to my visit for the better part of his whole life.

'Welcome welcome welcome!' he cries, pumping my fist like he wants to take my arm home with him. 'Hello-how-are-you? I-am-very-well-thank-you. My-name-Major-Hassan. I-am-pleased-to-meet-you. Luvvly-jubbly!'

I glance at Suleiman. I might not need him after all.

'I am also pleased to meet you. My name is Lieutenant Mulligan. You are the quartermaster for this battalion, is that correct?'

'I-am-very-well-thank-you. Luvvly-jubbly.'

Maybe not.

With Suleiman's help we get the pleasantries out of the way and establish that I have come to inspect the stores. Major Hassan looks suddenly hurt. This is clearly not very luvvly-jubbly information. He leans forward, clearing his throat.

'This battalion,' Suleiman translates, 'is a *good* battalion. An *honest* battalion.'

Major Hassan picks up a pistachio nut and holds it in front of me.

'In this battalion, not so much as a *pistachio* has ever gone missing . . .' After he has translated this one, Suleiman coughs politely, and mutters something in Arabic.

152

'. . . apart from twenty rifles,' continues Major Hassan, without missing a beat. 'And they are not really lost. We will find them soon.'

Then he eats the pistachio, presumably for emphasis. I have to hand it to him; he has the oratory down pat.

And he needs to, because within about twenty minutes it's evident that Major Hassan is presiding over a web of embezzlement and fraud that would have made Imelda Marcos look like a Carmelite nun. It starts with the vehicles; according to my paperwork, 3/4/10 should have fifteen brand new Ford trucks. There are only five in the vehicle park (and we count together, twice). According to Major Hassan, with a vague gesture to the outside world in general, the other ten are 'on patrol'. Perhaps. But if I'd been asked to find them, I'd probably have started with the Ford dealerships of Baghdad.

Fuel is equally interesting. 3/4/10 are being sent enough diesel every week to power a small and lively city, but I've yet to hear a single generator since we got here. Well exactly, Major Hassan tells me; that's the whole point. He can't very well keep the generators on the whole time if they're using – he checks his notes – 200 gallons an hour. Good point, I concede, but shouldn't the actual consumption be – now it's my turn to check my notes – 70 gallons an hour? Old generators, smiles Major Hassan. They all get like that. I think about the long queues of dinar-wielding drivers at every petrol station from here to Basra, and smile back.

It doesn't matter what we check – armoury, clothing store, workshops – it's the same story everywhere. By the time we finish I wouldn't have been at all surprised to open a door and find Lord Lucan playing cards on the Ark of the Covenant. Major Hassan is running this place like Trotters Independent Traders and not even trying to fake the paperwork. But I'm finding it hard to get too exercised about it.

Despite 3/4/10's somewhat shambolic appearance on parade, the Iraqi Army is awash with cash. Literally; since the invasion, the US has flown in something like $12bn in shrink-wrapped banknotes, quite a few of which appear to have fallen down the back of the sofa immediately after arriving in Baghdad (as evidenced by the recent Congressional Inquiry into where the fuck it's all gone). So it's hardly surprising that Major Hassan has reacted the only way which makes sense; grabbing as much as possible and stuffing it down his shirt like a Crystal Maze contestant, before someone comes along and turns off the luvvly-jubbly money tap.

I can hardly blame him. Take away the NHS, the state pension, and every other form of social safety net from your average Brit, then watch how long it takes before they start creaming a little off the top for their autumn years. About a New York minute, I reckon.

We go back to Major Hassan's office to wrap up, and he takes the opportunity to present his wish list. He makes a commendably bold start, asking me to approve $200,000 for two new accommodation blocks. The men, he explains, are having to sleep practically on top of one another. Not to mention shit all over the garage floor, I reflect.

I explain that $200,000 is some way above the amount I am authorised to approve (about $200,000 above as it happens). Anyway, we can't just go handing out cash willy-nilly. No, if Major Hassan wants new accommodation blocks, then he will have to submit an invoice. What's one of those, asks Major Hassan deflatedly. Oh, you know, I tell him; a breakdown of the request, with itemised costs, bills of materials, and so on. Major Hassan brightens, then seizes a pen and paper and scribbles for a moment. Suleiman takes the proffered sheet.

'What does that say, Suleiman?'

'It says: One accommodation block – $100,000. Another accommodation block – $100,000.'

'Thank you.'

Sunday, 6 August 2006 – Kumayt

I'm not the only one who's discovering that not all is as it seems in 3/4/10. According to Mike, they're being sent wages for about 150 soldiers whom he's almost certain do not actually exist. Brooksie has uncovered a scheme whereby the CO is sending *jundis* on a promotion course in Tallil, then busting them back to *jundi* for some made-up infraction when they get back and pocketing the extra pay himself. And Godders has spent the best part of twelve hours in an increasingly heated debate with the 3/4/10 ops officer about exactly what it is that the battalion actually does all day.

At one point he'd queried the almost total lack of any patrol reports in the ops room. Returning after lunch, he'd been heartened, and even a little remorseful – perhaps he'd just been a bit too quick to judge – to find two lever-arch files full of them. He'd been a bit less remorseful when he opened the first file to find fifty identical patrol reports, each written in the same pen, all of which when translated turned out to say, 'We went on patrol. It was good. Everyone really liked us.'

The training isn't going all that well either. No one is completely sure about what training 3/4/10 have already received, but what is rapidly becoming clear is that they have all the military skills of the Children's Crusade. Sgt Mason is being a bit tight-lipped about the map-reading lessons, but his face – not to mention the Silva compass he appears to have snapped clean in half – tells its own story.

Cpl Robbins meanwhile has been in charge of battlefield first aid. He took Cameron with him as his assistant and demonstration model, which has turned out to be a huge mistake. If we thought Cameron had been a hit with the DBE, as far as 3/4/10 are concerned he is every member of Boyzone rolled into one. Almost every scenario, says Cpl Robbins – sucking chest wound, gunshot to the arm, small abrasion to the head – quickly evolves into an excuse for half a dozen Iraqi soldiers to stroke Cameron lovingly on the cheek and then bandage him very, very tightly around the groin.

I see Cameron later, sitting on his cot bed and staring at nothing very much at all. The rest of B Squadron have similar tales and Jonty's looking grim. I can understand why; if the Iraqis think they'll be sending these lads to duke it out with JAM in Basra, then they'd better have a back-up plan.

Tuesday, 8 August, 2006 – Kumayt

Today the NCOs are running a lesson on anti-ambush tactics. In truth, there's not much you can do if you end up in someone else's Killing Area (after all, they've picked it for a reason). But we run through a few drills anyway: try to punch through the ambush and then hit them in the flank if you can, but if not then dismount and fire and manoeuvre towards the enemy until everyone gets killed. As ever, 3/4/10 listen to the lesson, watch the demonstration, and then do a version that includes the tiniest of nods to what we've just spent four hours exhaustively explaining under a blazing sun, but otherwise is exactly what they'd have done anyway.

After a couple of days in Kumayt, we seem to have reached a kind of unspoken understanding with 3/4/10. For our part we've realised that we can rant about professionalism and punctuality until we're blue in the face; 3/4/10 are not suddenly going to turn into the Prussian Guard. For their part 3/4/10 seem to have accepted that no matter how hard they pray, we're not just going to disappear and leave them alone, so they may as well humour us until the training's over.

It's the kind of resentful accommodation that is doubtless being reached between trainers and trainees up and down Iraq. And it's hardly surprising. After all, we're only here for seven months and must come across as unbearably full of piss and vinegar to 3/4/10, who for the most part will be soldiering here until they are killed, wounded, or (much less probably) they win.

So better to let them knock the edges off you, you off them, and then meet somewhere in the middle. As T.E. Lawrence himself once said, 'Better the Arabs do it tolerably than that you do it perfectly'. Or as most of B Squadron would probably put it, 'Jesus Christ. Jesus *Christ*. Actually, fuck it, that'll do.'

You might argue that we should be pushing them harder; tightening their drills, sharpening their tactics, and practising again and again until they can do it by the book. Because in a few weeks they'll probably be facing off with JAM in Basra. But then again it's not like JAM are exactly Navy SEALS either.

There's also an open question about whether our book is even the right one to teach them. At the moment the standard drill for a British Army patrol that ends up in trouble is to whistle up a Warrior, then hide behind it and rely on the fruits of the Western military-industrial complex to pulverise the enemy with a 30mm autocannon. But 3/4/10 won't have any Warriors. They won't, God love them, have much of anything. And if that's the case, then perhaps a *jundi* reversing his pickup at 25mph back through the ambush, while his cousin stands in the back firing his machine gun from the hip, is genuinely a better bet.

15

Captain Fantastic

Thursday, 10 August, 2006 – Kumayt

Jonty decides to mix it up, and tells the troop leaders to run some training for a change. I've been given Vehicle Check Points (*VCPs*). The idea is to give the 3/4/10 platoon commanders a short session on the basics, then they can use what they've learned to do a short patrol, set up a VCP a mile or so away, and search a few cars. Easy, says Jonty, clapping me on the back and sending me on my way. That's what you always say, Jonty, and it never fucking is, I don't reply.

The lesson itself goes well enough; I stand at the front of a stuffy classroom with Suleiman and wang on for half an hour about route cards, actions on, and all the rest of it. Only four platoon commanders have turned up and there should be at least ten, but that's actually not a bad hit rate for 3/4/10 (unless it's first aid with Cameron, in which case it's like Justin Bieber at the O2).

They're not exactly model students – all four of them spend most of the lesson yawning hugely, and the one at the back is completely absorbed in scrolling through Japanese pornography on his mobile – but at least they're quiet. Eventually I declare the lesson finished and that it's time to put it all into practice. The platoon commanders stretch unhappily then shuffle out into the sunshine.

I give them an hour to come up with their plans and prepare their soldiers (or at least wake some of them up). Then we gather on the parade ground and I tell them that one of the platoon commanders will give his orders while the rest observe. I nominate a captain with a pencil moustache who looks a bit like a young David Niven. Though I suspect he probably doesn't have quite the same twinkly charm; he responds to the nomination with a look like I've just suggested he fuck his grandmother.

Sgt Mason, who has come along to watch, whispers that his name is Abdallah, but B Squadron have privately dubbed him, 'Captain Fantastic'. Captain Fantastic is of the firm belief that he is Mr Maysan. He is particularly attached to his moustache; his all-time favourite pastime is staring lovingly at his own reflection and gurgling happily while he strokes it with a special comb.

He is also astonishingly thick; during Sgt Mason's map-reading lesson he'd somehow got it into his head that all you had to do was follow the north arrow on a compass and it would eventually take you wherever you needed to be. He'd refused to hear anything different in fact – despite repeated attempts to explain to him what a magnet is – and had eventually just raised his hand haughtily in the air, palm outwards (which might have been when the compass got snapped in half, admits Sgt Mason). Suleiman has heard that he's the nephew of a government minister, which would explain the diva-like behaviour. He certainly looks like he's ready to throw a *dolce* soy skinny *latte* over me now, anyway.

Captain Fantastic stalks to the front, muttering darkly. Barely looking at his soldiers, he rattles off a dozen short sentences, pausing only to shrug expressively and shoot more venomous glances in my direction. He finishes with a brief tirade (according to Suleiman this is a vicious warning not to lose any more rifles – evidently they're not proving as easy to find as Major Hassan reckoned), then dismisses them with a disinterested '*Yalla*.'[35]

About twenty soldiers start to pull on body armour. I take Suleiman and walk over to where Captain Fantastic is standing, eyes closed, and presumably wishing he could hurl me, Sgt Mason, and anyone else who presumes to get between him and 'tache time, right into the heart of the sun. I clear my throat.

'Thank you for the orders, Captain Abdallah. That was quite . . . short. Are you sure the soldiers were told everything they need to know for this patrol?'

His lip curls. Why will I not just die and leave him alone?

'We are walking, then we search cars. What do they need to know?'

'Well, there's a few things really. Like timings, and what they need to bring, and where the emergency RV is, and . . . I mean, there's a lot. All the things we talked about in the lesson.'

'I told them everything. All the things in the lesson.'

'Right. OK. OK, well, can you show me on the map where you are going?'

'I know where I am going.'

'Yes, but if I could just check, can you just show me on the map?'

'But you know where I am going.'

'Well . . . yes, I do, but still, just so we're on the same page, can you just show me on . . .'

'I have no map.'

'But I gave you a map in the lesson. I gave all of you a map in the lesson.'

'The lesson was a long time ago.'

'The lesson was this morning, Captain Abd . . . oh, look, never mind, just show me on here.'

Captain Fantastic brushes his hand vaguely over my map in a gesture that easily covers an area of ten square kilometres.

'Here.'

'Well, that's quite a big area, but . . . alright. What is your route to the VCP?'

'We do the VCP on the road, there.'

'OK . . . wait, what? No . . . no, that's just outside the camp. You're supposed to go a mile away.'

'No, we cannot go there. The men are very tired.'

'The men haven't done anything all morning apart from sleep. They can't be tired. Look at them; they don't look tired. And they're putting on their kit.'

'We have no water.'

'Yes you do. We gave a thousand litres to the QM yesterday.'

Captain Fantastic sighs. Then stares at me, hard.

'Someone died there yesterday,' he whispers.

'What, at the VCP? At the place you're supposed to do a VCP today? But . . . it's just a random road. How can someone have died there yesterday?'

'I am so tired. My life is very hard. Why are you persecuting me?'

'I'm not persecuting you, Captain Abdallah, I'm just trying to help you plan a patrol and run a very simp—'

'I do not want to be in the Army anymore.'

Eventually, of course, Captain Fantastic does the VCP exactly where he said he would; fifty yards from the front gate of camp. Sometimes, I muse to Sgt Mason, you can't even lead the horse to water, let alone make the absolute fucking bellend drink. Captain Fantastic sits in the shade of one of the Ford trucks alternately sleeping and gazing at himself in a wing mirror. Sgt Mason and I watch as his men desultorily search a few cars, occasionally helping themselves to the odd choice item from the boot when they think we're not looking.

About an hour in we're both somewhat surprised to hear the telltale *crack-thump* of a dozen AK rounds passing very close over our heads. Once we've peeled ourselves off the tarmac and established that we are not, in fact, all about to die, I ask Suleiman to find out what in the name of fuck that was in aid of. He comes back after a couple of minutes and tells us that one of the cut-offs – soldiers who are posted a few hundred metres either side of the VCP to catch anyone who tries to just drive through it – wanted to come out of the sun. They hadn't got any radios so decided to apprise the chain of command of their request by firing a long burst of 7.62mm straight over their own VCP. I look at Sgt Mason, who just closes his eyes.

The only consolation is that Captain Fantastic was clearly as surprised as we were, and dropped the watermelon he had just pilfered from a passing truck. It has burst open on the tarmac and painted his boots and shins a very gratifying shade of red. I feel my mood soar. Sometimes, that's all it takes.

Saturday, 12 August 2006 – Kumayt

It's our last night in Kumayt; we'll be leaving at the crack of dawn tomorrow. Not that we've told 3/4/10 that. No one's tried to kill us yet, but Jonty isn't going to take the risk of someone letting the local militia know to put out the EFPs. Luckily we've got the perfect excuse for turning in early to do some discreet packing.

We've taken to playing a bit of knockabout baseball on the parade ground with 3/4/10 after dinner. It's their second favourite evening activity, only slightly less popular than sitting on the roof of the surrounding buildings to observe us during what passes for our leisure time here. The boys are all playing up to it outrageously of course. And if you close your eyes on one of those warm summer evenings you can almost imagine you're back in England, on the boundary of some bucolic village cricket green. Until you open your eyes and realise the polite smattering of applause you just heard isn't for an elegant square drive to the boundary, but rather for Womack pulling a Charles Atlas front double-biceps pose in his hot-pink 'PIMP' crop-top.

Anyway, during this evening's game, one of the *jundis* put an absolute pearler straight through the windscreen of their commanding officer's brand new 5 Series. I have never seen soldiers move so fast – I didn't know 3/4/10 had it in them, frankly – and the parade ground is deserted before the baseball bat has even stopped spinning. It makes sense, I suppose; this is still an army in which three years ago they'd have wired your testicles to a car battery for telling the one about Saddam and the geese.[36]

It's the small hours. Most of B Squadron is fast asleep, but I've picked up a radio stag;[37] two hours sitting in a makeshift ops room with the duty signaller, reading *Nuts* and periodically reassuring CAN that everyone's still alive. Griffiths and Buxton happen to be in the roof sangar when I start, so I climb the ladder and sit with them for a while, bluffing my way through the constellations and chatting about their plans for when we get home.

These are my favourite times in Iraq, I think. No map-reading in a superheated Snatch, no Jonty in your ear asking where you are and what you're doing. Just me and the boys, sitting companionably in the warm night air, yakking away with that peculiar freedom you only get when you're talking to someone in the pitch-black.

Buxton is going to be a paramedic, he tells us. Taking care of the wounded the night it all went sideways in CAN gave him more satisfaction than three years of soldiering. Griffiths will be staying in. There's nothing for him where he comes from; most of his mates are either in nick, addicted to something or other, or both. Anyway he reckons there's a war on the horizon – could be Russia, maybe China – and he's always wanted to blow up another tank.

They ask what I'm going to do. I say something about teaching again. Will I hell – the truth is I don't have a clue – but what I do know is that I'd rather end my days working as a harem maid to 3/4/10 than go back to Enfield.

I leave them to it – if war films have taught me anything it's that wanging on about your plans for after all this is over is a guaranteed sniper round between the eyes. I'm at the bottom of the ladder when there are two gunshots, obscenely loud in the darkness. Then in my earpiece, Buxton.

'CONTACT WAIT OUT!'

I'm back up that ladder like I've been strapped to an ACME rocket. I haven't got a clue what's happening, but it's the lizard brain in me; when there's trouble you want to get up high. Either we're under attack by the militia or 3/4/10 have finally decided they're going to have a go on Cameron whether we like it or not. Or possibly both. I crash into the little sangar and collide with someone, who must be Buxton because it's like falling into a soft play.

'What the *fuck* is even happening?' I enquire commandingly.

'Two rounds, hundred metres, from the road, some bloke . . . can't see him now . . . just drove up and fired at us,' says Griffiths breathlessly.

'At us? Two rounds at us?'

'Yeah.'

It's all I need. Bent double, I run back to the ladder and stick my head over the low wall there.

'STAND TO! STAND TO! Smith – can you hear me? Get on the net to CAN *now*. Tell them contact, as at . . . ,' I check my watch, '. . . as at 0245. Two rounds, small arms, am investigating, wait out. Got it?'

I can hear the tumult from the garages below as every man in B Squadron simultaneously sits bolt upright then falls out of his cot bed wrapped in a mosquito net. I return to the sangar.

'Where is he now, boys? Eyes on?'

'No boss, he's fucked off. Can't see him at all.'

'Pass me those NVGs . . . and keep that road covered.'

I scan the road, a strip of black against the green, pixelated sand. There's a car. No movement though. What's that next to it? It's big, whatever it is. And boxy.

'Can't see anyone . . . something next to the car though . . . did he go into the ditch?' I ask.

'Dunno, boss. All I saw was him getting out of his tractor, then I think he said something, and then we heard the shots . . .' replies Buxton.

'Got it. I think he must have crawled up the . . . hang on, what did you say? Tractor?'

'Yeah. That one. Next to the car.'

I think for a moment. The militia use Toyota pickups. Or police cars, when they're allowed to borrow them. I haven't heard of them using tractors. It's conceivable, I suppose, that in the complete absence of *any* other options you *might* try to carry out a drive-by from the back of a Massey Ferguson. But it doesn't seem very likely. I hear someone clattering up the ladder. Then Jonty squeezes into the sangar.

'Where are they?' he asks urgently.

'Um . . . out there on the road, I think. Maybe in the ditch?' I say.

'Right. That their car? Fuckers. Mr Kite's getting a team ready to go out. We'll get another team on the roof. If they move, we'll drill them.'

'No, the car's not theirs. They . . . actually, I think there might only be one gunman . . . anyway, he came in a . . . tractor,' I say, uncertainly.

I feel Jonty twisting round to look at me.

'A tractor?' he asks, the beginnings of incredulity in his voice.

'Um. Yes. Apparently,' I reply. Buxton and Griffiths – the absolute bastards – have by this point clearly decided to take an impromptu vow of silence.

'They don't use *tractors*,' says Jonty, witheringly.

There is a garbled shout in the darkness.

'They don't start fucking chit-chats, either,' Jonty grumbles. Then he cups his hands around his mouth and addresses the night.

'Now, whoever that is, come out from wherever you are hiding. Right now. This is a British Army location you've been shooting at. If we see any weapons, we will open fire. Do you understand?'

There is an answering shout. Then another. It sounds like there are actually two of them out there. We don't have an interpreter yet, so Jonty deploys the standard British Army Officer Universal Translation Tool; speak English loudly, get even louder, then go as loud as you can, with a clear undertone of irritation that your interlocutor has inexplicably not learned so much as a lick of English in the whole thirty seconds you've been shouting at him. Oddly it doesn't seem to be working. The ladder clatters again. Suleiman joins us in the sangar. It is getting quite crowded.

Suleiman conducts a lengthy exchange with the voices on the road. I catch the words *Britani* and *Klashnikuf*, but that's about it. Then one voice says something and Suleiman laughs loudly. I swallow nervously. It doesn't sound as if he's coaxing some pair of desperate insurgents to come out with their hands up. In fact the three of them sound like they're having a fine old time. I try to remember exactly what I'd told the signaller to radio in to CAN. Then Suleiman turns to the rest of us in the sangar.

'These men, they are not terrorists,' he chuckles. 'This man has a *tractor*. The JAM, they do not use *tractors*.'

Alright Suleiman, I want to say; we've been around that particular buoy quite enough for one evening, thanks very much. Then it gets worse.

'One man is a farmer. He is driving to the fields in his tractor – it is too hot in the day now to work – and then he has hit a car. There is another man in the car, who has been sleeping. He has got out of the car with his gun, and there has been an argument. Then the first man – the farmer – has gone to his tractor and he has taken his gun. Then *bang bang*, he has fired into the sky, because he is angry about the crash. Then, they heard the shouting from here, and they hid in the ditch. They did not know there were British here. They were scared you would shoot them.'

As well they might be; one false move and they'd have had half of B Squadron on the roof trying to blow them away. You couldn't write it though; an RTA between a nocturnal farmer and Kumayt's answer to Rip Van Winkle, who apparently can't think of anywhere better to take a nap than in the middle of a main road. And instead of just swapping details like normal people, they've decided to duke it out like Old West gunslingers a hundred yards away from a British Army sangar. Iraqis, I decide – not for the first time on this tour – are out of their fucking minds.

It doesn't matter though. All that matters is that two locals have had a minor fender bender and I've reacted by charging about the ramparts like Michael Caine in *Zulu*. The fact that Buxton and Griffiths called it first – not to mention missed what sounds like it was quite a lively exchange of views out on the road even before all the shooting – is neither here nor there. I was in charge, and so as far as the Army's concerned, it's all on me. It's why they pay you the Elton John wages, I suppose.

In the end there's no official sanction; when I see Jonty the next morning he just smiles wryly and suggests that as a rule, we probably shouldn't put a thousand-man armoured battlegroup on high alert because a tractor's hit a car thirty miles away. The boys' reaction is a different matter. Naturally – inevitably – every farmer in southern Iraq seems to be put-putting around on his fucking tractor during our drive back to Shaibah. And every single one, without fail, is greeted over the radio with a falsetto, 'Stand tooooooo!' and 'Don't shoot, Mr Mulligan, I'm a *friendly* tractor!' by the B Squadron chorus line. It is a very long eight hours.

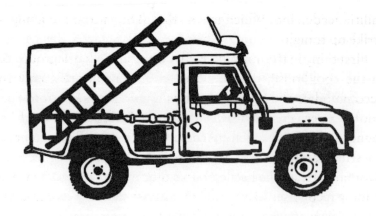

16

Strike

Sunday, 13 August 2006 – Shaibah / Basra City

We've heard about strike ops, of course. It's usually in the form of a terse little update from Jonty in our nightly O Group: 'Significant contact in Al Muwafiqina during a strike by the Basra City South Battlegroup last night. 2 x friendly T2 casualties, and 1 x Bravo (*human target*) killed; 800 rounds of 5.56 and 7.62 fired.'

You connect the dots to the sudden flurry of tracer you saw while you were sitting on top of the Hesco in Tiger Lines after dinner, and wonder briefly what it must have been like out there in the narrow streets, with the rounds arcing towards you from the pitch-black night. Then you go back to your tent to watch the next episode of *Glee* and forget all about it.

Well, now we're going to find out what it's like for ourselves. We have a new General, an energetic, hard-charging cavalryman, and he is determined to clean house in Basra. Starting with the militia leadership. Which means that B Squadron are going on a strike op tonight.

First thing in the morning, we troop along to battlegroup orders in the cookhouse, the only tent in Tiger Lines big enough to accommodate the full cast for this evening's production. On the floor is a perfect scale model of northern Basra, the size of half a tennis court, with carefully cut-out cardboard shapes representing streets and blocks of houses. It must have taken someone days. Around it are all the battlegroup's officers, as well as a few people I don't recognise, like a pair of aircrew and a bearded dude in scruffy civvies who couldn't have been more obviously Special Forces if he'd been sitting there taking notes for an explosive autobiography called, *Fucking Have Some of That; My 25 Years in the SAS*. This is clearly quite a big deal.

The PWRR CO stands up and starts running through the plan. We are going after a JAM company commander, he tells us. He leads a rag-tag bunch of a hundred or so militiamen in al Latif, a truly nasty district in the north of Basra. It looks hideous even on the model; a rat run of twisting, narrow streets just made for ambushes.

The PWRR intelligence officer flashes the target's photo up on a TV next to the model. He certainly looks the part. In fact, he looks like the live action version of Jafar from *Aladdin*. Apparently his specialism is executing women by the side of the road for breaking whichever imagined tenets of sharia law JAM's more mental clerics have come up with in their fever dreams this week. I feel a stirring in the room at this. Then again they used to tell Lancaster crews there were poison gas factories in the middle of the cities they were bombing; you just never know with the intelligence lot.

Next comes troops to task; who will be doing what in the CO's plan. A Company are on the inner cordon, with Recce Platoon doing the strike itself, and C Company in reserve. (I wonder what the CO really knows; you don't keep a whole armoured infantry company in your back pocket unless you're expecting trouble.) B

Squadron will be something called 'outer cordon and strike delivery'.

I feel suddenly a bit deflated. In spite of the obvious potential for tonight's little jaunt to turn into *Apocalypse Now*, it's still a bit disheartening to be left out entirely. But this will be an armour job all the way; a couple of Challengers on the outer cordon to keep an eye on things, and maybe one or two to lead the Warriors carrying Recce Platoon onto the target. I wonder if I can at least hang around in the ops room to listen on the radio.

Once the CO has finished, we file out of the cookhouse and Jonty tells us to meet him in the Squadron HQ tent in two hours for his own orders. Then he tells me to go and pick out the six least-fucked Snatches we have, for tonight.

'Sorry, Jonty . . . tonight? What, for . . . hang on, is there a patrol or some . . . what do you mean "for tonight"?'

'For the strike op. The one we're doing tonight,' replies Jonty, frowning. 'You've just had a two-hour Battlegroup O Group about it, if that helps. Strike delivery. That's you, and Third Troop. You're taking Recce Platoon to the target.'

Oh. Christ.

After lunch we reconvene and Jonty lays it all out in detail. Which doesn't help much, because it's actually even worse than I've spent the last two hours imagining. The battlegroup will leave Shaibah in a single column of sixty vehicles. Fifty-four of those vehicles will be armoured, covered in the most sophisticated ceramic composites British science can develop. Six of them – my ones – will be chipboard Snatch Land Rovers, covered in their own crews' cerebrospinal fluid if anything goes even a tiny bit wrong.

As we enter the city, the armoured vehicles will peel off one by one and take up positions in overwatch. Eventually all that will be left will be a single Warrior, with my Snatches following closely behind. Three hundred metres from the target this Warrior will also peel off, leaving us to turn off the main road and into al Latif. Alone.

Assuming I can find the target (which is far from guaranteed – the satellite photo map looks like a fucking Magic Eye picture), we'll drop off Recce Platoon. They'll kick in the door, and once they're finished we'll come back the same way we went in. Except this time with a JAM company commander in the back of my Snatch. Who will be either very upset or dead, depending on how the evening has gone.

On the walk down to Third Troop's tent after Jonty's orders, I think about the various different ways it could all go wrong tonight. It's a short walk but I still come up with about twenty, ranging from the terminal (like an RPG-7 through my windscreen the minute I drive into al Latif) to the merely embarrassing (like dropping Recce Platoon off at the wrong house; it happens more than you'd think).

This is the real deal. Soldiers die doing what we are about to do. In fact there's been one recently; a corporal from the Devonshire and Dorset Light Infantry shot dead in some backstreet ambush on the way to the target a few weeks ago. He'd been in a Snatch, too.

I give the boys the brief. They take it reasonably well. In the sense that once they've all told me it's the worst fucking plan they've ever heard, and Buxton has offered to just shoot himself at the end of the CO's bed if it saves the CO the bother of sending him to al Latif in a Snatch to get killed there, the moaning subsides to a quiet roar and they start packing their kit. They know there's precisely diddly squat I can do about it anyway; the Army's in charge now.

After a subdued dinner, we head down to the tank park and meet up with the PWRR's Recce Platoon. Recce Platoons tend to be the best soldiers in their battalion, and for tonight they'll need to be. The films make it look easy; it's all 'Room clear!' and shimmying artfully around corners while the baddies obligingly stay where they are and wait to get shot. That's not how it works in real life.

These boys will be assaulting a breeze-block compound they've never laid eyes on before, in the pitch-black, carrying 30kg of kit each, with a not insignificant chance that behind the next door they kick down will be a militiaman waiting to empty an AK magazine into their face from three yards away. And that's if he hasn't already opened up through a wall and shot them all dead while they're stacking up[38] for entry. Frankly I'm having fucking kittens, and I'm only dropping them off outside.

The Recce Platoon commander is Steve; tough, squat and commissioned from the ranks. He's a professional soldier to his core; indeed every time I've met him before I've got the sense that he's a bit bemused – in the nicest way possible – about what the hell someone like me is even doing in Iraq. And tonight he's not the only one.

With everything prepped, we settle down next to the Snatches. Sgt Mason has bribed one of the REME (*Royal Electrical and Mechanical Engineers*) vehicle mechanics with a case of Cokes to give them a once over, and I've bagsied the one he gaped least disbelievingly at. We aren't going anywhere for a while yet; this is classic Army 'hurry up and wait'. It's symptomatic of a work-place culture in which everyone's main career objective is to avoid pissing off the guy above him by being late for anything.

It's also an excellent way of broadcasting your intentions to anyone who happens to be watching. Like Shaibah's entire LEC population, who are currently sitting on their haunches and staring at us. Knowing the Army, there is probably a whole team of staff officers wondering vexedly why it is that the targets always seem to know we're coming, without ever *quite* making the mental leap to the sixty vehicles sat on the tank park for three hours before every strike op with ladders and grappling hooks strapped all over them.

I don't mind the wait myself; it gives me a chance to stare obsessively at my map and wonder whether, if I press it really, really hard against my forehead, the route will somehow sear itself into my brain. I'm not worried about the first bit. All I have to do is stick to the Warrior in front like he owes me money, then at a given signal – we've agreed on a blue cyalume thrown out of the turret – turn off into al Latif.

It's the bit that comes afterwards which I'm flapping about. There aren't any roadsigns in al Latif, and they don't go a bundle for house numbers or twee little plaques saying 'Acorn Cottage' or 'Hollydown House' either. So it's left at the fork, left *again* just after the road widens, right just before what looks like a pile of car tyres, then the house is on the left, and if it does have a plaque it'll presumably say 'Wonky Shack Next to Wasteground or Possibly Enormous Puddle'. It's enough to make fucking Magellan sweat.

Eventually the order we've been waiting for crackles over the radio: 'All callsigns, mount up, and prepare to move.' Steve nips out his cigarette and jumps into the back of my Snatch. I get into the cab with Griffiths. Mine is the first vehicle in the troop; I couldn't look Cpl Robbins in the eye and tell him to take this one in. I see the black shape of the Warrior in front of us lurch. And then we're moving.

It's lights off all the way, so as we roll out of the front gate I flick down my NVGs (*night vision goggles*). The militias would have to have all the situational awareness of Ralph Wiggum not to know we're coming anyway, but there's no sense in making it easy for them. The Army does have some outstanding NVGs; lightweight, adjustable, and with visuals like something out of *Call of Duty*. But they're for pilots and Special Forces, and for showing to visiting politicians while glibly pretending that everyone's got them. They're not for proles like us.

In fact, we don't even get one for both eyes. Presumably by issuing monocular NVGs the MoD can cut the unit cost by half; unfortunately it also means that any wearer has the depth perception of a pissed bat, and is why most British Army night operations feature at least one participant being abruptly clotheslined by a doorframe they could have sworn was still six feet away.

We cross the motorway bridge outside the Air Station and chug into the city. Now and again someone darts out of an alley to throw a brick at a Warrior, but otherwise the streets are empty; there's been a curfew in place since it all started going noisy a couple of weeks ago. I listen on the radio as the other troop leaders peel off into their cordon positions in their tanks. They sound keyed up. God knows why, I think uncharitably; JAM has never so much as scratched a Challenger 2. Their biggest problem tonight is going to be running out of hot water for a brew.

We press on north towards al Latif. My eyes are flicking back and forth in a constant pattern now; road, GPS, map, road, GPS, map. We're 500 metres from the turn-off. The road up here is a mess and I can barely see the Warrior in front of me through the thick clouds of dust from its tracks. Christ, what I wouldn't give for headlights. Three hundred metres. I begin to croak the distances over my PRR to the rest of the troop. Two hundred metres. That must be the little roundabout I'd noticed on the map. One hundred metres. I feel the Snatch start to slow. Fifty metres.

I press the GPS into my thigh, trying to shield its dim glow, and stare into the blackness in front of me for the Warrior turret and a little blue cyalume. Any minute now. Any minute. We must be right there. The Warrior slows to a crawl. Then it stops. There is a moment of silence. Then my earpiece crackles.

'Er, Hotel Charlie Three Zero, this is Hotel Bravo One One – you're . . . er, a hundred metres past the turn.'

Suddenly there's a shrill ringing in my ears. And for half a second it feels like I might actually be frozen; somehow physically immobilised by a few short words and the shattering horror of what they're implying has just happened. Then the world crash-zooms around me, and I can hear Steve's fist hammering on the roof above my head.

'YOU'VE MISSED THE FUCKING *TURN*!' he roars.

'OH *FUCK*!' I yelp in reply. Then, on the PRR, 'ALL CALLSIGNS. STOP STOP STOP!'

This is about as bad as it gets. There might be bigger, more spectacular ways to fuck up a strike op – reversing over Jonty on the tank park, for example – but I wouldn't bet on it. I'm the first vehicle, with a whole battlegroup shepherding me onto the objective, and every ops room from here to al Amarah listening in on the net. And I've missed the motherfucking, bastard, *cunt* turn-off.

What the bloody hell happened to the cyalume? How the fuck was I supposed to see the turn when I couldn't see three feet past the front of the Snatch? Not that it matters, of course. All that matters is that I – and God alone knows how many of the vehicles following me – have missed the *fucking* turn-off. I feel like curling up into the footwell. Jesus Christ, what a mess.

Griffiths is ten seconds ahead of me and already has the wheel hard over. He pulls forward and we start to turn. Then I see the looming blackness of a ditch in front of us and shriek at him to stop; if we put the Snatch in there it really will be game over. I hear the gearbox protest as Griffiths wrenches the vehicle into reverse and we jolt backwards, then promptly crash into the central reservation. I am close to bursting into tears; this is rapidly turning into *Carry On Up the Strike Op*.

We're only a couple of hundred metres from the target's house, too; if he's got any sense he'll be in his car and halfway to Tehran by now. Unless of course he's glued to his bedroom window and waking up his kids to come and have a look in the belief that some kind of travelling circus has just arrived in town. Above me Steve is keeping up a steady stream of invective; if he found me vaguely amusing before, he definitely doesn't now. He's drilled Recce Platoon for months in anticipation of their first strike op, and here they are, trapped in the back of Snatches while Griffiths practises his three-point-turns in the dark.

After what feels like several lifetimes, we're pointing back down the road. Griffiths floors it and we race towards the turn-off. It looks like the whole troop has missed the fucking thing; I can see them struggling through their own three-pointers as we roar past. There is another Warrior parked up ahead of us, its commander standing up in the turret and waving frantically towards a side-street. As we screech past he throws a blue cyalume onto the road, and I have to fight down a very strong urge to open my door and shoot him in the head. I settle for opening it to let him know he's a useless twat, and we take the turn-off practically on two wheels.

Of course the next bit – the complicated bit, the bit that I'd fretted endlessly about – goes like a dream. We snake through al Latif's winding backstreets like we're on rails. Steve, all trust gone, roars out the directions anyway. Then I see a patch of waste ground to our right, and beyond it a small, breeze-block house. Jesus Christ. This is it. We roll to a halt.

'*Debus, debus, debus,*' whispers Steve on the PRR. I feel the Snatch bounce on its axles as he and the other Recce Platoon boys jump down. They jog past and I hear a whispered but heartfelt, '*wanker*', which feels fair in the circumstances. Then I watch as they join the column of kneeling figures already lining up on the roadside. At a hand signal from Steve, the column rises and begins to file carefully towards the house, each soldier with his weapon in the shoulder, covering the opposite arcs to the man in front of him.

I get out of the Snatch and take up a fire position. The column reaches the house and starts stacking up outside the front door. Then pairs and threes start to detach themselves, slipping round the sides and back to cut off any squirters.[39] I scan the rooftops around us through my NVGs. The whole neighbourhood seems dead to the world. They can't be really – we've just recreated the pile-up scene from *Bourne Ultimatum* at the end of their road – but if they are awake then they're keeping their heads down. For now anyway.

Back by the house, I see the entry man swing back his Enforcer, the small steel battering ram that will put three tons of force through the door lock. Behind him kneels his cover man, weapon pointing directly at the doorway. His change lever will be set to A for Automatic; if there is anything waiting on the other side of the door, it will be his job to hose it down with everything he has. Then Steve counts them down.

'3 . . . 2 . . . 1 . . . GO GO GO!'

I can't see the actual door go in, but it must have flown off its hinges because Recce Platoon pour into the house like water. I hear shouts and see brief flashes of white light through the gaps in the breeze-block wall. They'll be moving fast, trying to fill the room while the target is still tangled up in his duvet, dazzling him with torches before he even thinks about going for the AK next to him. Then it'll be plasticuffs over his wrists and straight into a quickfire round of questions while he's still trying to process the fact that he's got a dozen squaddies standing at the end of his bed.

The Army calls this 'the shock of capture', but I've met the guy in Recce Platoon who does the tactical questioning and I suspect in this specific case it's more, 'the shock of being woken up at two in the morning by LCpl "Skeletor" Jones, quite probably the ugliest man in NATO.' I can hear him going at it now; the bellowed question, followed by a rather more sedate translation – it doesn't sound like Steve's interpreter is really getting into the spirit of things – then a plaintive wail from whoever it is they're talking to. They don't sound much like a JAM company commander. Then again, Jones's face startles people in the lunch queue at Tiger Lines; spotlit by an Army torch at 2 a.m. it must be like being questioned by Darth Maul. So it's not impossible that they've got the right guy after all.

You could argue that this is all a bit inhumane. And admittedly, it's not how they did things in *Dixon of Dock Green*. But then again those lads never had to worry about someone emptying an AK into their panda car while they were serving a warrant. The streets might be empty now, but it's a sure bet that the militia will be getting their act together, and fast. This is their neighbourhood. I scan the rooftops again. There are already a couple of heads bobbing around on top of a house about fifty yards away.

The intelligence officer had reckoned we'd be OK for about fifteen minutes before the local militia could try something on, but presumably he hadn't accounted for us using at least five of those playing bumper cars in the Snatches. I wonder briefly whether a firefight would be the worst thing in the world at this point. It'd take people's minds off my galactic fuck-up anyway.

And with any luck I'd get my head blown off, so I wouldn't have to explain what's just happened to Jonty. His promise back in Germany to sack me if I turned out to be shit suddenly feels very real again.

But there won't be a firefight tonight; a minute or so later Recce Platoon begin emerging from the house, jogging back to the Snatches in ones and twos. I stand up as Steve passes me.

'Moved away. Months ago apparently. Fucking Slime,' he says, disgustedly.

I make all the right annoyed-sounding noises, but as I climb back into the Snatch my heart is singing. I'm probably still going to get hanged, drawn and quartered for missing the turn-off, but not nearly as much as if the target had still been living here. In fact there's a good chance the grown-ups will reserve most of their ire for the intelligence boys, who appear to have chalked up yet another absolute blinder – in what is by now quite a long list – by sending nearly a thousand people on a strike op against the wrong house.

The drive back to Shaibah is uneventful. After we pass the main gate, we stop by the unloading bay to clear our weapons. I stand next to the Snatch, waiting for the boys to finish. Steve walks slowly up to me. I don't dare look at him at first. I've put a size eleven boot straight through his plan, not to mention placing him and the rest of Recce Platoon in very real danger. Strike ops are dicey at the best of times, let alone when you give the target a spectacularly noisy five-minute warning that you're about to kick his door in.

Steve stares at me and raises an eyebrow. I open my mouth to say something, and without any warning whatsoever – and to my utter horror – feel my bottom lip start to wobble.

Steve wraps his arms around me in a bear hug, and tells me not to worry about it. Then he calls me a wanker again. But a lot more gently this time.

Later on, as it happens, I do have a bit of a cry; in the shower block, with the water on as high as it'll go, and only after checking three times that there's no one else in the building. Perhaps it's just because it's been a harrowing night. Or maybe the sense we're running out of lives is starting to catch up with me. But if I had to guess, I'd say a lot of it might actually be because of Steve. Whether he understood that I was punishing myself enough as it was, or could see that I'm starting to get to the end of my tether, it took him all of a forty-minute drive back to Shaibah to forgive someone who could very easily have got him killed.

And if that doesn't make you well up, then I don't know what will.

17

Cedar II

Tuesday, 15 August 2006 – Shaibah / Dhi Qar / Camp Abu Naji

If we'd thought Basra was spinning out of control, Maysan has meanwhile gone full *Ragnarök*. Route Six is now seeded end to end with IEDs and al Amarah is like the Thunderdome; patrols can't get more than a couple of hundred metres in without half the city trying to kick the shit out of them. CAN itself is getting IDF'd five or six times a day, and the mortar crews have clearly remembered to write down the range because they're starting to hit stuff. A couple of weeks ago they blew up the fuel bladder, the same one that Godders and I had once tried to use as cover, abruptly sending 80,000 litres of aviation fuel up in smoke. Then they waited a week or so for it to be replaced, and duly blew it up again.

As a result of all of this, the Army has been forced to face into the realities of the situation – not always a given; this is after all the team which brought you both Gallipoli *and* the Somme – and close

CAN for good. We are moving out. From now on, the General has declared, no longer will we force a whole battlegroup to live cooped up in the most IDF'd square kilometre on the planet.

Instead they will be set free, like doves at a slightly down-market wedding, to range up and down the border with Iran. They will live like their forebears in Eighth Army and master the desert as they did. They will stem the flood of lethal weaponry from across the border, and keep a bewildered enemy at a constant loss as to where they will pop up next. Most importantly, they will no longer require nearly a thousand soldiers every two weeks to keep them supplied with Fruits of the Forest cheesecake, and a dozen tankers' worth of kerosene whenever the militia decide it's time to blow up the fuel bladder again.

It will need a lot of careful managing though. When we pulled out of al Muthanna after PIC, our camp there was looted bare by the locals in about five minutes flat. There had been a camera crew present too, so the whole country had watched it happen. CAN will be different, Jonty tells us. CAN will be wound down in an orderly, soldier-like manner, and handed over to the Iraqi Army looking like new. I think about the footage I've seen of jubilant al-Muthannians pulling air-conditioners out of the walls with their cars and reverently bearing away tattered copies of *Nuts* and *Zoo* like they're holy texts, and don't say anything.

The General's plan means we have exactly twenty-one days to empty CAN. The staff officers in his HQ, who have a tenuous grasp on the limits of human endurance at the best of times, have promptly issued a task list that would have made a Roman galley slave gulp. Today we are on our fourth convoy escort to CAN in two weeks.

It's a long old route; dog-legging from Shaibah all the way to Nasiriyah, the capital of Dhi Qar province, 150 miles to the north-west. There we will resupply at some American base called Camp Cedar II (what happened to Camp Cedar I is never explained) before travelling another 150 miles north-east and into CAN. The militias must have discovered the back roads we were using before, because Nasiriyah isn't exactly a picnic; the Italians lost nineteen blokes there in a single car-bombing a couple of years ago, and there has been a steady trickle of nastiness ever since.

The first half of the trip is a cinch; the motorway we're on isn't used much and there's endless desert in every direction, so we don't have a lot to do except VP check the occasional bridge and wonder idly what had possessed some Saddam-era official to install a concrete parasol and some plastic cartoon animals every five miles or so.

I'm hesitant to lay into the Iraqis' taste in roadside facilities – we are, after all, the nation which brought the world Little Chef – but it's hard to imagine why you would ever pull over for a picnic with the kids in the middle of what is effectively a gigantic long-jump pit. We stop for a break at one anyway, and the boys carry out the usual rituals of the British soldier at leisure – taking photos of each other pretending to fuck the cartoon animals, then trying to knock over the parasol.

Jonty watches, smiling tolerantly. I'd found him the previous evening crouched over his desk in the Squadron HQ tent, carefully marking up every likely VP from Shaibah to CAN. I left before he noticed, and would never dream of telling him I'd seen what he was doing, but it has confirmed yet again that he's one of the good ones. Nine out of ten squadron leaders would have just winged it on the day. And when you're two-thirds of the way through the tour and the close shaves are mounting up, you hang on to that kind of thing. If we do get whacked one of these days, it won't be because Jonty phoned it in.

A few hours later we arrive at Camp Cedar II. It's enormous, and we drive along the perimeter fence for miles before we find the main entrance. Third Troop is doing its turn at the front and I take it slow as we roll through their anti-car-bomb chicane. I haven't got this far only to get flat-packed by some dip-chewing hick from Toad Suck, Alabama.

Eventually we reach the massive front gates. A door opens in one of them and a small, round American, turtle-like in helmet and full body armour, steps out. I climb out of my Snatch and tell him that we're a British convoy from Basra and that we're scheduled to resupply here before continuing north.

The American stares at me. Or at least I think he does; he's wearing a pair of wraparound shades and I can't actually see his eyes.

'Nobody tole me 'bout that,' he says doubtfully. 'Where d'you say y'all are from?'

'We're the UK Force Reserve. From Basra. Can you open the gates?'

'Hawd on,' he says, turning away. He starts mumbling into a radio handset. I start to get a throbbing sensation in my temples.

'Look, can you please just open the gates?' I interrupt. 'Half the convoy's still stuck on the main road. It's not safe for them just to sit there, and they're blocking traf—'

'Hawd *on*,' he repeats, and this time there is a hand, index finger raised.

I fight down a sudden urge to reach out and cut it off with my Leatherman, and take a deep breath. Behind me I can see people getting out of their vehicles to see what's going on. One of them is Jonty, who raises his arms in the universal gesture for, 'Why are you standing in front of a closed gate while an entire convoy sits on the road with its arse in the breeze, you fucking bubblehead?'

I shrug demonstratively. The American finishes his muttered conference and turns back to me.

'Ah'm gonna need to see some ID.'

For a moment I think I can't possibly have heard him correctly. It must show, because he says it again, this time slower, as if talking to a small – and not particularly bright – child. Wordlessly I reach into my pocket and hand over my ID card.

'Nope,' says the American. 'Ah'm gonna need to see *all* y'all's IDs.'

I gape at him.

'But that's . . . ridiculous. You can see . . . I mean, we're obviously British? Just look at how I'm dressed! And how I talk! Look at them!' I say despairingly, pointing at the top cover in a nearby Snatch. 'I mean, that guy's *black*!'

The soldier in question, who is from Second Troop, stares at me. I mouth an apology.

'Y'can get black Eyeraqis,' the American replies stubbornly. But he doesn't sound sure.

'Just open the fucking gates! For Christ's sake – I'm British, this is a British convoy, and . . . just fucking open the gates!' I argue eloquently. At this, the American's lips take on a noticeable pout.

'No,' he says, shortly. 'Git them ID cards, and then y'all can come in. Y'all could be in-fil-trators.' He says 'infiltrators' like it's from a foreign language. Which it's increasingly clear it might be.

I give up; we really don't have time for this. No one has given us a briefing on the calibre of the enemy round here, but if this clown thinks they're capable enough to assemble a dozen Snatches, sixty sets of British uniform, and a spokesman able to pass himself off as a shrill subaltern from just south of High Wycombe, then ambushing a convoy that hasn't moved in fifteen minutes will be a piece of cake.

I storm off down the convoy to collect a squadron's worth of ID cards, or failing that, driving licences. Either would have been fine as it turned out; in fact I could have handed the guy on the gate a sheaf of cereal box tops for all the scrutiny he affords them. I snatch them back after the last vehicle has rumbled through. He hasn't taken his shades off the whole time. Maybe he's blind. It would certainly explain a lot.

We park up on a large expanse of gravel. A jut-jawed US lieutenant straight out of central casting gives us an orientation brief. We are presently on Freedom Lot Alpha, we will be fed in Victory Hall Dining Facility, and we are welcome to snatch some sleep in Patriot Lines. Any questions? Greene, who appears to believe he's on *Live at the Apollo*, asks where he might find the Urinals of Destiny. He is rewarded with a blank stare from the American, and a withering glance from Mr Kite, which says very clearly that it had better have been fucking worth it, Chuckles.

'That is, ah, not the name for the ablutions,' explains Lt ChiselledChin slowly, 'but should you need them, the correct facilities are, ah, over that away.' Then, still looking a bit confused, he leaves us to it.

It's lunchtime, so we head over to the Dining Facility, or in US Army Newspeak, the DI-FAC. Or as B Squadron dub it once we've seen what's inside, the DIE-FAT. It's no secret that the Americans have more stuff than us; we've all seen their vast five-mile-long logistics convoys crawling past Basra, and the rows upon rows of their aircraft parked on the tarmac in Qatar. But for a visual representation of the sheer immensity of the US war effort in Iraq, the Camp Cedar II cookhouse takes some beating.

There are burger bars as long as tennis courts and soft drinks fridges the size of walk-in wardrobes. There is even – Baskin-Robbins be praised – a 51 Flavor (*sic*) ice cream stand. In fact the only modest thing about it is the salad bar, which is getting a very stiff ignoring. Tonight is Surf 'n' Turf night, the smiling chefs inform us, and we shouldn't be shy about seconds.

Compared to the cookhouse at CAN, with its laminated signs warning '**One** Sausage per Man **Only**' and chefs who act as if slapping together a chip butty for troops coming off a night patrol is like the miracle of the loaves and fishes, it's no wonder the boys look dazzled. They also behave like we never feed them at all, and I hear nothing for the next hour or so except for happy little moans and the occasional lavish burp.

There's a downside to all this abundance, of course. And it's sitting all around us, happily eating seconds on plastic chairs that look as if they're one more portion of Freedom Fries away from snapping like matchsticks. At first glance Camp Cedar seems like a heavily militarised version of *The Biggest Loser*. In fairness it's mainly a logistics base, so it's not like anyone here is rappelling out of helicopters and shooting people in the face. But even so, some of them are so massive it's difficult to conceive what the heck they *are* doing. Unless it's wrapping their generous folds around high value assets during mortar attacks or something; the lads on the next table over would make Hesco look dainty.

I chat with a couple of our hosts while I wait for my second wind and another go at the Surf 'n' Turf. They seem pleasantly surprised to see us here. In fact, several of them seem surprised that there are Brits in Iraq at all. Perhaps they think this is just the latest in a long series of conflicts where they've had to go it alone. Like Vietnam. Or both World Wars and Korea, probably.

There are also a remarkable number of references to Osama bin Laden. By this point it's been pretty clear for at least a couple of years that the Iraqi regime had precisely dick all to do with Islamist terrorists, so it's quite odd to hear some of our hosts claiming that this place is as much a frontier against al-Qaeda as Afghanistan. Don't get me wrong, B Squadron's takes on the war and its underlying causes aren't likely to feature in the *Chatham House Quarterly* any time soon, but we are at least aware that Saddam Hussein didn't fly a 767 into the Twin Towers. The longer the conversation goes on, the more I begin to wonder whether my friend on the front gate is actually at the right-hand edge of Camp Cedar's intellectual bell curve.

It's easy to take the piss, though. For all that these guys' BMIs would give their IQs a good run for their money, you can't deny that they're part of the most formidable war machine on the planet. And it's very noticeable that this same war machine is in the middle of a surge that is starting to kick the enemy's arse all over the Sunni Triangle, while we're basically standing back and watching the militias take over Basra by inches. Then again, maybe if we had unlimited access to as many 500ml cans of Monster as we could pour down our throats, we'd be a bit livelier too.

Eventually we manage to prise the boys away from the DI-FAC and back out to the Snatches. Under the supervision of a sergeant from Camp Cedar's quartermaster department, we refuel and top up our water. Then with a benevolent smile, the sergeant beckons us over to a shipping container. He opens the doors and I catch a brief glimpse of pallets of Gatorade and Coke and chocolate bars, piled ceiling high. Why don't we help ourselves, he winks. Just a little thank you for your service.

I'm not sure what kind of money US Army sergeants are on, but I hope it's a decent wedge, because otherwise they're still going to be deducting the losses from his paycheck when he hits the retirement home. The words have barely left his mouth when half of B Squadron surge past like it's Black Friday at H&M. Seconds later they're streaming out again, bent double under slabs of soft drinks and chocolate.

I can just about hear the sergeant's stunned protest in amongst the hubbub, but he doesn't stand a chance. He has said to help ourselves, runs the boys' reasoning, and that's all they need to hear. This is B Squadron all over; they'll graft for days on bottles of lukewarm water and ration packs if you need them to, but give them an inch and they will – as the old saying goes – take fifty boxes of Gatorade, a dozen 36-packs of Coke, and enough plundered chocolate to make Hershey's call a board meeting.

We leave the sergeant standing forlornly next to an empty shipping container, his pen dangling uselessly from his clipboard. Then we mount up for the drive to CAN. Most of the Snatches are so full of loot that the top cover gunners have to stand on top of it all. My own vehicle looks like the Popemobile, with Greene and Womack poking through the roof almost from the waist up, waving stately goodbyes. We drive back through the main entrance and onto the road. Then I almost have a stroke as someone on the perimeter abruptly opens fire with a heavy machine gun.

I can't see the gunner, and for a panicked moment think that he must be shooting at us. Then I dismiss the thought as too improbable. Then I remember the way Einstein of Elk Gulch on the gate had pronounced 'in-fil-trators', and start to panic again. It certainly wouldn't be the first time a very obviously British unit has been enthusiastically engaged by the US Army.

For a lot of US reservists on convoys from Kuwait up to Baghdad, Basra is the first patch of Iraq they have ever set eyes on, and they are all twitchier than meerkats with a Costa card. Only last week one of them put a random burst straight into a British vehicle. It was never clear what prompted this; perhaps the gunner felt that the vehicle – half a mile away and on a completely different road – was somehow too close. Or maybe he was spooked by the enormous Union Jack on the antenna. But it goes to show that being hosed down by an American who has literally just seen you leave the same camp he's guarding might be a bit unlikely, but it's not impossible.

In the end we never do find out what they were shooting at; ten minutes later Cpl Robbins puts his Snatch into a ditch filled with raw sewage, which takes everyone's mind off everything apart from how to avoid being the dude who has to attach the tow strap (Greene in the end; apparently the gag about the urinals was definitely not fucking worth it).

Possibly it was just something they didn't like the look of; at the moment they're losing seventy soldiers a month – killed – so you can understand a bit of jumpiness. Or maybe it was just their way of saying goodbye. Either way the 'Great Gator-Raid' is probably the last time we'll visit Camp Cedar II; it's very unlikely we'll be back this way again.

Which is a shame. Not least, as I realise rummaging through my pockets after we leave Nasiriyah and head north towards CAN, because the guy on the front gate still has my fucking ID card.

18

Rest & Recuperation

The return journey from CAN to Shaibah was uneventful. Which was just as well, because it meant I was back in time for my flight home for R&R. Your fourteen days' leave included travel; a bit of a sore point given the RAF ran the air bridge with all the élan of narcoleptics running a DVLA branch office. Apparently on a previous tour one soldier from a Highland regiment had, through a combination of appalling weather and even worse luck, made it to his mother's home in Inverness in just enough time to have lunch and then start the journey back again. That said, I've been to Inverness, and at least Basra gets the sun.

The other curious feature of R&R was how abruptly you could find yourself back in normality. At the end of the tour there was normally decompression; a couple of days in Cyprus unwinding over two cans of warm Fosters per man per day, listening to a talk by the padre that may as well have been titled, 'Please Don't All Kill Yourselves Lads', and discovering that there is literally nothing which the Army can't suck all the fun out of with a twenty-minute safety brief, including banana-boating and ten-pin bowling.

But for R&R there was none of that. So it was quite common-place for young infantrymen in Basra Palace to be fighting for their lives in the back of a cordite-filled Warrior one minute, only to be deposited, blinking, in the Oxfordshire countryside less than forty-eight hours later. About twelve hours after that, it was also quite commonplace to find lots of them in a headlock on the floor of a custody suite, after sticking the nut on some civilian who had jogged their pint or looked at their girlfriend or something. It's not an excuse, of course, but it is at least an explanation. If you train teenagers to kill and then stretch them to breaking point for months on end, thousands of miles from home, it should hardly be a surprise when one or two of them come back and beat someone up in an All Bar One.

I noticed a bit of it myself, on that first drive back to my parents' house from RAF Brize Norton. They'd met me in arrivals, smiling a bit uncertainly, and we'd all piled into Dad's battered old Volvo. I wasn't seeing JAM militiamen parading down the high street or anything, but I still found myself unconsciously resting my hand on the door handle, about where the pistol grip of my rifle would be in a Snatch.

I tensed as we drove under bridges without checking their pillars for command wires. And when we stopped in a queue of traffic, I almost found myself reminding Dad to leave a car's length in front, just in case an RPG gunner should pop up in the alleyway next to Boots. All the while I could sense my parents glancing at me now and again. I had taken care to leave out some of the details in my emails and phone calls, but the evening news had been fairly lurid, and I'm not sure they knew what kind of son they would be getting back.

I wasn't sure either. I certainly couldn't gauge how much to say about what I had been doing, or how I felt about it. During dinner at home or when relatives popped round to see the tanned, much thinner version of the nephew or cousin who'd gone off to Iraq four months previously, I kept it light, telling them about the boys' obsessions with the nurses who worked at the field hospital in Shaibah, or Womack and his 'PIMP' crop-top.

Other times, mostly with mates in nightclubs and kebab shop queues, I could barely contain myself, and babbled endlessly about the night we'd been IDF'd for a whole lifetime in CAN, or how it was only a matter of time before we lost a whole Snatch crew to an EFP. But even as I yelled earnestly into their ears – over whichever bangin' bass beat wouldn't stop reminding me of how a 120mm mortar makes your chest vibrate when it lands – I could see that none of my friends really knew what to make of it.

And who could blame them? They were out for a good time and a few drinks before Monday in the office. The last thing they wanted was someone coming over all heavy and reeling off statistics about crew survivability. After a couple of nights of their gamely nodding faces, I resolved to keep my mouth shut.

I thought a lot about the squadron. It wasn't the old trope of feeling guilty for not being out there with them; even the General took R&R. And the five minutes I spent sitting on the bathroom floor at a house party, with tears streaming down my face for no reason I could remotely understand, told me that I needed a break from the tension as much as anyone. No, it was pure worry. The drawdown in CAN was ending and enemy activity was through the roof. They knew we'd be leaving soon, and every militia in Maysan wanted to be able to claim that they'd been the ones who'd made us do it.

I got an email from Godders a couple of days before I was due to fly back. Third Troop were fine, he reported, if groaning a bit under the iron fist of Sgt Mason's merciless Fourth Reich. CAN, on the other hand, was becoming very unhealthy. On their most recent visit, B Squadron had been bombarded by what sounded like a fucking railway howitzer, he said, and Mike had earned a lifetime of notoriety by pushing Brooksie out of the way to get to his body armour.

The camp itself was an empty shell; they'd even packed up the Maysan memorial wall, brick by brick, along with the little brass plaques listing the twenty-eight men who'd died there. Ben the Goat had been shipped off too – not, disappointingly, to an al Amarah *shish* joint – but rather to spend his autumn years trying to cripple people in the Air Station. All that was really left was to hand the place over to the Iraqi Army. Apparently there was 'a plan' for that bit. Not that anyone had told Godders about it. Wish us fucking luck, he'd said.

They'd have needed more than luck. By pure coincidence the withdrawal happened on the same day that I started my journey back to Iraq. As usual RAF Brize Norton were doing a very faithful impression of people who'd never actually seen a plane before, so I was slumped in departures counting the hours and watching Sky. Then there it was on the breaking news ticker: 'British forces pull out of Iraq base.' Then about an hour after that: 'Large crowds gathering outside Iraq base abandoned by British forces.' I could have written the next bit for them. And a few hours later, sure enough: 'Locals loot then destroy ex-British base in Iraq.' From orderly withdrawal to the Sack of Constantinople in under three hours; that had to be some kind of record, even for Maysan. I wondered what had gone wrong.

Everything, as it turned out. When I saw Godders a few days later, he told me that the crowd – four to five thousand strong – had arrived at dawn and then camped patiently outside CAN all morning. We hadn't actually announced that this was the day, but then you don't need to tell a Maysani the game's afoot when there's the scent of a new office chair and a late 1990s Xerox colour photocopier in the air.

At about lunchtime, the CAN commanding officer held a brief handover ceremony with his opposite number from the Iraqi Army; our flag down, their flag up, 'partnership', 'forward-together-as-brothers', 'leaving-it-in-a-better-state-than-we-found-it', bit of bugling, and into the Warriors while they still could. Then they drove off.

The crowd took that as their cue to pelt towards the front gate like highlanders at Culloden, cheering ecstatically. The Iraqi

Army had fired a couple of rounds into the air before surrendering to the inevitable and joining in the plunder. In fact they had got so into it that when the governor sent another Iraqi Army unit to restore order, there had been a minor gun battle between the two. Then the new arrivals were themselves assimilated, Borg like, into the gleeful crowds. In the end they got away with a couple of million dollars' worth of equipment, then burned the whole place to the ground.

The footage is still available on the internet, if you look hard enough. We found it later, in Shaibah, and watched agog as balaclava-clad militiamen rampaged through camp – over the tank park, past the cookhouse, past the same Welfare Sauna where we'd lain and prayed for their mortars to miss on so many nights – shouting the *takbir*[40] and firing their AKs exultantly into the air.

There was something deeply unnerving about seeing all those familiar spots filmed on that shaky handheld camera, the dubbed-in chanting almost drowning out the gunfire. The balaclavas were odd too; it was almost as if their wearers were hedging their bets, like we might be coming back.

Well we weren't. Not ever. A week or so later I think they must have realised it too; Moqtada al-Sadr himself came down to al Amarah to lead the parade celebrating victory over the *kafir* occupier, and his JAM militiamen marched openly on the city's streets with their weapons.

To nobody's great surprise PIC in Maysan was quietly moved a few months further to the right.

Saturday, 2 September 2006 – Basra Air Station

When I get back to the Air Station, I'm touched to find Third Troop there to pick me up. They greet me with ironic cheers at the arrivals shed and I suddenly feel a fierce jolt of pride. No one else on my flight has this, that's for sure. For most of them – including that snooty staff colonel who'd pushed in front of me in the boarding queue without a second thought – it'll be into a little white minibus then off to whichever anonymous corner of the Air Station they'll spend the rest of their tour in. I can sense them watching as I take my rifle from Griffiths, while the troop climb aboard the Snatches, all practised ease and just a touch of swagger.

Fuck spending the war moving little flags around a wall map; *this* is what it's all about. Though obviously if someone had offered me a comfy chair in a brightly lit ops room while we'd been cowering under the mortars in CAN, or waiting for JAM to come over the walls in Kumayt, then I'd have bitten their hand off. But what can I say; I must just be in the moment.

It hadn't been Third Troop's turn to do the Shaibah to Air Station run, explains Sgt Mason, but given that all the boys had in their diaries was a packed day of playing *FIFA 05* and wanking, he'd voluntold them to come and pick me up. It's good to see them again – I'm surprised by quite how much I've missed them – and they seem quietly happy too. But then again they're probably just looking forward to having a soft touch in charge again.

We drive back to Shaibah, but according to Sgt Mason we won't be there for long. Rumour has it that the CAN battlegroup, now responsible for covering 250 kilometres of Iranian border on their own, are finding it rather like being the little Dutch boy who plugs the hole in the dyke with his finger. Except there are about a thousand holes and their hands are made of caster sugar. He reckons we'll be heading up to the border to reinforce them soon.

As usual he is bang on the money. I've barely dropped my bags in the troop leaders' tent before Jonty summons us for orders. We'll be leaving for Maysan tomorrow, he says, and should expect to be out for a while. The CAN battlegroup's effort to stem the flow of rockets and IED components into Iraq is going even worse than the rumours. They're being run ragged by the local smugglers; apparently it's like one of those exhibition matches where they get a couple of professional footballers to play against a hundred seven-year-olds, turning them inside out with heel taps and Cruyff turns while the kids just pelt madly towards wherever they last saw the ball. In two weeks they've managed to intercept the grand total of one AK-47.

There was a BBC crew filming when they found it, which must have made the CO happy. I imagine he was a bit less pleased when their report then cut straight to a grinning trooper, who cheerfully admitted that someone in his section had accidentally dropped their own rifle in a river the other day, so this 'basically just makes it evens, like'.

The Americans aren't too thrilled either. The MoD's spin doctors, never ones to let the facts get in the way of a good story, have been a blur of activity ever since CAN closed. So the red tops are running a lot of headlines like, 'The New Desert Rats' and 'Our Boys Use The Tactics Which Beat Rommel'. This has gone down like a cup of cold sick with the Yanks up in Baghdad, who know very well what's actually going on, and are presumably thinking that if these really are the tactics we'd used against Rommel, then it's a wonder that he didn't kick our arses all over the Western Desert, and that Hitler's not on a plinth in Trafalgar Square.

Tuesday, 5 September 2006 – Shaibah / Iran–Iraq border

We leave Shaibah in the early hours; we're in stripped-down Land Rovers again, so Jonty wants to be well into the desert before JAM wakes up. We're moving in two half-squadron columns using parallel routes, meaning there's a decent chance that 50 per cent of us will get to Maysan without being atomised by a daisy-chained IED. Route Six is now officially closed; after another two soldiers killed in a Snatch yesterday, someone has finally decided enough is enough. But by this point the militia IED teams are active on anything bigger than a goat track, so splitting us up makes a grim kind of sense.

Our route takes us through the Central Marshes. They're a shadow of what they were when Thesiger was here, poling through the reed beds and gazing wistfully at his more nubile canoe boys. They've been reflooded since Saddam drained them in revenge for the 1991 uprising but you can tell just from looking at the sagging reed houses that life here is still about as tough as it gets. Not for the first time I thank my lucky stars for being born such a cossetted little Home Counties Fauntleroy; a slightly different flick of a sperm's tail and I might easily have started here, driving an emaciated water buffalo slowly down the road in sandals made of old car tyres. It's got to the boys too; I can see them lobbing rations out of the Snatches every time we pass a village.

We arrive at the RV with the other half of the squadron in the late afternoon. Excitingly, it transpires that they've managed to blow up one of their supply trucks on the way. Apparently it had abruptly burst into flames about three hours after they left Shaibah. The driver and commander had tried gamely to put it out with their hand-held extinguishers, before simultaneously remembering all those five-foot gas canisters they'd loaded that morning and putting in a very respectable time for the 100 metres.

The canisters had taken a while to detonate, but when they did it had been like a Michael Bay film. Most of the boys had spent a productive ten minutes taking moody selfies for Facebook in front of the burning hulk, while Jonty delicately broke the news to HQ that he'd managed to blow one of his own vehicles to smithereens before most of the Division had even had breakfast.

There are lots of rumours about how the fire started, from sunlight refracted through a shard of glass, to a cigarette tossed carelessly out of the window (which is where the smart money is; the truck's driver isn't nicknamed Sponge Lungs for nothing). But however it happened, losing a supply truck is a royal pain. Not least because a lot of the boys' personal kit had been on there. I imagine they'll be devastated.

Which shows how much I know, because when Third Troop find out what's happened they all look thrilled. I only work it out later on, when I see the list of what they're telling their insurance companies was on the truck. It's like they've copied out the Argos catalogue consumer electronics section by hand. I'm sure if their claims departments really thought about it, they might reasonably wonder what Greene was planning on doing with a PlayStation on the Iran–Iraq border. Or how Womack had been able to get a 50-inch TV into an issue Bergen. Or indeed how the truck had even got out of Shaibah; as Mr Kite notes darkly when he sees the list, it must have been carrying about eight times its maximum fucking payload.

I should probably say something. But then again I'm very aware – not least because they spend all day telling me – that junior troopers like Womack and Cameron are paid a pittance; just over £16,000 a year in fact. On a busy day, which might include everything from guard duty in 50-degree heat, to combing the verge for roadside bombs, they'll be clearing just over £2 an hour. So if they want to claw a little back from Norwich Union then it's fine by me. Anyway, I've now said I'd had a pair of binoculars on there which I'm pretty sure I lost in Kumayt, so it's not like I'm squeaky clean either.

Dusk is falling, so Jonty hurriedly gives his orders. Our mission, he tells us, is to choke off the militia's arms supplies at source. The Iranians are shuttling rockets and IEDs over the border almost faster than JAM can use them, and having the time of their lives fighting a risk-free proxy war against the Little Satan. They're being ably assisted by local tribes on both sides of what our government still fondly imagines is an actual border, who have been doing this so long that they could probably get a Trident missile across if the price was right.

To stop them we have assembled more manpower than this place has seen since the Iran–Iraq war. On the ground, two British battlegroups in Land Rovers, armoured vehicles, and even a few airboats with those big fans on the back for the marshes. In the air, 24-hour coverage from a fleet of US surveillance aircraft, scouring the border with their electronic eyes, and ready to trigger us onto anything even remotely suspicious.

Jonty's map is covered in ally-sounding boxes: Target Areas of Interest, Rattrap VCPs, Kill Areas. We should mostly expect to find Chinese 107mm rockets and EFP components, he reminds us, but there are rumours that Quds Force are on the ground too.

Quds are the Iranians' best; Revolutionary Guards special forces, trained in guerilla warfare and reporting directly to the Supreme Leader. If we find anyone who looks like they fit the bill, we are to detain them immediately. Proof of any kind of direct action by Tehran in Iraq would be politically seismic. While the orders continue, I imagine myself uncovering a pantomime villain Iranian, like the big reveal at the end of *Scooby Doo*, and delivering him to a weepingly grateful Jonty, while Mr Kite hangs a garland of flowers round my neck and tells me not to worry about those binoculars. It'd absolutely bury any previous fuck-ups, that's for sure.

I force myself back to Jonty's monologue. We'll leave immediately, he's saying. Troop locations are marked up on the map; we're to go straight to them and wait for the surveillance aircraft to find us a target. It all sounds completely epic and I'm almost skipping as I head back to Third Troop's vehicles to brief the boys.

From the looks on their faces, I can tell they're as up for it as I am. Given their usual reaction to a new tasking (dramatic sighs, moaning weakly on their cot beds like shipwreck survivors) this is very encouraging stuff. After a quick kit check to ensure we have enough plasticuffs to arrest the entire Iranian Revolutionary Guard, we drive out to our designated location. Then we sit back to wait for our first customer.

We don't see a single vehicle all night. Elsewhere First Troop's only stop is on a watermelon truck. Second and Fourth both intercept the same car, two hours apart, which is being driven by a DBE officer going on leave. But otherwise it's a complete washout. After a couple of hours the surveillance aircraft are reporting that there isn't so much as a pushbike within a hundred miles. It's clear we're not going to be spear-tackling any Quds Force commandos tonight. Instead, it looks a lot like we'll be sitting by the side of an empty road in the middle of a desert, for the next ten hours.

Before tonight I thought I'd understood what boredom is. I've had enough practice, that's for sure. It's a core part of the Army really; for every day you spend getting thrashed like a 1930s Stakhanovite shock-labourer, there'll be at least a dozen when you're bored silly, waiting for something – anything – to actually happen. But those experiences have been only a taster – an *amuse-bouche*, if you will – for quite how desperately I'd like to slam my own head through the Land Rover's windscreen if it means not having to spend a single minute more sat by the side of this road.

I look at my watch: 03:33 (it is always 03:33 in these kinds of situation). Then I begin to ponder whether this might genuinely be the most pointless mission in British Army history. I'm sure I'm not the first either. There's a lot about being a soldier which is the same no matter what era you're talking about; the comradeship, the occasional moments of mortal fear, the humping heavy weights for fucking miles on end. But the one thing that I am sure binds squaddies across the ages like nothing else is this; the cast-iron belief that *no one else*, past, present or future, could *ever* waste their time in quite such a spectacularly fatuous fashion as they themselves are doing at that moment.

It never makes it into the history books, mind you. And British cavalry breaking a French square is always going to make a much better oil painting than a sodden redcoat leaning on his musket in an empty field muttering, 'I mean, what the *fuck* . . .' But not that many people break French squares; everyone who's ever been in the Army has been the redcoat.

Eventually the horizon begins to glow. We clamber back into our Land Rovers and drive back to the squadron RV. As we park up, I see Jonty wave apologetically. As well he fucking might. We drag out our cot beds and zip ourselves into our sleeping bags against the cool dawn air; the plan is to rest up all day before trying our luck again tonight. I fall asleep almost immediately.

I wake up what feels like thirty seconds later, gasping for air and soaked in enough sweat to fill a child's paddling pool. Eyes screwed shut against the brilliant glare, I thrash around feebly, fumbling for the zip on my mosquito net. All around me I can hear the boys going through similar agonies. Sleeping bags are flung aside, and the occupants lie on their cot beds, heaving like freshly landed fish. Someone sits upright and calls the sun a 'prick'.

I look at my watch. Half past seven. Oh my Christ.

19

Lady in Red

Wednesday, 6 September 2006 – Iran–Iraq border

According to the BBC the average daily high in al Amarah for
September is about 42°. And that's the city. According to the
interpreters – who reckon this is a hot one, even for them –
50-degree days aren't unheard of in the desert. And 50° isn't just
uncomfortably warm; it's a legitimate oven temperature. Five
hours in it will get you a Heston Blumenthal slow-roasted rib of
beef with bone-marrow sauce described by one critic as a 'master-
piece of low-temperature cooking'. B Squadron are about to do
two weeks.

Indeed, the easiest way of conveying it for people at home probably would be for them to set the appropriate temperature on their
oven, then just stick their heads in. They could be joined by a
couple of friends, taking it in turns to release low, lingering moans
– something like, 'Fuuuuck *me*', or 'For fuck's *saaake*' – every
three minutes, all day. Ideally these moans should have a note of

vague reproach, as if it's the other person's fault that they have their head in an oven. As opposed to the other person just being a pond-life second lieutenant with no more say over who has to put their head in an oven than anyone else (and who, by the way, also has to spend the whole day with his head in the fucking oven).

Intermittently they could set light to a plastic bag to recreate the lingering aroma of sixty people's rubbish being burned all day long. If thirst's an issue they can drink as much water as they like, but only from the hot tap. Finally, when it's all over they should pay themselves £53 for the day. Then remind themselves that this was technically the 'rest period'.

Real rest is impossible. And we try everything; from putting up ponchos for shade, to making fans out of ration-pack boxes, to lying totally still in the hope that just not moving will somehow shave off a couple of degrees. Finally we resort to stripping completely naked and covering ourselves in spare clothes, with a designated 'water-boy' whose job it is to go around the whole troop keeping them wet.

Quite what the Quds Force will make of it if they're in the area is unclear. Maybe even now there are surveillance photos on some-one's desk in Tehran, showing Buxton reclining like a Roman senator in the Baths of Diocletian, a wet Army sock draped on his forehead, while Cameron solicitously pours Evian all over his heaving belly. I bet they'll leave us alone then.

Monday, 11 September 2006 – Iran–Iraq border

We've been here almost a week trying to stop the torrent of lethal weapons that the intelligence boys still swear blind are flooding over the border. And yet somehow we are still to intercept so much as a water pistol. That first night we'd been the epitome of readi-ness; gunners loaded, drivers in their seats, commanders primed meerkat-like next to their radios. By now our VCP looks like Custer's Last Stand, with most of the troop slumped pathetically up against the Land Rovers, moaning softly.

We're joined each night by Maysan's entire mosquito population, as well as about a billion sandflies that traverse every crevice of our bodies like tiny, dogged Victorian explorers. And so we sit, and scratch, and grunt sadly at one another like chimpanzees in an Albanian zoo.

And still we see no cars.

Wednesday, 13 September 2006 – Iran–Iraq border

We're starting to hit our limits here. You can put Third Troop through a lot before they lose their Zen-like amiability, but after a week of baking heat, bottomless tedium and snatched sleep, I bet even Buddha himself would have wanted everyone to just fuck the fuck off.

Morale isn't helped by some genius in Battlegroup HQ, who has divided up the rations by the simple expedient of assigning each sub-unit the menu which corresponds to their name; Menu A for A Company, Menu B for B Squadron, Menu C for C Company, and so on. I'm sure it made life very simple for whichever mouth-breather was using his fingers and toes to count the boxes. It better have done, because it's also meant sixty men eating nothing but corned beef hash for seven days on the trot, and you could probably detect the methane cloud from space.

Between that and the sheer pointlessness of our task here, we're in exactly the kind of situation in which young officers like me are supposed to step up and earn their wages. But in practical terms there's not a great deal you can do, other than bob around the squadron like Lt George in *Blackadder*, smiling idiotically and murmuring encouragement to the boys; privately I want to rip my own head off just as much as anyone else.

Perhaps they know we're all about one more spoonful of off-brown goo from mutiny, because this evening the Iranians started jamming our radios. At first it's endless stretches of some kind of high tempo Farsi-pop. I've always been vaguely aware that music can be used as a weapon; apparently the main reason the

Americans managed to winkle Noriega out of the Vatican embassy after Panama was that he literally couldn't bear another second of 'Never Gonna Give You Up'. Before tonight I'm not sure I ever bought it. But after fifteen minutes of listening to a man who sounds like he's plasticuffed to a jukebox while someone kicks him rhythmically in the testicles, I'm more or less ready to surrender the whole troop to the Revolutionary Guard.

As a tactic you have to admit it's genius. Consequence free – you can't go to the UN and complain because 'they're playing music at us' – but stunningly effective. No matter how many times we switch frequency, Ayatollah FM finds us within minutes, and our multi-billion-pound radio systems immediately go all to fuck. After two hours of *Now That's What I Call Someone Being Clubbed to Death With an Electronic Keyboard* they change the CD. And at this point I have to check what I'm hearing with Sgt Mason, because it feels so surreal that I wonder if I've just had too much corned beef hash. It's Chris de Burgh.

Quite why the Iranians have settled on Chris as their chosen tool of psychological torture isn't clear – I mean, he's not *that* bad – and we can only sit and stare blankly as the chorus from 'Lady in Red' floats tinnily out of the radio handset. I don't mind admitting that I'm spooked; it's a vaguely disconcerting song at the best of times, let alone when you're standing in a moonlit desert 3,000 miles from home. The Iranians play it on loop for an hour and forty-five minutes, by which point I realise exactly why they have settled on Chris as their chosen tool of psychological torture.[41] Then it's time for Talk Radio.

I imagine the Iranians think this is the most disturbing bit of the whole programme; their version of Lord Haw-Haw or Tokyo Rose, chilling British hearts all over Maysan. Unfortunately for them, after listening to Chris de Burgh doing the breathy bit on '. . . cheek to *cheek*' twenty-six times in a row, almost anything else is light relief.

That includes a scratchy monologue by a GCSE-level English speaker in which he tells you repeatedly that you and everyone else in your infidel army are all going to die. That you're fighting under false pretences for the Jews. That you're being ruthlessly exploited by an evil, mafia-like organisation bent on chaos and based in Tel Aviv (dead wrong – the Army's actually based in Andover). And that you will surely burn forever more in hellfire. Which frankly sounds alright compared to another week in Maysan, as long as they've got Menu A down there.

Luckily it's all too ludicrously overblown to have any real effect. If the Iranians had the slightest clue they'd be playing on the boys' actual fears. 'When you get back to Shaibah, the RSM will have organised another Fun Run . . . there will be a compulsory Inter-Unit StairMaster Ultramarathon . . . Aviva are going to ring up and ask you about that electric guitar you said you'd lost on the supply truck . . .'

We pass the handset round so everyone can have a listen. When I give it to Greene he gestures for quiet, then pushes the pressel switch and sings them all eight verses of 'The Fresh Prince of Bel Air'. I haven't got a clue if there's anyone sat in Tehran listening. But I'd like to think so.

Friday, 22 September 2006 – Iran–Iraq border / Shaibah

Finally – Yahweh be praised – whichever supranational Zionist cabal is actually running things has decided that enough's enough. We're going back to Shaibah. In the two weeks we've been up here the entire battlegroup has managed to intercept the sum total of two AK-47s and a 1950s-era hand grenade, which the scowling owner apparently claimed he used for 'fishing'. They don't fuck about in Maysan.

The road move down is uneventful; we do most of it at night, and by the time dawn breaks we are well into the Rumaylah oil fields to the west of Shaibah. They're the third biggest proven oil reserves in the world, and the stuff has bubbled up into the desert all around the road for miles; black, sulphurous lakes the size of football pitches. They're also the same reserves that Iraq accused

Kuwait of tapping just before the Gulf War, meaning a lot of B Squadron's current problems can be traced exactly to this evil-smelling patch of sand. There was industry here once; abandoned derricks lie all over the place. But it's as quiet as the grave now and we don't see a soul. We are back in Tiger Lines for lunch.

At orders that evening Jonty has news. An hour after we'd passed through the oil field, a Danish patrol had happened upon a group of Facilities Protection Police, nominally responsible for looking after the place, on the same road. In a departure from their normal practice (lounging on little plastic chairs at their checkpoints and falling asleep in the sun), they were instead furiously digging something up from the verge. It turned out to be a mixed bag of half a dozen EFPs and 155mm artillery shells, which had been wired together in an IED array covering the best part of a hundred yards.

Naturally, says Jonty with a tight smile, the police immediately claimed they'd found the whole thing quite by chance and were busy 'defusing' it. The Danes, who've heard that one before, are pretty confident that in fact the police had put it there themselves, and were digging it up to use somewhere else. Whichever story's true – and my money's not on the version where the Iraqis accidentally tripped over a command wire on their morning jog – it doesn't change the fact that we've just blithely driven through the biggest IED array of the campaign so far.

That night I lie in my cot bed and think about what a hundred yards of IEDs would have done to B Squadron. Wiped out a troop at least, I expect. Then I wonder how we'd got away with it. It wasn't our drills, that was for sure; we'd barely stopped in the oilfields. It had to have been a technical issue. We're alive because someone had crap reception on their mobile, or let the detonators get wet. Either way, it's another life used up.

And for the first time all tour, I find that I can't fall asleep.

Monday, 2 October 2006 – Shaibah

The squadron spends the next week or so catching up on sleep, and lolling around the Welfare Village trying to look windswept and interesting for the baristas. Jonty advises us to make the most of it; while we've been pootling aimlessly around Maysan, Basra has finally slipped into anarchy.

The three British locations in the city, Basra Palace, the Shatt al-Arab hotel and the Old State Buildings, are now being hit so much that they've started staggering meal times, lest a rocket hit the cookhouse and wipe out half a battlegroup. The boys on sentry there are having to 'balloon' for hours on end – crouch down and stand up repeatedly to make themselves a harder target – because half the city seems to have taken up sniping as a side hustle. And more or less every patrol that goes out can look forward to getting Swiss-cheesed by platoons of enthusiastic rooftop gunmen.

Worst of all are the logistics convoys; what was once a job for half a dozen Land Rovers is now a battlegroup operation. And when Warrior commanders are having to fire more rounds on a weekly resupply than they did during the invasion, even MoD Media Ops are having a hard time spinning it into a good news story.

It's clear we'll need to do something. Third Troop have got a few ideas, most of which involve either nuking the entire city from space, or lowering an enormous glass dome over it and letting the militias fight it out. But fortunately the Army doesn't do suggestion boxes. Instead we'll be carrying out Operation SALAMANCA, otherwise known as the Basra Security Plan.

The idea is to carry out a series of 'pulses' across the city, one district at a time. Each pulse will see us cordon off the district, then flood it with British troops to clear out the militias, while simultaneously carrying out quick-win reconstruction work; ditch clearing, road repairs, and so on. The kind of stuff *Challenge Anneka* might have got up to if they'd made her refurbish a community library while the locals repeatedly fired large calibre machine guns at her big blue truck. This will, the theory goes, build civic confidence in us and the Iraqi authorities. Not to mention reassure the locals that there is more to the British Army than enormous running gun-battles through their city every time we need to escort the Portaloo truck into Basra Palace.

Jonty holds his O Group after dinner. He begins by introducing us to the 'Basra Consent Survey'; a big map on which each district has been colour-coded according to how its residents are likely to react to the presence of British troops. There's no key, but presumably the green means 'well', and red is 'like a blood-drunk Zulu impi'. Op SALAMANCA will target the red districts first, says Jonty. We stare at the map. That doesn't narrow it down much.

Pulse number one will be in al Sukuk, towards the north of the city. We'll be based out of the Shatt al-Arab hotel. I listen as Jonty reels off our various tasks; Godders will be guarding some engineers while they clear ditches and Mike is to escort the RMP to the local police station. Brooksie might need to provide security while some specialists visit a hospital, but he'll have to wait and see; someone's just worked out that it's the same hospital where JAM take all their wounded fighters. Apparently HQ are trying to decide whether donating medical equipment to a hospital full of people you have recently shot is a really good look, or a really bad one. I will be visiting a school to help assess what their needs are. That doesn't sound too bad. Then Jonty glances back at his notebook.

'Oh, actually, Third Troop, extra one for you. The locals have been in touch about a couple of anti-ship missiles – Silkworms – down by the river. Apparently they've been there for years, and they're rusty as fuck, but still live. If they did go off they'd flatten half the district. You're going down there to provide security while the engineers have a go at defusing them.'

I just nod, not trusting myself to speak. There's no point anyway. It's what all the shouting at Sandhurst is about, not to mention the endless drill; instinctive obedience to orders. Which is exactly what you need when so much of this job involves telling people to do things that go completely against their better judgement. Like breaking cover to charge a machine gun. Or standing next to a 2-ton missile in God alone knows what kind of condition while someone who has almost certainly never even seen one before fiddles about trying to defuse it. Anyway, that's how you end up just nodding idiotically, rather than throwing your hands into the air like an Italian bartender and asking, 'What the fuck do you mean "have a go", Jonty?'

20

SALAMANCA

Tuesday, 3 October 2006 – Shaibah / Shatt al-Arab Hotel

We leave Shaibah after lunch in a full battlegroup convoy. Third Troop are nestled comfortably in the middle, so I'm able to soak up the sights. They are unedifying. Baswarians appear to have the same approach to litter that anyone would if their bins hadn't been properly collected since 1979 and there was a good chance of being shot dead on the way to the dump. Properly disposing of a Solero wrapper is clearly not high on anyone's list of priorities.

The streets are choked with colourful rubbish of all kinds. Dozens of stray dogs, few of which seem to have the full complement of limbs, are happily sorting their way through it. Every other street is a bustling warren of shops; metalworkers just visible in a dark recess, crouched over something red hot and sparking, dusty washing machines stacked three high on what passes for the pavement. And everywhere I look, pyramids of watermelons.

Then the buildings peter out and we find ourselves on a sweeping concrete road that curves towards the Shatt al-Arab hotel itself. It had probably been a taxiway once. Back in the day 'Hotel Shatt' was quite the destination and had even sported its own mini-airport. It was all very *Thunderbirds*, or would have been had Tracy Island been filled with cigar-toting Iraqi pleasure seekers, rather than a mildly tedious family of international do-gooders. Wealthy gamblers could land on the runway and be inside the casino boat moored next to the hotel without ever having to go into the city itself.

I wonder what they'd think if they were here now, with the casino boat resting on the bottom of the Shatt and the hotel's small control tower bristling with heavy weapons. Probably about where they could fit a baccarat table in the wreckage; for a nation where gambling is technically against the law, it still seems that Iraqis will bet on just about anything.

After parking up we find our allocated tents, dump our kit, and are mortared almost straight away. We immediately drop flat and start communing with the floor tiles; there is no Shaibah-style insouciance here. JAM hit the jackpot two days ago, landing a round right in the middle of the accommodation and killing a medic in the process; we'd driven past the blackened mess of tents on the way in. And from the way our cot beds are rattling with every explosion, they're clearly after the bonus ball too.

It's also strongly suspected they have spotters hidden on a small strip of sand called 'Cigar Island', which lies midstream in the Shatt behind the hotel. Unfortunately for these spotters, the mortar crews are quite nervous about accidentally dropping anything in the city itself – JAM prefer to kill their civilians hooded and covered in cigarette burns – so tend to err on the side of overshooting. As the rounds slam down around us, it's some consolation that if there are any militia hidden on Cigar Island, then the little fuckers are catching almost as much incoming as we are.

What's more, the spotters don't have all the resources of the world's fifth-biggest defence budget to protect them. Shortly after we've stood up and dusted ourselves off, Mr Kite tells us to muster by the vehicle park for a briefing on the Shatt's new anti-IDF measure. As we walk over, I wonder what it might be. Perhaps they're installing those Phalanx radar-controlled guns which the Americans use to shoot the mortars out of the sky. Or maybe we're getting hardened accommodation pods like the Foreign Office used to live in at Basra Palace.

Whatever 'it' is, it's about time. Even for the Army, which generally shows the kind of disregard for employee health and safety that would make the foreman in a Liberian diamond mine blink, allowing soldiers to live in tents while being mortared six times a day is fucking ridiculous.

What 'it' is, in fact, is breeze blocks. When I first see the great heap of them on the vehicle park, I assume it's building works or something; new accommodation to replace the stuff JAM levelled a couple of days ago. Then Mr Kite tells us to take twenty-four each and stack them around our cot beds. There is silence.

'Say that again, SSM?' says Godders.

'Not my decision, sir,' says Mr Kite quietly. 'Straight from the RSM here. This is their new anti-IDF measure. They're doing the same thing down in the Palace.' He shrugs.

There's not much to say to that. We all line up dutifully, then start carrying our allocated breeze blocks back to the tents. The boys are unusually quiet. But if I had to guess, I'd say they're thinking along the same lines as me; they're 3,000 miles from home and in a warzone, and they've done everything asked of them for months. But when it comes to asking for a little something in return, from the self-same government that has sent them here – something which might mean they can snatch some rest between patrols without wondering if they'll be killed in their beds – they've been given twenty-four breeze blocks per man.

I once read somewhere that the first time Siegfried Sassoon ended up in Craiglockhart, he confessed that he no longer hated the Germans, but if he came across a government minister he would kill them. I think I know how he felt.

We spend a couple of hours operationalising our new anti-IDF system. Half a dozen breeze blocks break while we're stacking them, so I expect they're only really going to be useful for stopping our internal organs decorating the inside of the tent if we do get hit. When we're finished we head into the hotel itself for dinner. It has been stripped of furniture but the gilt fittings and intricate wood friezes are all still there. And whoever designed it appears to have answered the question, 'How many gargantuan acrylic-diamond chandeliers would you like?' with, 'Yes.' I'm half tempted to clap my hands to see if the lights dim and a disco ball drops out of the ceiling.

The Army has completed the look with sandbagged windows and mass casualty medical packs hanging from every wall; the whole place looks like Liberace's house battening down for the end of the world. The cookhouse itself is in what must have been the ballroom. It's now full of squaddies at Formica tables, shovelling as many chips down their necks as they can before the next shift comes in, or JAM lands a rocket on the hotplate. I contrast the scene with the one in my head; the same room, filled with Iraqis in black tie and floor-length gowns, smoking cigarettes in holders and gazing out over the Shatt while a string quartet fills the warm night air.

It doesn't exactly feel like progress.

Wednesday, 4 October 2006 – Shatt al-Arab Hotel

If we're expecting to spend much time relaxing in our breeze-block mausoleum, HQ has other ideas. Apparently they're worried that JAM will work out that we're planning something out of the Shatt. Given they've recently ordered the best part of a thousand squaddies to drive into it in broad daylight, I can just about follow their reasoning. So we'll be 'increasing our operational tempo' to make sure we 'keep the enemy on the back foot'. This is presumably the foot they're not currently using to repeatedly kick the entire British Army in Basra very hard in the balls. Third Troop have been tasked with a night patrol.

According to Jonty we've got two missions. The first is to prevent anyone digging in any IEDs nearby. The second is to deter mortar attacks. Fortunately, both missions can be achieved using more or less the same tactic; driving slowly around the local area in an aimless and unpredictable fashion. And with the standard of map-reading I've shown so far, that should be right up my alley, ha ha ha. I smile thinly – you have to, when it's your squadron leader telling the joke – then go off to find the ops room.

After handing in my flap sheet,[42] I stand in front of a large map of Basra while a bored lance corporal from the Shatt's intelligence cell gives me a briefing. As usual it contains not a jot of useful information about what might happen on my own patrol, but is instead an endless litany of terrifying things that have recently gone wrong on other people's. After ten heartening minutes hearing about Snatches flipped like Duplo toys by IEDs, and RPGs fired through the back doors of Warriors, the lance corporal wraps things up by showing me a photobook of militia personalities from the area.

Every intelligence cell in Iraq has one of these; they're meant to help you recognise the local celebrities so you can detain them on sight. In some cases the profiles are quite useful; colour photos, full names, notes about distinguishing features and so on. In others you may as well flick through a copy of *The Beano*; profiles where the photos are from a hundred metres away, or where there's no photo at all, or where the individual in question is either FNU (First Name Unknown) or SNU (Surname Unknown). And occasionally both. Up in CAN this had once prompted Schofield to remark how strange it was that no one had caught that Fnu Snu fella yet, given it seemed like we'd been looking for him all fucking tour; a statement that had at once entered Third Troop folklore.

I meet Third Troop on the vehicle park along with a Warrior and its crew. Every patrol in the city now has to have at least one armoured vehicle leading it, a recent policy change that has only taken half a dozen dead Snatch crews to enact. I brief them on the route, remind Schofield to keep an eye out for Fnu Snu (to gentle cheers from the rest of the troop), and we mount up.

I haven't been in Basra at night since my starring role in *National Lampoon Presents a British Army Strike Op* a month ago. It doesn't look as though I've been missing much. The streets are deathly quiet and almost completely dark; the city's only getting about six hours of electricity a day at the moment and municipal lighting isn't a priority.

I think back to Tin City and shift uncomfortably in my seat; it all feels a lot like the quiet moments before a new serial. Except this time the flash in the blackness and the sudden, battering cacophony of shots will be for real. And if someone steps out of one of these alleyways with an AK-47, they'll be able to turn our Snatch into the Bonnie and Clyde car before we even know what's happening. It's no fun at all.

We drive around for an hour or so. I can tell Griffiths is as nervous as I am, because he maniacally whistles the chorus from 'Colonel Bogey' through his teeth for almost all of it. Then Cpl Robbins announces that his engine is starting to miss; he thinks it's the fuel injector. It's hardly a surprise; most of our Snatches have done more miles towed than they have under their own steam by this point. But if anything does kick off I don't particularly want to be dragging four tons of fucked Land Rover through an ambush; fighting with a troop of Snatches is dicey enough even when they're all working.

We're only due to be out another ten minutes anyway, so I call up the ops room and ask if we can come in early.

'Hotel Charlie Three Zero, Zero. No, you're to stay out there,' comes the reply. 'The multiple leaving Basra Palace has broken down at the gate and we need at least one callsign on the ground, over.'

I turn to stare briefly at Griffiths in the darkness. Then push the pressel again.

'Hotel Charlie Three Zero. Just confirm, we're the only callsign on the ground, over?'

'Zero. That's correct. Out.'

Next to me I hear Griffiths swear softly. Between the troop and the Warrior crew there are fourteen of us out here. Basra has a population of about 1.5 million. Not to mention a pretty lively militia of at least a few thousand. The British Army is used to being outnumbered, of course; Rorke's Drift was forty to one, and we won that one. But this kind of ratio is just asking for trouble.

There are supposed to be almost 10,000 British soldiers in Iraq, yet somehow we can't even scrape together a rugby team for patrolling the city we're supposed to be responsible for. You have to wonder what the fuck everyone else is doing all day. And all of a sudden, I can understand why we're always getting mortared so much.

Thursday, 5 October 2006 – Shatt al-Arab Hotel / Shaibah

The next morning I wake up to find the boys packing their kit all around me. SALAMANCA is cancelled; we're leaving this evening. Apparently the General never actually got the sign off from the Iraqis. Even I can see that this is quite the cock-up; the Army will all but flog you for taking your dessert out of the cookhouse without permission, let alone forward-mounting a thousand men into Basra City for an operation you haven't cleared with the locals.

It seems that when the Iraqi prime minister was briefed, he'd immediately pulled the plug on the whole thing. If Iraq is going to slip into all-out sectarian war – and frankly it's looking odds-on at the moment – then he will need all the support he can get from his fellow Shias. He certainly isn't about to let the British Army start rampaging through Basra arresting them all. As far as he's concerned, JAM might be a pain in the arse, but they're not al-Qaeda.

My own feelings are mixed; now that we're in the city it seems a shame not to do what we came here for. On the other hand, 'what we came here for' in my specific case was standing next to a missile designed to take out aircraft carriers while someone dicked around with its innards trying to work out what all the wires did, so I'm not missing much. And if I'm truly honest, I'm starting to feel an increasing sense of dread.

I'm long past the stage where getting mortared is a novel, semi-frightening-but-also-semi-cool experience, and with every barrage I'm finding it harder and harder to fight down the panic. More to the point, we must be about the only Snatch unit in southern Iraq which hasn't yet had to jetwash the remains of a couple of close colleagues out of the cab. So perhaps returning to the relative safety of Shaibah is no bad thing after all.

We spend the rest of the day lying about on our cot beds. Or on the floor; JAM must have noticed that the Shatt is full to bursting and it looks like they've put the mortar crews on overtime. Eventually it gets dark and we roll out of the front gate. It's a moonless, overcast night and I can't see a thing even with NVGs, but with any luck we'll be back in the Welfare Village for last orders.

Cpl Robbins's fuel injector has by now ascended to the great Halfords in the sky, so Griffiths hooks him up to our vehicle with a tow rope. Twenty minutes later he drives us straight off the side of a leveed road, and we plummet like an airborne piano fifteen feet into the desert floor. I find out what my last words are likely to be (a small, sad noise which sounds a bit like '*mip*') before my face smacks resoundingly off the windscreen and I become briefly the most confused man in southern Iraq.

Cpl Robbins's Snatch is pulled smartly into the abyss behind us, and hits the back of our vehicle with a crash which sounds like a day of paperwork and a month's pay. We have to use a Warrior to pull the Snatches back onto the road. Jonty watches with his hands on his hips and a face like one of Attila the Hun's less friendly henchmen. We miss last orders by a country mile.

Saturday, 7 October 2006 – Shaibah

At morning orders Jonty announces he's giving the squadron a couple of days off. At first we're suspicious. This is the Army after all; most of the time you get treated like a lab chimp in some CIA-sponsored experiment from the 1950s about the effects of repeated crushing disappointment on the human psyche. I am particularly wary; Jonty has been impressively icy since I swan-dived two-thirds of my troop off the road a few days ago. So we just stare at him, then scamper back to our tents to wait uneasily for the inevitable kit inspection or 100 per cent rifle-cleaning parade. Only after a few hours do we start to believe it might not actually be a wind-up.

The British Army's off-duty pastimes have changed a bit over the years. They're not as literary as they once were; apart from some couplets in the toilets about the RSM (his surname is Hunt, which helps the battlegroup's lyricists tremendously) I'm not aware of our tour having generated much in the way of poetry or literature. Instead, we watch DVDs. *The O.C.* has quickly become the troop leaders' world; quite what draws us to the travails of angsty teens in Californian high society isn't clear, but we all know we have to keep it quiet. If the boys ever catch us racing back to our tent after orders, practically fitting at the idea that Marissa might have slept with that trustafarian bastard Johnny, our lives won't be worth living.

The boys watch their share of DVDs too, of course; indeed Buxton has been motionless in his pit for so long that he's managed to create a fairly credible replica of the Turin Shroud on his bedsheets (though Jesus obviously didn't have a laptop balanced on his chest, or an orange stain by his right arm where he kept the Cheesy Wotsits). But theirs are *proper* films – *300*, *The Departed*, *Mission Impossible* – with tits, or death, and preferably tits *and* death. And they're more into gaming anyway, spending long happy hours hosing down the Wehrmacht in *Call of Duty*. They're good at it too. Which would be quite useful if only JAM were also sporting enough to goosestep around in the open firing *Panzershrecks*, instead of hiding half a mile away and trying to blow us all up via mobile phone.

Sadly for the boys' kill-streaks, we also have to use some of the spare time to catch up on the various briefings, career courses, and other bits of Army trivia that we've missed while we've been busy. For them it's absorbing lessons like 'Equipment Care and Management', while for the troop leaders it's endless revision for promotion exams. Clearly some people in HQ aren't going to let a small thing like a raging insurgency stop them from wasting everybody's time with admin. I imagine in another life they'd have been clucking about checking the tyre pressures on their Mitsubishi Zero, while everyone else wrapped Rising Sun bandanas round their heads and got ready to spank into a US aircraft carrier. It is, in its own way, quite impressive.

The highlight of our catch-up training is an interactive DVD on ethics, which gets handed out by Jonty. Every soldier in Iraq has to watch it; an order that comes straight from the US Commanding General in Baghdad. And he has his reasons; earlier this year a US platoon south of Baghdad went rogue, raping a fourteen-year-old child then murdering her and her family. They were swiftly caught, tried, and their sentences ran to hundreds of years, but the incident has sent shockwaves through their army.

And in that light I suppose the DVD makes sense; it means the General can look the Press in the eye and tell them that lessons have been learned, that every man has received an unambiguous briefing, and so on. Although whether the next PTSD-riddled US grunt, driven mad by his third year-long tour in a row, will be prevented from going postal just because he's watched a cartoon called *Janet and John Agree Not to Do the Village, Just Do the Whole Fucking Village, Man*, is another question entirely.

It's not really called that of course, it's called *Living the Warrior Way* or something equally tragic. We watch it together in the Third Troop tent after orders one night. It comprises a series of short animated vignettes, each leading neatly to a situation where you have a clear choice between Doing the Right Thing, or alternatively Doing Something Else Entirely. There isn't a tremendous amount of subtlety in the choices.

An Iraqi whose car you are searching is complaining. Do you:

(A) Remind him that you have the right to conduct searches and provide him with paperwork recording your interaction?

(B) Beat him up?

Inevitably the troop insist that I click the Something Else Entirely button. This in turn generates a sadface emoji, and a mournful reminder that asking Iraqi children to dig up IEDs for you, or executing people for trying to steal your sunglasses, Is Not Living The Warrior Way.

On balance, I think I prefer *The O.C.*

Sunday, 8 October 2006 – Shaibah

Just because we're ensconced happily in our little Tiger Lines cocoon, every day feeling pleasantly like the last, it doesn't mean that life has stopped in the outside world. It certainly hasn't stopped for Schofield's child support arrears, which are now up to an impressive £15,320.25.

He finds me in the troop leaders' tent. He's white-faced and brandishing the letter from the Child Support Agency. He remembers the girl, he thinks, but the fact he's apparently got a three-year-old daughter in Birmingham is a new one on him. What the fuck's he supposed to do, he asks shakily; fifteen grand's more than he takes home in a year. A lot more.

I can see why he's flapping. And frankly I'm outraged on his behalf – for all that he should probably have been more careful, whacking the guy with three years' worth of accumulated child support payments without so much as a by your leave feels hideously unfair. How the hell was he supposed to know he had a child to pay for? And to do it while he's on active service for his country . . . well. I grasp Schofield's shoulders and tell him we'll sort it out together. Then I stalk over to the ops room to place what I'm planning to be a polite but withering call back to the UK.

On the walk over I'm still seething. I like Schofield a lot. Troop leaders aren't supposed to have favourites – it's a bit like a parent having a favourite child – but I can't help it, he's mine. Like most of the Army, he wasn't exactly beating off job offers from NASA when he joined. And he's clumsy to the point of disaster. Two weeks ago I could only watch as he popped the bonnet on a Snatch and opened a still-boiling radiator; the cap exploded off in a burst of steam and hit him so hard in the face that he had a tiny Land Rover logo embossed on his forehead for three days. But by God he tries. He tries so hard as to break your heart. Reaching the ops room, I punch in the number for the UK very firmly indeed.

After an hour and a half on hold I get through to a very nice CSA caseworker called Jacqui, who helpfully talks me through the thirty-six letters, fifty-odd phone calls, and several hundred emails which she has fired off at the mysterious ether which she knows only as 23646335 Trooper D. Schofield, over the past three years. I march straight back to Tiger Lines and find B Squadron's answer to the Scarlet Pimpernel still hanging around outside my tent.

He looks downcast; presumably disappointed that his honey-tongued troop leader has somehow failed to just talk him out of fifteen grand's worth of nappies and formula he hasn't paid for. Quite what his contingency plan was for when I found out the CSA have actually been running him down like the Pinkerton Agency for three years now is unclear; he just mumbles and says he hasn't been opening his email much. I sigh, then pull out a pen and paper, and we start working out which decade we'll be in by the time he's finished paying it all off.

21

Shark-Infested Custard

Monday, 9 October 2006 – Shaibah

The good times – for everyone except Schofield, anyway – don't last. At breakfast this morning Jonty brings us all crashing back down to earth by informing us that we're going to spend another week training the Iraqi Army. This time it's 2/4/10, the sister battalion of our pals in Kumayt.

2/4/10 have recently been warned off for operations in Baghdad. And if we think Basra's going haywire, Baghdad is making it look like Scrabble at the WI. Indeed, the US general running it has recently been moved to admit that without a substantial number of fresh troops, he is probably going to lose control of the city.

This is a bit of an eyebrow-raiser. Not least because in the British Army, any questions to our generals about how the campaign is going – you know, *actually* going – tend to be met by the kind of manic enthusiasm more normally associated with teenage girls at a high school cheerleading try-out. Every six months we have been in Iraq to date has apparently been a 'new turning point', and every operation a 'significant blow'.

Our generals also appear to believe, with quite spectacular cognitive dissonance, that JAM only fight when they feel under pressure. As opposed to because they have – probably correctly – guessed that they're on the verge of kicking us out of Basra. Or indeed just because it's fun. And so every time there's a four-hour-long, hideously violent firefight in the middle of Basra, it will routinely be cited as a sign of JAM 'running out of options'.

You can't help but think these are the same kinds of characters who'd have hung around the *Führerbunker* right to the bitter end, telling everyone that Twelfth Army was *just* round the corner, and that Downing Street would soon be levelled by a gigantic sonic catapult. Presumably they'll continue to claim JAM are 'running out of options' right up to the point that they overrun the Welfare Village.

2/4/10 were told that they would be heading up to Baghdad a couple of days ago. They had listened quietly to the news, seen the empty trucks pull up outside, and then promptly mutinied. A small faction of officers took the CO hostage in his own office and said they'd only release him when the orders sending them to Baghdad were rescinded. In case he hadn't noticed, ran their argument, people were clacking themselves off like Chinese New Year up there, and frankly they didn't much fancy being part of it.

The commander of the 4th Brigade, hearing about the mutiny, had gone down to 2/4/10's camp himself with the intention of personally banging a few heads together. Only to be rather neatly ambushed as he approached the main gate in his staff car. After sitting in a ditch for an hour while his bodyguards duked it out with the 2/4/10 sentries, he decided that the order to Baghdad would be rescinded after all.

Instead 2/4/10 would come to Shaibah to do some training with the British (and, I suspect, to allow them to be more easily bundled into the trucks up to Baghdad when the time did come). This sent a very clear message to the rest of the Iraqi Army. Namely that if you're ever told to do something you don't want to do, then taking your CO hostage and attempting to murder your brigade commander may very well get you out of it. For a while, anyway.

Frankly it seems like they might be onto something; Third Troop get at least one tasking a week that makes me feel like killing the CO, or at least lightly maiming Jonty. Spending a week teaching patrolling and doing 'reconstitution activities' (whatever they are) with the Iraqi Army is probably one of them.

Jonty hands us all a training programme and tells us we'll be kicking off later today. In the meantime Godders and I are to go and find the person running the Shaibah MiTT. This stands for 'Military Transition Team', with the emphasis very much on the 'Transition' bit. Given Iraq is costing the US something like $50bn and 1,000 dead GIs a year at this point, you can understand why. The idea is that the MiTTs will train the Iraqi Army to at least hold their own in combat, meaning we can start to get our own little pink bodies off the streets.

The more technical aspects of soldiering, like logistics, planning, and command and control, are taking a back seat. Eventually the Iraqis will have to learn that stuff too – even at the very highest levels their approach is still straight out of the Golden Horde playbook. ('We're going *that* way, lads, and if you need anything you haven't brought with you, just nick it off the locals.') But it can wait until the militias are back in their box. I don't envy whoever will be doing the technical training. If 3/4/10 are anything to go by, much of the Iraqi Army still considers the concept of taking a map on patrol to be up there with quantum string theory; I'd rather not be around when someone starts trying to teach them Clausewitz.

Godders and I find a Corrimec with 'OC MiTT' on the door and go in. It takes a moment for my eyes to adjust to the gloom; the blinds are closed and it is Stygian. On the ceiling a single fan spins slowly. There is a desk at the far end of the Corrimec and behind it, a slump-shouldered figure wearing a major's crown. Godders clears his throat and the figure starts suddenly, then stares at us. He is a late-stage Hamlet in DPM (*disruptive pattern material*); deathly pale, with deep circles under his eyes and what appears to be the beginnings of a nervous tic in one of his cheeks.

We introduce ourselves and the major motions for us to sit. Godders gently proffers the training programme we've been given by Jonty and asks what 'reconstitution activities' means.

'It means just that,' says the major. He is practically whispering. 'Reconstitute them. They were trying to kill each other a few days ago, and they've got to go to Baghdad in a week. Do some team building. Races, games, that kind of thing. Here . . .' he plucks feebly at one of the towering stacks of paper on the desk in front of him, then pulls out a handwritten sheet. 'I've got some ideas. Try some of those.'

'Oh . . . OK,' says Godders, gingerly taking the sheet. As he folds it away, I see the words 'Raft Building Competition'. Jesus. 'What are they like, anyway?'

A huge shudder seems to pass through the major's body and he closes his eyes for a moment. Then they snap open again.

'*Terrible*,' he hisses urgently. 'I thought I'd seen the worst of it – I've been in the MiTT five months already – but I think this lot might actually break me.'

'Oh . . . right. That bad? We were with 3/4/10 for a bit, and they were alright. In their own way.'

'See for yourselves,' says the major, his eyes flashing. 'They're in the camp next door. Just follow the music; they've turned one of the accommodation tents into some kind of cabaret. I don't even know how many of them there are. They're just a . . . herd. We took them on the range yesterday and it was like the invasion all over again. My sarn't major had to have a lie down afterwards, and he's ex-Hereford.'[43]

I glance at Godders. He looks meaningfully at the door. Time to wrap it up. God knows what this guy has done to deserve this. In the old days, if you really fucked up they'd just make you take a Forlorn Hope through the breach at Ciudad Rodrigo. Or put you in charge of a telegraph repeater station on some bare-arsed island in Antarctica. Both sound like immeasurably better options than running the Shaibah MiTT. We thank the major for his advice and head for the exit.

'They burned down a shower block, yesterday,' he continues, as if we're not there. 'I mean, how do you burn down a *shower* block?'

We leave him to his nervous collapse and head back to Tiger Lines. He isn't the first trainer to have been driven to psychological meltdown by the Iraqis, and he won't be the last. We like to think of the British Army as having some kind of special connection with the Arabs; something to show for all those years charging around the place in pith helmets and drawing the kind of nice neat borders Nanny would have liked straight through the middle of their ancestral territories.

But if this campaign has shown us anything, it's that there aren't actually many T.E. Lawrences or Wilfred Thesigers left. For every British trainer who can sit comfortably round the evening campfire with his charges, bantering easily in pidgin Arabic over a steaming cup of sweet *chai*, it seems there are ten or more who would happily fling themselves – and perhaps a couple of chosen locals – right into the heart of the flames.

Wednesday, 11 October 2006 – Shaibah

To give him his dues the major was not wrong about 2/4/10; it takes us all of a couple of days to work out that these lads would make 3/4/10 look like the Praetorian Guard. And they're sullen with it, in a way 3/4/10 never had been. It's fair enough I suppose; they've had a brief stay of execution, but they know very well what's coming next. And if I was three or four days from being dumped in probably the most violent place on earth with nothing but a rusty AK and a hearty pat on the back, I expect I'd be pretty fucking moody too.

After a futile couple of mornings trying to teach patrolling to whichever 2/4/10 *jundis* didn't manage to hide in the toilets quickly enough, we decide to take the path of least resistance and do the lessons inside their accommodation. At least it guarantees most of them will be there. Only about a quarter are ever paying attention, of course; the rest are either playing noisy games of *Snake* on their mobiles, or sunk into some kind of existential torpor with their berets over their eyes.

It might just be that some of them are a bit sceptical about what there is to learn about soldiering from someone who was still smearing rusks all over himself while they were facing down Iranian tanks on the Al Faw. Or maybe they're just convinced that whatever happens in Baghdad is in God's hands now anyway. A firm belief in predestination would certainly explain the staggering individual acts of heroism which some *jundis* will occasionally pull out of the bag. Like the ones already up in Baghdad, currently kicking in the most dangerous doors on the planet with their US mentors. Unfortunately it might also explain why they routinely get vaporised trying to pull IEDs out of the ground with bits of string. But you can't have it both ways, I suppose.

Occasionally, when it seems I really am losing the audience, I fling open the door and announce we're going for a run outside. It's like throwing open the curtains in a teenager's bedroom on the first morning of a new term; once the agonised groans, plaintive hand-wringing, and covert attempts to slip quietly away under a tent flap have subsided, the lesson can continue.

Most days pass in a sort of soporific blur. Although there is a stirring interlude when half a dozen *jundis* abruptly push a flaming wheelie bin into the tent halfway through a session on VCPs. Warbling with surprise, I pull an extinguisher off the wall and douse the fire with ten pounds of dry powder, of which I immediately swallow about five. My students shriek with laughter and applaud like it's the curtain call for *Billy Elliot* – it's the first time I've seen them genuinely excited all week – before promptly picking up every other extinguisher in the tent and letting them all off in my face.

If this was a film, that would have been our plot pivot. The moment when we looked at one another, each man indistinguishable under a floury white coat, and realised that we weren't so very different after all. Then we'd have slapped each other on the back, wiped the powder from our grinning faces and agreed that we'd make a go of this fight, as brothers.

But this isn't a film. So instead I have a quite spectacular Violet Elizabeth meltdown, then stumble from the tent and throw up lavishly all over myself. According to Ali, the interpreter, the fire had been caused by a cigarette butt, and the Iraqis had pushed the wheelie bin inside my tent on the basis that they knew that was where the extinguishers were kept. I can only nod mutely; for 2/4/10 that makes perfect sense.

Five minutes after I've restarted the lesson another group push a different wheelie bin, similarly aflame, into Godders' tent. Ali just shrugs. Maybe it's a regimental tradition or something.

But if patrolling lessons fall a bit flat then 'reconstitution activities' are the biggest flop since *Titanic II*. We give the major's sheet of ideas an honest try, but twenty minutes is more than enough to show that treating combat infantrymen like a group of sales reps on a teambuilding weekend in the New Forest is not going to help us win this war.

'Tell them that the aim is to get this box out of the taped-off area using these planks and ropes. But the area inside the tape is mined. So if they touch it with their feet they're dead, and the whole team has to start again.'

'They say it is not mined. We are in the middle of a big British base. How can it be mined?'

'No, sorry, it's not really mined, it's just so they don't step on it, and use the planks instead.'

'If it's not mined, they want to know why they can't walk on it.'

'But . . . no, wait, hang on, it's really only so they use the planks to walk on.'

'The planks will also set off the mines, they say.'

'Alright, tell them it's not mined, it's shark infested custard. Either way, you can't touch it.'

'What is custard?'

Sunday, 15 October 2006 – Shaibah

It's the end of the week and we take 2/4/10 to the ranges at the back of Shaibah. It's fair to say that marksmanship is a bit of a blind spot for the Iraqi Army, in much the same way as it's fair to say that Saddam Hussein had a bit of a problem with his temper. Some of it's an equipment issue; one look at the AK-47 will tell you everything you need to know about the designer's thoughts on accuracy. The sights themselves are basically welded on, and unlike on most Western rifles, where the first click down on the safety catch sets the weapon to single shot – on the AK-47 one click down takes you straight to rooty-toot, Baghdad unload, thirty-rounds-in-three-seconds, Fully Automatic, Baby.

Between a rifle that's almost custom-designed for 'spray and pray', and an inherently macho culture which is convinced that only wets use the sights, it's little wonder that most Iraqi Army battles have historically been characterised by everyone planting the butt of their AK somewhere around the sternum, then holding down the trigger and screaming imprecations until the firing pin goes *click*.

The range itself is standard; a large, three-sided earth enclosure with a row of 25-metre lanes inside. The targets are traditional NATO Figure 11s, depicting a charging Soviet infantryman. For realism's sake we should probably be using a picture of a sullen man in a 'Rebok' tracksuit, who fires three rounds from an AK then drops it and claims to have been running a watermelon stall the whole time. But needs must.

The one departure from normal practice is Cameron and Womack, who are quietly cradling their Minimis on top of the earth walls at either side of the range. Insider attacks – 'green on blues' – aren't nearly the problem in Iraq that they are in

Afghanistan, but they also aren't completely unheard of. Given 2/4/10's recent form for abruptly drawing down on one another, Jonty isn't taking any chances. It's not clear what the Iraqis themselves make of it. We're making all the right noises of course, telling them we're 'shoulder to shoulder', 'working as brothers' and all the other platitudes. But after watching us post two sentries with orders to blow them all away if they so much as look at us funny, you have to wonder how much they believe us.

Godders takes the first eight *jundis* through the range package. It's a basic zeroing shoot; twenty-five rounds single shot, in separate five-round groups. That's the idea anyway; in the end it's more like the lobby shootout in *The Matrix*. We can only watch as the *jundis* either hose down a target two lanes over, fire everything they have into the clear desert sky, or simply wait until Godders asks if everyone's finished, then abruptly blast twenty-five rounds on automatic off to the side.

What 2/4/10's own range days are like is anyone's guess, though there's a clue in the reaction to Godders' 'unload' command at the end. In the British Army that's the cue to clear your weapon carefully and put down the magazine with any unused rounds next to you. In 2/4/10's world it's the cue for anyone with any ammunition left to casually fire it one-handed into the earth wall at the end of the range.

Later on the same day 2/4/10 get their marching orders. They seem to go quietly enough, but I suspect that after what happened the last time they won't be issued their ammunition until *after* they get to Baghdad.

According to Jonty, while it's still early days, the US-mentored battalions already up there are starting to help turn the tide. I hope 2/4/10 will too. But if they do, it won't be because of anything we've done. The last week has followed the standard modern British Army approach to mentoring; the days of Glubb Pasha living and breathing the fight with his men are long gone. Now all we seem to do is deliver a bit of nugatory training, pat ourselves smugly on the back for 'finding Iraqi solutions to Iraqi problems', then step smartly away and leave the locals to get on with it themselves.

In fact it's quite ironic that our generals have spent the last three years blithely lecturing their US counterparts on counter-insurgency (as if they're somehow all too thick to work it out without someone regurgitating half-baked anecdotes about Malaya and Northern Ireland at them). Because the Americans not only train their Iraqis – properly – but then they actually go on operations with them. And you don't need to be Sun Tzu to know that this will probably get more out of a soldier than making him build bridges across shark-infested custard, before retiring for a *latte* in the Welfare Village, while he climbs on board a truck to Armageddon.

Thursday, 21 October 2006 – Shaibah

It's about ten to six in the morning and I'm lying in bed trying to work out whether I should roll over and go back to sleep, or get to breakfast early (no contest really; it's the Tiger Lines cookhouse, not the Ritz Carlton Central Park.) Then the lights abruptly snap on and Brooksie strides in, covered in dust and wearing his body armour. This is something of a turn up; last time I checked he was sleeping peacefully in a cot bed three feet away.

'Get on thy knees, STAB. For I am Brooksie of Basra. Behold my mighty works, and despair!'

I stare at him.

'I've just been in a massive contact in the city,' he clarifies, grinning.

This is big news. For all that this tour has been the most violent in years, we're closing in on the finish line and somehow no one in B Squadron has so much as fired their weapon yet. Personally, that doesn't worry me too much; I have a sneaking suspicion that in ten years' time I'll be pretty content knowing that there's no chance I've ever killed anyone,[44] (unless you count boring 2/4/10 into a coma). But testosterone's a hell of a hormone. And B

Squadron is full to bursting with it. There are probably at least a few dozen people who would give six months' pay, no questions asked, just for the chance to squeeze the trigger and say they'd fired a real live round in Iraq. Brooksie, it seems, has just fired several thousand.

It had started with an ambush on a Danish patrol near the Qarmat Ali bridge, in the north of the city. One of their boys had been killed almost straight away and the rest were pinned down. The QRF from the Shatt had been crashed out to help, but within minutes it had been obvious that a couple of Warriors weren't going to cut it tonight; it seemed like half the city had picked up an AK and joined in the fun.

So the order had come down to deploy Brooksie's troop in their tanks; he must have tiptoed out of the tent like Rudolf Nureyev, because none of us heard him leave. It was a big call, but a good decision too; by the time they roared onto the bridge like *The A-Team*, the firefight was so intense that Brooksie ended up having to use his main gun.

He'd fired training ammunition – inert rounds with the high explosive taken out and replaced with concrete – to minimise collateral damage, but it was still 17.5kg of tank shell travelling at 5,000 feet per second. He's pretty sure that Qarmat Ali now has a couple fewer houses – and several dozen fewer people – than it did yesterday.

By now we're all sitting at the end of Brooksie's bed like toddlers at circle time, pressing him for details. The strategic implications of a full-on tank battle in a city that we've been claiming is under control for three years now don't even cross our eager little minds. We just want to know what a 120mm main gun does to a house. Or what it looks like when someone gets cut in half with 7.62mm.

Pretty gnarly, Brooksie tells us. And interestingly, the blood stays warm for a surprising amount of time. He knows because he'd seen it glowing bright white through his thermal imaging sight when one militiaman had dragged himself into a house after having both feet blown off by the tank's chain gun. We murmur, and nod, and envy him. Because he has seen it, and we have not.

That night I climb up onto the Hesco behind Tiger Lines and look out across the desert towards the north of Basra, where Qarmat Ali is. There's no green tracer arcing through the sky this evening; the Garamshas and Halafs must be having a night off. Brooksie is quite rightly the hero of the hour, and has spent all day either being slapped heartily on the back or answering a million questions about what it's like to fight in a Challenger 2 for real. He's still crowing about being in a full-on contact, and looks like he's lapping up all the attention. But I noticed at lunch that his hands are still shaking slightly.

And no wonder. He'd mentioned the bit about warm blood and his thermal imaging sight as if it was a quirky little anecdote about his weekend. And we'd all reacted the same way, with interested nods and murmured, 'Yeahs'. But when you really stop to think about it, that must have been about as horrific as it gets. A pixelated figure on a dark TV screen, clawing his way into cover in agony, with his stumps dragging on the dirt and a pool of warm, white blood getting ever bigger around him. I think about what it must be like to see that, and to know that it was you who did it to him.

And all of a sudden, I don't envy Brooksie anymore.

22

SINBAD

Saturday, 23 October 2006 – Shaibah / Basra City

Op SALAMANCA is back on. Except it's not called that anymore. Now it's called Op SINBAD, after the eponymous sailor-hero who's supposed to have been from Basra. I haven't read *One Thousand and One Nights*, but I'm pretty sure that Sinbad spent his whole career being shipwrecked, getting tortured by unspeakable locals, and escaping death by the skin of his teeth. Perhaps the General's trying to tell us something. Anyway it's almost exactly the same plan as before, although with a bit more emphasis on reconstruction, and a bit less on kicking in the doors of people whom the prime minister might need to make into MPs in a few months' time.

At orders yesterday Jonty briefed us on the plan. This pulse will be in the University District, which is one of the few green-shaded bits on the Basra Consent Map. Apparently the residents are quite supportive up there. Or at least they don't all want to use our entrails as bunting, which by Baswarian standards counts as quite supportive. This was encouraging stuff. So far most of Jonty's briefings about places he's sending us have been about as chipper as a *King Lear* monologue.

The district is centred on a cluster of campuses in the north of the city, on the banks of the Shatt al-Arab. Basra University had once been quite the institution, but between a funding collapse and the local militiamen publicly flogging students they catch doing anything immoral (which apparently covers everything from skipping prayers to eating an ice cream too suggestively), the shine has rather come off it. For most of this pulse, B Squadron won't be too involved; in fact we'll mainly be sitting back in the Air Station acting as the reserve in case it all goes sideways. Apart from Third Troop. Third Troop will be taking the General to visit the troops.

I had just taken a big gulp of Coke when Jonty dropped this little bombshell, and the rest of the O Group watched with interest as most of it came straight back out of my nose. Spluttering, I stared at him wildly. He couldn't be serious. Taking out the General? He knew for a fact I'd got lost at least six times this tour (and those were just the ones I'd told him about). Even when I was the middle of a convoy I'd shown that I couldn't necessarily be relied on not to launch my Snatch into oblivion. All things considered, he'd be better off sending the General out with Mr Bean. The other troop leaders stared at me with a kind of fascinated horror, like someone who's just stepped on a landmine but hasn't lifted their foot off yet. But Jonty was deadly serious.

He also knew what he was doing, because he kept me running around like a blue-arsed fly for most of the rest of the day, leaving me no time to dwell. That evening I briefed the boys, more or less begging them to behave. No cheeky catnaps in the back of the Snatch, no rap battles on the troop radio net, and for fuck's sake no one have an ND (*negligent discharge*).[45] They nodded back, impressed. I probably hadn't looked this highly strung since meeting them all for the first time in Sennelager.

Today is the great day; we leave Shaibah at dawn to head to the Air Station and pick up the General. The boys look pristine and so do the Snatches. Sgt Mason has promised them that if he finds so much as a cigarette butt – or indeed another item of niche interest German erotica, like the one that Jonty discovered with a strangled yelp during an OC's inspection last week – he will falcon punch the responsible individual to death. I feel my spirits lift. You couldn't fault our appearance at least.

The General lives in Divisional Headquarters, inside one of the Air Station's old terminal buildings. It's a seriously high-powered venue; the kind of place where they have a soldier at the door whose sole function is to salute people going in and out, while he daydreams about flaying his recruiter alive. I follow some flunky through a maze of corridors, enjoying the stares from passing staff officers. By this point in the tour my body armour is looking gratifyingly ally. I even have a carabiner attached to the bottom of it, which I use to clip on my helmet (and which the boys occasion-ally use to clip me to my Snatch, or nearby fences, or other troop leaders, when I'm not paying attention). They don't see many carabiners in Divisional Headquarters.

We arrive at the General's office where he briefly destroys my hand to remind me that he is the alpha silverback, and I his pocket-holding prison wife. I make all the correct submissive subaltern noises, then we walk back out to the Snatches where his Close Protection team are waiting with the boys.

Army CP teams all come from the RMP, who occupy a slightly incongruous niche in the British Army ecosystem. On the one hand the RMP are technically soldiers. On the other, they also dedicate their entire careers to stopping other soldiers doing things they love; to wit, getting so plastered they shit themselves, and then sticking the nut on someone in the RMP.

They like to think they're nicknamed Redcaps (because of the scarlet hats on top of their heads), but to everyone else they're just Monkeys (because of what they've got inside them.)[46] Outside the confines of the RMP they are all utterly friendless, not least because the only encounter most of the Army will have with them is a brief exchange of pepper spray outside a German nightclub at three in the morning, followed by a trip back to camp in a squad car. Several members of Third Troop have played a starring role in these kinds of productions back in Sennelager, and I can almost taste the resentment in the air.

Their leader struts over. He is a small, bald sergeant in a pair of wraparound Ray-Ban sunglasses. For a guy who must spend 95 per cent of his working day standing outside an air-conditioned office while the General has meetings, he has kitted himself out as if he's about to storm the *Reichstag*.

'You the patrol commander?'

I admit it.

'OK, here's how we'll run it – first off we're meeting up with the Basra Chief of Police, just outside the city. Then we'll go with him to visit a couple of schools we're renovating. The boss wants to get out, meet the kids, press the flesh, that kind of thing. When we get there, we'll go with him, you lot can stay outside. And keep your head on a swivel; we do not, repeat not, want to come out and find they've got any surprises for the boss. Once we're done, you'll bring us straight back here. Any questions, fella?'

I pause, then jab him very hard between the eyes with my rifle, his Ray-Bans snapping neatly in half. As he folds to the floor I butt-stroke him briskly to death.

I don't, of course. I just stare at him for a moment, then in the iciest tones I can muster, tell him that it's my troop and while he can wander round with the General strapped to his chest in a BabyBjorn for all I care, I will deploy my own soldiers however I see fit, thanks very much 'fella'. He just smirks and walks off.

With our friendship firmly established, I stalk to my own ve-hicle. The General is already standing in the back chatting away to Womack and Greene. I shoot them a pleading look. Generals always try to ask you what you're really thinking; deep down they all want to be Bill Slim and they must enjoy the 'man of the people' vibe it gives off. If you've got any sense, you just smile and nod and tell them that the mail is getting through and your boots fit really well, thank you, sir. This is Womack and Greene, though; knowing those two they'll be chanting their various woes like the orphanage chorus line in *Annie* before he's even finished the question. But I needn't have worried; when I see their faces, they look as nervous as I feel.

We set off towards the city and after a couple of miles park up by a motorway bridge where we're supposed to be meeting the Chief of Police. It's going to be a complex bit of diplomacy for the General, I expect. There are various estimates for the penetration of the police force by the militias, but according to the only western journalist to be based in Basra at least 50 per cent are affiliated to one group or another. A week after saying so, the same journalist had been abducted off the street in broad daylight by men in police uniforms and shot dead on the city's outskirts. Which rather reinforced his point.

The police are certainly not keen on SINBAD, and were a driving force behind SALAMANCA getting binned. They're claiming it makes a mockery of their jurisdiction in Basra and will only serve to inflame tension on the streets. They may have a point, but I suspect the real reason they don't like it is that doing SINBAD properly would probably involve one half of the force immediately arresting the other half.

By now we all know that the more senior the Iraqi, the more their sense of punctuality will evoke the cocaine-addled lead singer of a 1970s glam rock band. So no one is surprised that the Chief hasn't arrived yet. A fleeting forty-five minutes later, we hear the faint sound of sirens, and a convoy of a dozen police cars appears in the distance.

Say what you like about the Chief (and given his track record, you might reasonably say, 'this man is intimately involved with several vicious sectarian militias, and quite possibly leading one of them'), he knows how to make an entrance. After barrelling past us at something like Mach 9, all the drivers simultaneously stand on their brakes as if at some unseen signal. Crashing sounds announce that at least one or two of them might have missed it. Even before the tyre smoke has cleared and the last crumpled fender fallen off onto the road, dozens of policemen are swarming around us waving their arms and yelling importantly into walkie-talkies.

The police cars themselves look more like carnival floats; they've all been garlanded with flowers and have gaily coloured ribbons fluttering from the radio antennae. Either today's the inaugural Pride Basra and we've missed the flyers, or these guys are really, really thrilled about visiting some schools with us. At no point does anyone look remotely inclined to turn off any sirens.

I spot the Chief of Police instantly; he is the size of a T-55 tank, with an enormous moustache, aviator shades, and shoulder boards like a Marshal of the Soviet Union. He and the General shake hands briefly, our man beaming and saying how delighted he is to be working so closely together on such an important day, theirs saying something I don't catch but which is presumably along the lines of, 'I am very aware that the only real change you have made to the plan we rejected in outrage three weeks ago is to call it by a slightly different name.' He doesn't look happy to be there. Neither do the General's CP team. There are a lot of pistols being waved around.

We set off into the city with Third Troop leading the way and the Notting Hill Carnival bringing up the rear. For once I'm not scanning the roadside wondering which pile of sand's going to fire a molten jet of copper through my head; there's no way JAM will dare take us on while we're in convoy with their pals. After a couple of kilometres we start passing parked-up Warriors, their dismounts waving us through with all the bubbling enthusiasm of men who've been standing on the same bit of sand for six hours, and know they probably have another six to go. We've arrived in the pulse area.

We turn into the street where the school is supposed to be. But I can't see it. I feel a little ball of unease start to form in my gut. Then a pair of anonymous black metal gates fly open and approximately 200,000 small children come barrelling into the road. We stop the vehicles and they surround us, pressing their grinning faces up against the windows of the Snatch and shrieking with glee. Here and there I can see a teacher grappling with the forest of little waving arms but they're not even making a dent. It's like being rushed by a horde of demented pygmies. And it's wonderful.

I get out and fight my way with difficulty to the back of the Snatch. The General is already out, patting small heads and smiling benevolently. For a man whose visits normally involved a saluting dais and guard of honour, he's taking the mobbing remarkably well. His CP team, on the other hand, look very flustered. I don't know what they're so worried about; no-one within twenty yards of the General is much over three feet tall, so unless JAM have an Oddjob-style assassin up their sleeve then he probably isn't going to get whacked by anyone in this crowd.

Eventually the CP team manage to bundle the General and the Chief of Police inside the school gates and the tumult in the street dies down. Sgt Mason and I give the sentries their arcs and warn them to make sure they change their fire position every minute or so. Last month a top cover gunner from the artillery was shot and killed just north of the city doing exactly what we're doing now; stagging on in the street waiting for one of the grown-ups to finish a meeting. He'd been standing in the back of a Snatch when he'd taken a single round straight through the neck. His mates had done all the right things; throwing smoke, clearing any likely firing points and all the rest of it, but they never even came close to working out where it had come from.

There have been several close shaves since, and now the intelligence people think there may be a sniper in play. It makes sense; there's one up in Baghdad called 'Juba' who's supposed to have killed nearly forty Americans, and it won't have taken long for JAM to sit up and take notice. Snipers are particularly keen on officers, who are easily identifiable by the enormous 6' x 6' maps of southern Iraq they're often seen wrestling while they try to work out where the fuck they are now.

They also give me the screaming heebie-jeebies. The thought that there might be someone out there now with a set of cross-hairs over my head – a head which has felt about the size of a comedy Halloween pumpkin ever since we heard about Juba – is enough to keep me bobbing about like a Thunderbird with Parkinson's every time I'm out of the Snatch. The street we're in is the standard Basra rabbit warren; there could be a dozen of the fuckers within a hundred yards and we'd never see a single one. And you don't need to be Annie Oakley to get a headshot from a hundred yards.

On the other hand there are still plenty of kids around, which is a reasonably good sign that nothing is imminent. Basra is a staggeringly young city; according to our briefings on PDT, 40 per cent of the population are younger than fifteen, and 10 per cent are younger than five. A good chunk of that 10 per cent appear to have turned up on the street we're in, and are busy trying to use my Snatch as a Wendy house.

The boys are dressed in the usual grubby singlets and knock-off football shirts, the girls in brightly coloured dresses (JAM are quite relaxed about waiting for them to hit puberty before they start thrashing them in the streets for dressing immodestly). They're also thin, and although this is a primary school, quite a few of them still look very small for it. This shouldn't come as a surprise, since all of them would have been born while the UN sanctions were still in place.

These sanctions had been meant to contain Saddam militarily after the first Gulf War by denying the Iraqi government access to world oil markets, and hence their major source of funding for weapons purchases. Which in fairness had more or less worked. Unfortunately the same funding also paid for food and medicines, so the sanctions had indirectly killed several hundred thousand children, and meant that the average height of an Iraqi five-year-old went from being the same as one from southern Italy in 1990, to being the same as one from northern Sudan by 2003.

These kids still seem lively enough, though. They also make Damien from *The Omen* look like Christopher Robin. It isn't our first encounter with the children of southern Iraq, so as soon as the cries of 'Mistah, mistah! WELLY GOOD!' go up, we swing straight into the time-honoured rituals.

'Gimme gun.'

'*La*. [No.] No gun. You are too small. Gun not for children.'

'Saddam bad!'

'Agreed. You're still not having the gun.'

'Look gun?'

'OK, we can look gun.' [*Kneel down with assault rifle. Six children all try to look through optical sight simultaneously. Realise what you're doing, and that a little fist has just clicked off the safety catch and set the change lever to 'Automatic'. Hastily retract assault rifle.*]

'Gimme . . . camera?'

'What? No. *La*. Are you mad?'

'Photo, photo, photo!'

'OK, we can do a photo.' [*Original audience joined by further eleven enthusiastic parties. All start throwing what appear to be LA gang signs. Take photo. Mobbed immediately by seventeen children, desperate to confirm that they're in shot. Recall tribal belief they told you about on PDT that cameras steal the soul of the subject. Observe that it doesn't bloody well appear to be the case here.*]

'Gimme . . . light stick.'

'No, I need those. Here, have a boilie.' [*Watch as child sucks sweet briefly, then screws up face and spits it into the dust. Reflect that it would take more than UN sanctions to make Army-issue boiled sweets acceptable.*]

'No sweet. Gimme pen.'

'Ahhhhhh, pen. Pen we can do. Here you go.' [*Scatter spare pens into the crowd like an aquarium worker feeding the piranhas. Crowd roars with approval.*]

'Good pen!' Pause. 'Saddam GOOD! FUCK YOU!' [*Crowd departs, making more gang signs.*]

Shortly afterwards the General returns. His CP team appear to have been picked even cleaner than us; the little bald sergeant has even lost his Ray-Bans. Keep your head on a swivel yourself, fella, I think happily. We mount up and Basra's answer to *Police Academy* lose another dozen wing mirrors turning round in the road. Our reception at the second school is if anything even more rapturous than the first, and we're immediately mobbed by another thousand happy little faces. Snipers aside, it's very close to being a lovely day.

Eventually it's time to pack up and go home. This first SINBAD pulse is a short one – only today in fact – and it seems to have gone off brilliantly. Probably because we've deliberately started in the single poshest part of Basra. There will now be a week's pause until the next one, while our HQ staff assess various detailed social impact metrics, and theirs presumably work out how to kill absolutely everyone involved next time round.

When we get back to the Air Station, the General disappears inside Divisional Headquarters for a moment then returns with a slab of ice-cold Cokes for the boys. It's a pretty classy touch, even if they do prefer Snapples.

He's enjoyed himself tremendously, he says; riding around on top cover reminded him of his days as a young subaltern when he hadn't a care in the world. I rather suspect that he hadn't a care in the world because he was a subaltern in 1980s Germany – where the only real threat was a savage case of alcohol poisoning – rather than a subaltern in 2006 Iraq, where your cares might reasonably include mortars, EFPs, and being shot in the neck by a sniper because you weren't bobbing around enough. But I can see his point. It can't be easy; between Whitehall trying to wind the whole thing down, the Americans asking pointedly whether we are *ever* planning on getting a grip of Basra, and a police force riddled with militia, the man has got a lot on his plate.

It's the kids who suffer in the end though, I muse to Sgt Mason while we're unloading the Snatches back at Tiger Lines. You can't help but feel for them. It's not much of a life when you're sixty to a classroom and even a simple pen can make your day. The ones we met today seemed happy enough, but then again they're only small. If doing more pulses means we can help make their lives easier, even just a bit, then after today I'm all for it.

Yeah, mega sad, agrees Sgt Mason. Those kids clearly don't have two pennies to rub together. Still, it's not all doom and gloom, because what they do have is every single brake-light from three Snatch Land Rovers, two radio antennas, a pair of wing mirrors and a petrol cap.

The little fuckers.

23

Condor

Sunday, 24 October 2006 – Camp Condor

Al Amarah has been captured by JAM. It's not a total surprise; we haven't set foot in the place since we bugged out of CAN. But it's still one of the biggest setbacks of the war so far. It's a cast-iron rule of any counter-insurgency campaign – Vietnam, Malaya, Northern Ireland, you name it – let the rural areas go if you absolutely must, but start losing the cities and it's game over.

And that's not the only reason we need to do something about it. There are camera crews in al Amarah, and if people at home start seeing cheering JAM militiamen standing next to burning police cars in a city that we've told them is nearly ready for PIC, they might get the wrong idea about how well things are going out here. So it's no great surprise when we're summarily plucked out of Shaibah and deposited in an abandoned airfield twenty miles south of al Amarah.

The trouble all started when JAM – perhaps a touch rashly, in retrospect – splattered the al Amarah chief of police all over the inside of his customised Merc with a roadside bomb. While the police in al Amarah are, like their colleagues in Basra, at least 50 per cent militiamen, they're affiliated to something called the Badr Brigade rather than JAM. The two militias aren't so very different ('You say a woman without a headscarf is an irreligious slut, I say she's a godless whore. Potayto–potahto.') but they're bitter rivals nonetheless.

So when Badr-affiliated police promptly kidnapped a local JAM commander's brother in revenge, then gouged his eyes out with a spoon and buried him in a shallow grave on the Iranian border, you could probably have seen the next bit coming (well, unless you'd just been violently introduced to a police station cutlery drawer).

JAM did not beat about the bush, and immediately stormed al Amarah with 800 militiamen. It took them all of two days to burn down most of the police stations in the city and raise their flag over the governor's residence. They have since started building defensive positions and patrolling the city in captured police cars, and look a lot like they want to stay.

The government have sent down several Iraqi Army battalions in response, who are currently on the way to al Amarah and will try to take it back if that's what it comes to. One of them is said to be 3/4/10, and I wonder how Captain Fantastic's feeling about it. Suicidal probably; if he struggled with a VCP by the front gate of camp then he's going to find a brigade attack into a fortified city very emotional. And that's assuming Major Hassan doesn't flog all their ammunition to JAM as soon as they get here.

The current state of play isn't all that clear; there are rumours that the two sides are negotiating and that Moqtada al-Sadr himself is on the way down from Baghdad. Apparently he may not even have sanctioned the assault on al Amarah. This makes sense; if his real aim is eventually to lever his way into government, it's not a great look for his goons to be rampaging through major Iraqi cities setting fire to all the police stations. But the truth is that no one really knows what's happening. And since this is Iraq, it's at least as likely that they'll bin off the diplomatic niceties and start going at each other like Visigoths again within the hour.

That's where we come in. If al Amarah does go all Pete Tong again then we'll roll a squadron's worth of Challenger 2s into the city (assuming they don't all break down five minutes after leaving camp), and re-establish order at the point of a 120mm main gun. It doesn't matter how upset you are about your recently enucleated[47] brother; people tend to lose their appetite for messy acts of fraternal revenge when they're staring at the 75-ton main battle tank that has just turned into the end of their road. In the meantime, we are to stay here and make sure everyone knows that the Brits Are Back. Although probably Only For A Bit.

'Here' is called Camp Condor, and was once home to an Iraqi MiG-29 squadron. It has a runway and half a dozen hardened aircraft hangars, each with a neat hole in the roof and a much less neat crater in the floor, courtesy of the laser-guided bombs that unceremoniously deleted the whole place on the first day of the Gulf War. It's now home to 600 British soldiers and about ten times that many bats. They hang ominously above our heads all day, occasionally demonstrating that you can be the rufty-tuftiest Millwall-supporting Recce Platoon headcase you like, you're still going to scream like 1980s Michael Jackson if one of them falls off and lands on your face.

Condor is a hive of activity; the CO has ordered a 24-hour patrol programme. This is partly to make sure that no one sneaks up and mallets us while we're not looking, but also because if we show off all the hardware menacingly enough, it might persuade both JAM and the Badr Brigade that it's in their best interests to put down the RPGs and hug it all out. Or pretend to until we pack up and leave anyway. So most of the battlegroup spend all day driving round and round the perimeter in Warriors and Challengers, and running VCPs on Route Six so that everyone going in and out of al Amarah can get a good look at what will be coming to fuck them up if they don't simmer down.

I don't drive anywhere though. I sit on my cot bed. I'm still not allowed anywhere near a Challenger 2, and we haven't even brought the Snatches up this time. But it was this or stay in Shaibah helping the Squadron Quartermaster-Sergeant (SQMS) stack ration boxes, so here I am. My only real job is a daily stint as watchkeeper in the Battlegroup HQ tent. As the most junior officer up here by some distance, I have naturally been relegated to the shift no one else wants to do – midnight to 4 a.m. – like some superannuated Three Counties Radio DJ, playing obscure seventies bluegrass to an audience of long-distance lorry drivers and insomniacs.

It's not hard, but it is only marginally more interesting than counting the holes in my mosquito net. About the only real highlight is giving our mortars permission to fire. It's still just illumination rounds – the moratorium on using our offensive support weapons to actually be offensive remains in place – but if nothing else it's useful for lighting things up when one of the patrols outside Condor wants to check whether that small bush over there really did just start whispering in Arabic.

It's also quite good fun, because no matter how many times you're warned before bed that we'll be using mortars overnight, when one of them goes off thirty yards away just as you're slipping into REM sleep there isn't a warning on earth that will stop you firing your sphincter halfway back to Basra. So two or three times a night the signallers and I quietly give the mortar platoon the thumbs up, then enjoy the sight of a hundred people in our hangar all falling out of their cot beds simultaneously and trying to dig a shell scrape with their chin.

In fairness we have been mortared a few times ourselves since arriving in Condor, so I can understand everyone's reaction. Unlike most attacks though, these ones came with a warning of their own. The first morning we were here, the CO went to visit the commander of a police station down the road. There he had been pointedly reminded – in the typically lyrical manner which

Iraqis use when they're delivering difficult news, but are keen you don't shoot the messenger – of the Arab tradition of hospitality. But also of the Arab tradition of not outstaying one's welcome. In this case for more than twenty-four hours. Just in case anything . . . unfortunate should happen after that.

The CO had replied – in the rather blunter manner which infantry colonels use when a pot-bellied policeman in a Frank Spencer beret starts trying to channel Don Corleone – that if any of his men were killed or wounded by mortars while we were in Camp Condor, he would in fact return personally to shoot the messenger, 'in this office, in your fucking head' (*sic*). But it seems like the commander doesn't believe him, because we've had quite a bit of incoming since. Alternatively the commander has correctly assessed that there is almost zero chance of anyone actually getting hurt; the militia appear to have Mr Magoo on fire control this week and I'd be surprised if any of the rounds have landed within half a mile.

I am on another wee hours watchkeeping shift – once again the Alan Partridge of the battlegroup net – when there's a crackle on the radio and the sound of a small, falsetto voice clearing its throat. It's Condor Connie. For the last few nights, someone has taken to alleviating the tedium by putting on a girl's voice and broadcasting their various thoughts over the radio. These are normally on a theme of how very bored they are of Condor, Iraq, the PWRR, the wider Army, and if they're feeling brave, the RSM. They're completely unidentifiable; there's at least a hundred people with access to a radio in the battlegroup. And while it's not best practice, there's not much else going on at 3 a.m.

This evening, Connie has decided to strip her routine right back and just warble, '*I'm booooored!*' in High C every couple of minutes. I grin at the signallers in the gloom, and wonder how long she'll keep it up. Then the tent flap opens and the RSM lumbers in. God knows what he's still doing up, but he's evidently decided to make a 'morale boosting' appearance because he's all smiles with the signallers, and even pretends not to notice the copy of *Viz* that someone's left on top of the map board.

Then there's a particularly drawn-out warble from Connie, which floats out of the little radio speaker in the corner of the tent. The smile freezes instantly on the RSM's lips.

'What's that, sir?' he asks me.

'Er . . . I think . . . well, it's one of the lads, RSM. You know. Just messing about a bit, and . . . having a laugh, I suppose . . .' I tail off.

The RSM frowns. Like all sergeant majors, 'messing about a bit' and 'having a laugh' were wiped from his hippocampus, *Total Recall*-style, the day they gave him his rank slide.

'It's fucking around with a battlegroup net is what it is, sir,' he says reproachfully. 'Here, give me that handset.'

He puts it against his ear and pushes the pressel switch.

'Hello, unknown callsign, this is Zero. Minimise. I repeat, minimise. This is the battlegroup net; it is not to be used for chit chat. Out.'

There is a pause. Then:

'*Ohhh, hello, RSM,*' coos Connie. '*I've missed yooou. Do you miss meeeee? I'm booooored . . .*'

I feel the temperature in the tent instantly drop by five degrees.

'Unknown callsign, Zero. I say again, minimise. You are to clear the net, immediately.'

'*But I'm booooored . . .*' comes the ethereal, whispered reply.

Even in the faint glow of the radio's lights I can see that the RSM has gone a deep shade of purple. Behind him the signallers stuff their fists in their mouths, their shoulders silently heaving.

'Unknown callsign, this is your last chance. Get off the fucking net, right now.'

Another pause.

'*Are you booooored tooooo?*'

'THAT'S FUCKING IT, YOU LITTLE CUNT!' explodes the RSM. 'YOU FUCKING GET IN HERE RIGHT NOW! OR I'M COMING OUT THERE TO FUCKING FIND YOU MYSELF AND YOU CAN FUCKING STAND BY, BECAUSE I'M GOING TO BEAST YOU UNTIL YOUR FUCKING EYES BLEED!'

There is a much longer pause. Then just as I'm beginning to think that's the last we've heard of Connie tonight, a voice floats out of the speaker once again. Except this time it's not a lilting falsetto, it's in deep, gravelly Cockney.

'Alright mate, calm down. I'm not *that* fucking bored . . .'

Monday, 25 October 2006 – Shaibah

We are back in Shaibah. After six days of sitting about in Camp Condor we got word that JAM were leaving the city – they'd made their point – and an uneasy peace had settled on al Amarah. The Iraqi Army moved in to reinforce the police, and there was no longer any need for us to parade up and down Route Six showing everyone what a big, tumescent member we have.

Quite what it means for PIC in Maysan that JAM can apparently overrun the provincial capital whenever they feel like it is unclear. You'd assume it'd move to the right a bit – until the Sun turns into a Red Giant and absorbs the Earth, perhaps. But knowing the lunatics in HQ, they'll probably just claim that JAM capturing a major city inside two days is yet further proof that they're 'running out of options', and move it forward a couple of months.

If we were hoping for a reprise of the downtime that Jonty gave us after the last trip to Maysan, we're in for a disappointment. It's getting quite close to the end of the tour now; we'll be leaving in a month. For anyone half sane that's a Good Thing; a cue to get your head down and grizz out the last few weeks. And maybe, without jinxing it, start making tentative plans for when you get home. But for a special breed of senior officers, the end of the tour induces only a deep, nagging sense of unease. After all, you're only going to get one chance to command your battalion, or brigade, or division on operations, and the window's closing. If you haven't done something noisy and impressive yet, then now is the time; those OBEs won't hand themselves out.

It starts with a no-notice strike op with the Devonshire and Dorset Light Infantry (DDLI). They live in the camp next door and are responsible for everything south of Basra. Apparently they've got wind of a High Value Target in Az Zubayr, a large-ish town about five kilometres from Shaibah. For reasons no one ever bothers to explain to us, the DDLI don't have any vehicles of their own, so they need a lift from B Squadron.

Jonty only gets the heads up at eleven, so it's close to midnight by the time we've tipped the boys out of their tents and driven across to the DDLI. One look inside their ops room tells us that we probably won't be getting our orders round a carefully constructed scale model this time. The place is like the Bombay Stock Exchange meets *The Wurzels*, full of anguished Janners waving target photos around and wondering aloud who's got all the fucking Blu Tack. In the end we do it round a map spread out on the bonnet of Godders' Snatch, with the flustered DDLI company commander tracing out the route with his finger.

The target is apparently a Big Cheese in al-Qaeda in Iraq, he says, and he's staying overnight in one of Az Zubayr's several Sunni neighbourhoods before heading up to Baghdad in the morning for some unidentified – but almost certainly cartoon-ishly evil – purpose. We are to wait for confirmation that he's bedded down for the night then go and lift him. Oh, and he's got at least six bodyguards, so we can probably expect to be contacted. I look at the glum faces of the other troop leaders. Forty-five minutes ago our biggest problem had been whether it was worth starting a new season of *The O.C.* before bed.

We sit by our Snatches for an hour waiting to leave. Then I wander off briefly to find a loo. I return five minutes later to find the tarmac empty, and tail lights disappearing round a corner in the far distance. I take a brief moment to stare at them in goggle-eyed panic, then break into a sprint, squawking at the top of my lungs for someone to for Christ's sake stop.

They don't, of course, and I end up having to leap into my still-moving Snatch like Burt Lancaster in *The Train* (if he'd also been sobbing with exhaustion and trying to bollock the driver between dry heaves). Apparently Griffiths had just followed the Snatch in front when it moved off, on the basis that it's exactly what I'd said he should do in orders. A fair point, I concede, but equally I didn't remember the part where I'd said I'd start this strike op with a solo five-kilometre fun run across the fucking desert. We bicker for another few minutes, before remembering there's an al-Qaeda kingpin lurking somewhere out there in the darkness and lapsing into a bad-tempered silence.

Not that we get anywhere near him in the end. The DDLI company commander has decided we'll ignore the roads and instead go straight across the desert to Az Zubayr. On the face of it this is a pretty good plan. Any insurgent with half a brain will have 'dickers' out in force; lookouts on rooftops with a mobile to their ear and a tendency to scowl horribly then vanish if you ever get too close. If we use the roads we'll be spotted in moments, and our target will be halfway to Baghdad by the time we putter into town.

Unfortunately what had looked on the map like a flat expanse of desert turns out to have more craters than the Hindenburg Line. Within moments of leaving Shaibah one of the Snatches is buried bonnet first in some kind of trench, and another has broken an axle. After ten minutes of crashing headlong into invisible chasms in the pitch dark, the order comes to turn our headlights on so we can see where we're going. We won't be taking down any al-Qaeda overlords this evening. In fact our best hope is that he'll rupture himself laughing.

We eventually reach Az Zubayr an hour after leaving Shaibah. Unbelievably the DDLI company commander insists on pressing on to the target's house. I wonder if he's missed the bit where we've just spent forty-five minutes crashing about the desert like Billy Smart's Circus with our headlights on full beam. A bit of lunatic optimism is all very well – in fact it's a core Army value – but it's also a fairly reliable way of getting everyone massacred. But he won't be told. Despite everyone's best efforts to explain that unless al-Qaeda let you bring a guide dog on *jihad*, our target has probably seen us coming, it still comes down to a classic Army game of 'Rock, Paper, I'm The Fucking Company Commander'.

So we spend a deeply unpleasant half-hour moving at walking pace through Az Zubayr's twisting alleyways, our weapons made ready, and braced for six al-Qaeda bodyguards to pop up and mow us down like the rooftop ambush in *Clear and Present Danger*. It's hideous. But the ambush never comes – not least because we never actually find the right house – and eventually we end up back on the main road into Az Zubayr.

We're then ordered to set up roadblocks on all the exits out of town. We stare at the DDLI company commander. I can't actually see any hidden cameras, but at this point if he peeled off his face and re-emerged as Jeremy Beadle I wouldn't be the least bit surprised. Either that or he's actually a deep cover plant from the Republican Guard, sent here by Ba'athist diehards to bollocks up the war effort. Roadblocks on the exits are for when you've just missed a target; he's squeezed out of his toilet window while fifteen squaddies piled into his living room. Our target has presumably sauntered out of his front door an hour ago, having had time to pack a small overnight bag and grab a magazine for the car ride.

But we do as we're told – you never know, there's an outside chance this guy's opted to make his getaway on a skateboard – and set up the roadblocks. They'd be more effective if we knew what the target actually looked like, but the DDLI's photocopier packed up earlier and the company commander has the only picture. We could do a couple of things with the description he gives us over the radio ('Mid-forties Iraqi male, moustache, black hair, kind of a . . . monobrow. And . . . like . . . squinty eyes'); arrest the driver of every third car, or accept that the British Army don't always get their man. We opt for the latter. After an hour of waving every single car mechanically through our roadblock, we head back to Shaibah. On the road, this time.

24

Airborne

Tuesday, 26 October 2006 – Shaibah / Maysan

The next morning Jonty's head pops in the tent flap before I've even finished putting on my pants. He tells me C Company are doing a road move up to Maysan and they need someone for the ARF. I nod reflexively, hopping gently on one foot, and Jonty's head disappears again. I finish putting on my pants then spend the next half an hour – not for the first time this tour – trying to find out exactly what it is I've just agreed to.

It turns out that ARF stands for Airborne Reaction Force. It's based on the simple premise that nothing worries an insurgent like a mystery helicopter landing somewhere behind them. And with good reason; it could be the SAS. Or Delta Force. Alternatively it might be Third Troop, but either way it's going to give you pause for thought before you start digging that big hole next to the road for your IED. The idea is that we'll fly up and down C Company's route, landing ahead of them to clear VPs, check out suspicious activity, and generally lurk about in the darkness giving the enemy the willies for once.

We go to C Company's HQ tent for orders. Their OC is tall, rangy, and nicknamed 'Darth' for his habit of breathing weirdly heavily whenever he gets angry. Which is a lot. He hasn't actually Force-choked anyone yet, but his subalterns reckon it's only a matter of time. I trace the route they'll be taking onto my map then go to brief the boys.

I can detect a glimmer of keenness as I run them through the plan. Soldiers love helicopters, and none more so than those whose other option is a Snatch. I also know it'll be an outstanding opportunity for them to capture some action shots for their online dating profiles. Most of them have at least one account – I'm told Greene is currently exchanging messages with no less than forty-seven individual women – and they routinely spend hours duck-facing in front of the camera like thirteen-year-old girls.

I once found a memory stick of the results that they'd acciden-tally left in the Squadron HQ tent. Cameron with a belt of 7.62mm draped around his bare torso. Womack covered in baby oil and reclining on a cot bed like the Creation of Adam. And worst of all, Schofield sitting naked astride the main gun on a Challenger at sunset, pouring a bottle of water over his head with a look of what he presumably believed to be sensual ecstasy on his face. I am now half hoping that someone's brains *do* get splattered all over me, as long as it means those particular mental images get elbowed out of my amygdala.

C Company depart at dusk and we head to the helicopter land-ing site (HLS) to wait for our ride. We've been briefed to expect a Sea King, and earlier today we spent a full hour in the tank park with the rough outline of one chalked on the tarmac, rehearsing how to get on and off and where we'd sit. The boys whinged – they know what a fucking door is, and how to fucking sit down – but I'm not taking any chances. I love them all, like sons, but soldiers in general – and Third Troop in particular – can cause an accident inside a perfect scientific vacuum if you take your eye off the ball.

I remind them about PDT, and the briefing we'd had on our new radios. The instructor had warned us to wash our hands after handling the radios because they were all box fresh and covered in some kind of anti-chemical weapon coating which could be harmful if ingested. Within thirty minutes three of the boys were being carted off to the med centre, clutching their stomachs and groaning pitifully. After a brief investigation, the instructor had to add an extra bullet point to his PowerPoint slides, reminding users not to *lick* the radios either. Not even 'for a laugh'. Compared to that little jape, I tell them, walking into a tail rotor at night would actually be quite sophisticated.

The helicopter clatters onto the HLS and we clamber aboard. Then it staggers into the air and we start heading north. A prototype Sea King first flew in the 1960s, and from the look of the interior we might well be sitting in that exact one. I try not to think about the unidentified fluid that I can feel dripping onto my neck, and plug myself into the intercom.

'Oh, hello,' says a voice brightly. 'What are we doing tonight, then?'

I think for a moment. The Army's mastery of Stockholm Syndrome would make the Patty Hearst kidnappers look like rank amateurs, so I have by now completely accepted that no one ever tells me what's happening. I am, after all, just a shit-eating grunt. It hasn't occurred to me that they don't tell pilots either.

'Well, there's a convoy moving up to Maysan, and we're supposed to just . . . land a bit, in and around them, and . . . well, just make sure there's nothing going on.'

'Great!' replies the voice, as if it's the best news they've had all week. 'Where do you want to go first?'

I read out a grid reference a few miles north of where the convoy will be by now, on the outskirts of a little village where there have been a few minor contacts in the past. Then I sit back in my seat and reflect on what a very strange organisation the Army is. They don't trust you enough to let you pick your own haircut, and

won't let you use a cross trainer without a 45-minute safety briefing, but at the same time they'll happily give you your own helicopter to order around in the middle of a warzone.

I look out of the window as we thud low past a set of gas flares,
the jets of flame painting the interior of the Sea King a dull
orange. It is so ally I think I might cry.

We clatter on for twenty minutes, then spot the long column of
C Company vehicles trundling along the road. A few minutes
later the pilots inform me that we're approaching the grid I've
given them. Very good, I say, feeling like Jack Hawkins in *The
Cruel Sea*. Set us down, please.

The drop from the Sea King's door to the ground is further
than I remember. That or the pilots are still in the hover, holding
us off the ground in case they have to depart in a hurry. Either way
I leave the helicopter like a pub drunk missing the doorstep at
closing time, plummet through space for long enough to get as far
as, 'Oh fuuuu—,' and pancake squarely into the sand. The impact
knocks so much wind out of me that I barely register the Sea King
taking off, and it's a full minute before I can pull myself, gasping,
onto all fours. Not the start I'd hoped for.

The boys – once they're no longer folded in half laughing – are
as solicitous as ever (i.e., broadly at par with a hyena pack).
They've all managed to disembark like Olympic gymnasts, of
course. After I can stand up again without heaving we shake out
into a loose arrowhead and start patrolling towards the little
village in front of us. Nothing much has ever happened here; the
local tradition seems to be to fire a few desultory rounds after the
last vehicle in a convoy for form's sake. And it doesn't look too
lively now.

God alone knows what these people do for fun at night; I
can't see any lights, and certainly none of the satellite dishes
that festoon most houses in the city. Perhaps they have one of
those oral storytelling traditions I've read about, like the
Bedouin. I wonder if there'll be a verse passed down about us
one day: *They came in a helicopter / Like a hawk in the night /*

The first one fell out / And went Argh Fucking Hell Help Me Lads My Fucking CHIN.

It seems unlikely; the only living souls who appear interested in us are the village dogs, who are going off like it's the afterparty at Crufts. We wander around for another ten minutes. Then I call up the Sea King and ask to get picked up again.

Bringing in a helicopter at night is a nerve-wracking business. Lots of armies issue their soldiers with infrared strobes, which give off an otherwise invisible flash that pilots can see through NVGs. Our Army, whose attitude to spending money on that kind of thing could be a plotline in *A Christmas Carol*, does not. Instead British soldiers are told to tie an infrared cyalume to a piece of string and whirl it madly around their heads. This apparently imitates the effect of an actual strobe, as well as saving money that can much more usefully be spent on Herman Miller swivel chairs for civil servants in the MoD.

Once you've tied your cyalume to its piece of string and are waving it in frantic circles like you're trying to rope a Texas Longhorn, the next step is to kneel down and tuck your chin into your chest. The pilot then lands right next to you, so close that he could kick you in the arse if there wasn't a cockpit in the way (literally; he's trained to use your quivering lower back as an aiming marker). Your job is to keep waving your cyalume, while trying to stop your sphincter from producing a high-pitched whistling noise as five tons of whirling death misses your head by a foot and a half. It's not all that much fun.

Back in the air I give the pilots more grids and we repeat the exercise a few times. We don't find anything, but the boys look like they're enjoying themselves. C Company, on the other hand, are not. They have missed an important turn and are having what our pilots describe to me as a 'total gang fuck' in the desert below. They tune me in just in time to hear Darth vowing to the platoon commander leading the convoy that he will be working in a fucking Carphone Warehouse inside the month if he ever does that again. This is known as 'inspirational leadership' in the infantry, and can be traced all the way back to that time when the Duke of Wellington called his lads 'the scum of the earth' and everyone seemed to take it as a compliment.

We're running low on fuel by now, so the next landing will be our last. I glance at my map and pick a likely looking spot; a T-junction where the road nears the Euphrates. It's a classic VP and the convoy will be going through it in half an hour, assuming Darth hasn't light-sabred all his platoon commanders to death by then.

Shortly afterwards the engine note changes and I feel the helicopter beginning a slow descent. I take off my headset and unbuckle the seatbelt, ready to leap gazelle-like to the ground when we touch down. Through my window I can make out some orange lights in the distance. That'll be al Qurnah, a modest little town – 50 per cent breeze-block houses and 50 per cent open landfill sites patrolled by three-legged dogs – which we've driven through a few times on the way to Maysan. The locals claim, apparently with total seriousness, that it's the original site of the Garden of Eden. I hope for the sake of Abrahamic religions everywhere that they're making it up.

Then, just as I begin to stand up, there is a crashing drumbeat of monstrous *thwacks* that shakes the whole Sea King. My shrieks of alarm are drowned out by the sudden roar of the helicopter's engines; we are lurching upwards again and I can see the pilots' heads swivelling urgently from side to side.

This is it then; we've landed in the middle of an ambush meant for the convoy and someone has stitched the whole fucking helicopter from nose to tail with a machine gun. We must have been hit a dozen times. Jesus Christ. I grope desperately for the ends of my seatbelt; if I'm not strapped in when we crash then I'll either be flung out or break my neck on the inside of the helicopter. I jam the buckle together with nerveless fingers. Then I close my eyes. And wait.

Five seconds later I open them again. We are still in the air. The lurching has stopped. I look down the cabin. I can't see any gaping holes in the fuselage. Nor have any of the boys turned into the bullet-ridden, headless corpses I'd been expecting. In fact, like me, they appear to be peering wildly around the Sea King, eyes like Dobby the house elf, all mouthing something which looks a lot like 'What the *fuck?* What the *fuck!*'

Perhaps we haven't been machine-gunned out of the sky after all. I remember the headset next to me and snatch it up.

'. . . dusty as fuck. Ah well. That's it for the night anyway. Steer 175 for Shaibah.'

'What was all that about?' I practically wail.

'Brownout,' comes the curt reply. 'Palm trees next to your junction. Must have drifted into them with the rotors. No harm done. But we're going back now.'

That explains it. Brownout describes the almost total loss of visibility that sometimes occurs when you try to land a helicopter in a sandy or dusty area. Given Iraq is basically made of sand and dust, it's a fairly common occurrence here; barely a week goes by without either us or the Americans putting a helicopter on its roof because the pilot suddenly couldn't see which way was up anymore. We've been lucky to get away with some scratched rotor blades. Really lucky.

We fly back to Shaibah and leave C Company to it. They miss another turn later on, so presumably someone is going to be flogging Nokia 3210s in the Westfield Centre by the end of the month. But they make it all the way to Maysan without being contacted; I expect not even JAM want to mix it up with Darth when he's in one of his moods.

When I get back to Tiger Lines, Jonty claps me on the back and tells me how jealous he is of me cutting about in helicopters while his arse polishes a chair in Battlegroup HQ. I smile weakly and don't say anything. It had taken half an hour for my heart to stop pinballing around my chest after the brownout, and when I go to bed that evening I have a nightmare about being crushed underneath a Sea King. It's so intense that when I wake up I'm not completely sure that I haven't cried out. I wouldn't be the only one; by this point in the tour there are some nights when the troop leaders' tent is like the Vienna Boys' Choir.

There are three weeks left. And it's just as well, because I'm not sure how much more of this I can take.

Friday, 27 October 2006 – Shaibah

At evening orders, Jonty tells us to get ready for another Op SINBAD pulse. It almost feels like a relief. The little ad-hoc task-ings we've been doing for the past few days haven't shown any signs of letting up, and I am beginning to dread the appearance of his little gnomic face at the tent flap.

In the last forty-eight hours alone I've driven the regimental band to the Air Station (and almost had my head blown off by a trombonist trying to fire a warning shot at a dog), and spent a morning marshalling traffic around a collision between a Warrior and a jingly truck[48] (which had apparently contrived to 'come out of fucking nowhere', despite being multicoloured, covered in bells, and on a desert highway with roughly ten kilometres' visibility in all directions). And to cap it all off the SAS have just wrecked several of my Snatches.

Apparently they'd needed them for a strike op in the city. Which was a bit worrying; I'd rather hoped that the UK's warrior elite had better options than vehicles that would have been rejected out of hand by a Sudanese children's militia. Even so, when Jonty told me to hand them over I hadn't quibbled. This was Special Forces business.

I've previously only ever had fleeting encounters with the SAS here. It's easy to spot them; for a supposedly discreet organisation they seem to put in a tremendous amount of effort to ensure that absolutely everyone knows who they are. They're the guys who wear North Face jackets over their uniforms, silently daring any passing sergeant majors to tell them to take it off. Or who casu-ally roll out their thermarests on the floor of the Hercules while everyone else straps obediently into the bench seats. Most of them are in Baghdad hunting al-Qaeda, and they only venture south occasionally. Their most high-profile escapade in Basra was about a year ago, when two of them had definitively put the 'Special' into 'Special Forces' by getting taken hostage by the Iraqi police during an undercover surveillance mission.

They'd been following the head of Basra's Serious Crimes Unit – a man who'd allegedly committed quite a few more than he'd ever bothered solving – when they were stopped at a routine police checkpoint. Quite what their contingency plan was is unclear, since neither of them spoke a lick of Arabic and their 'disguises' were only slightly more convincing than the valmorphanization scene in *Team America*. Perhaps they thought they'd be able to nod and smile their way out of it, and hope that their eyebrows didn't fall off while they were talking. Bizarrely the police hadn't been fooled by two blokes from Hereford wearing a thin layer of L'Oréal Matte Bronzer and cotton wool balls glued to their cheeks, and had asked them to step out of the car.

This pair had responded by pulling out their rifles and riddling the nearest police car with bullets, thereby confirming that even the SAS can come up with a fucking stupid plan. They managed to shoot two policemen dead but were eventually captured, beaten, and taken to the local police station to be processed, presumably with a car battery and some lengths of rubber tubing. The Army, upon discovering what had happened, duly crashed out every man jack in Basra and levelled a small corner of the city trying to find them. Both men were on the verge of being handed over to JAM when the General ordered a Challenger 2 to drive through the police station wall, after which they were dragged out of the rubble by their hair and chucked in the back of a Warrior. The police had not been at all pleased. And for once I can see where they were coming from.

This time round the SAS were after an individual called Omar al-Farooq. He was core al-Qaeda, a right-hand man to bin Laden, and had actually been held by the Americans in a prison in Afghanistan for a while. Fair play to the bloke, he'd then pulled off the kind of getaway that would make Papillon look like a mewling infant; after picking the lock on his cell he'd changed out of his prison uniform, climbed a ten-foot wall, and then crawled through a Soviet minefield to a waiting vehicle. He was Iraqi by birth and had come back to carry on the fight in his homeland. He was, unsurprisingly, very unlikely to come quietly.

I'd given the Snatch keys to a bald-headed operator with a week's worth of stubble and a skull that looked like a relief map of the Pyrenees. Ordinarily when you borrow a vehicle in the Army it comes with more forms than most adoptions: drivers' hours, logbooks, maintenance records, and so on. The idea is to have a seamless audit trail so they can nail you to the wall if you so much as scratch it. Which is why most soldiers' instinctive reaction in a catastrophic vehicle accident is not to scramble out before the wreckage catches fire, but rather to grab a biro and immediately start backdating the paperwork. But with the SAS there was none of that. I didn't mind particularly, but Sgt Mason was in a quiet rage; vehicles and administration were his bag and this was the worst kind of heresy.

Six hours later the SAS dropped our Snatches off again. The same operator I'd given the keys to handed them back with the quiet smile of a man who truly enjoys his work, then strolled away whistling. I walked over to the first vehicle and blanched. It looked as though it had just finished the Dakar Rally; both wing mirrors were gone, and every single light on the front was smashed. I followed the reek of cordite to the back doors and opened them gingerly. The rear of the Snatch was ankle deep in empty casings and ammunition boxes, and what looked like a bloodied first field dressing. Evidently Omar had opted to go out like Tony Montana at the end of *Scarface*.[49] The other Snatches were in a similar state, and it had taken us a whole day to get them serviceable again.

It was worth doing a good job though. According to Jonty the next SINBAD pulse will be in a district called al Qibla. While there are probably worse places for your vehicle to break down – central Mogadishu, for example, or Croydon – al Qibla is near the top of the list. It's a dirt-poor little den of resentment in the south of the city, jutting into the desert as if the rest of Basra is slowly trying to vomit it out. It also features regularly in our daily intelligence summaries. Any patrols going in can guarantee a comprehensive shoeing by its resident militiamen, and most of the mortars and rockets that are currently raining down on Basra Palace are fired from al Qibla's many noisome patches of waste ground.

If Op SINBAD works there, it'll work anywhere.

25

Al Qibla

Saturday, 28 October 2006 – Basra Palace

We'll be based out of Basra Palace for this pulse, so shortly after breakfast the whole battlegroup forms up for the road move. We'll be one of several convoys nosing their way carefully into the city today. Some of the reconstruction projects will involve building work, so we're taking a troop of Royal Engineers with us as well. They've even got a JCB with them. I glance at the driver, perched high in his cab. He looks about as happy as you'd expect for someone who's just been told he's driving into Basra City inside a big glass box eight feet up in the air.

We reach the outskirts of the city and start moving south-east along the road that handrails the edge of the Shia Flats. It feels like ten years ago when we were here in the back of a Warrior on our handover patrol. Snug at the rear of our convoy and without any map-reading to do, I prattle away at Griffiths as per normal. But he seems a bit quieter than his usual self. In fact all the boys are. And I know why.

By now we're only about two and a half weeks from going home, and you wouldn't be human if the odds didn't start playing on your mind. It doesn't help that dying right at the end of your tour is such a common trope of film and TV – M*A*S*H, *Platoon*, you name it – someone always gets wasted just after they've got out their picture of Peggy Sue and told everyone about the kids they're going to have after this is all over. Now is about the last time you want to be told you're going to spend four days put-putting around Basra's single most violent neighbourhood in a Snatch, that's for sure. No wonder they're worried.

And they're right to be. We're about halfway to the left turn that will take us into the city proper when there is a distant *thump*, and we see a sudden cloud of dust and sand somewhere on the horizon. The vehicle in front slows then stops. We pull up behind, and Griffiths and I hop gingerly out, scanning the rooftops a couple of hundred metres away through our weapon sights.

Whatever has happened up front, now would be an excellent time for some enterprising gunman in the Shia Flats to stitch the entire convoy from end to end. There are about sixty vehicles sideways on to him, all sitting on top of a slightly raised road like tin ducks at a fairground shooting gallery. I wonder how the JCB driver's feeling about it all. Sitting in a glass cage of anxiety, I imagine. Probably muttering, 'Learn to drive a JCB, they said. Set you up for fucking life, they said . . .'

After a while, the news crackles over the net; the first vehicle in one of the convoys up ahead has hit an EFP. Fortunately it was a Warrior; the EFP was a decent size, and if it had been a Snatch then we'd have been shovelling four men into body bags before we'd even started the pulse. I shudder and offer up a silent thank-you for JAM's love of the cartoonishly spectacular.

It seems that they're desperate to bag a Warrior for the propaganda value, and so will often go for one of those even if there are much softer targets available. Like us. Not that it hasn't made a mess of the Warrior, mind you. The copper slug has gone all the way through the armour and most of the way through the engine block, before running out of energy just short of the driver. He ought to buy a lottery ticket; if it had been fired from the other side of the road, they'd have been scraping him out of his seat with a spoon.

Eventually they hook the damaged Warrior up to a recovery vehicle and the convoy moves off again. We seem to be going much slower than before; not particularly surprising given that whoever's now leading watched a molten copper slug hit the Warrior in front of him at Mach 6 about twenty minutes ago. In his shoes I'd probably be crawling too.

We enter the city and after a couple of kilometres hit the river, where it's a right turn onto the long corniche that leads to Basra Palace. It's lined with ninety-nine plinths which once bore bronze statues of commanders who Saddam thought had done particularly well in the war against Iran. They'd stood up there for years, each one looking suitably ferocious and pointing in the vague direction of the enemy across the water (thereby not only preserving their memory, but also rather neatly epitomising the sophistication of their tactics for most of the war). Almost all of them have been looted by now, but there are still one or two fierce-looking heroes with Ned Flanders moustaches hanging on grimly to their little platforms.

We pass through the front gate of Basra Palace, which resembles a scaled-down Arc de Triomphe, except covered in red-faced squaddies and heavy weapons. The Palace itself comprises a large number of individual residences, each with its own surrounding garden. They are separated by small canals and ornamental carp lakes, which Saddam's sons (whom even he must have worried were turning out to be wrong 'uns) are said to have used for the odd spot of hand-grenade-fishing, as well as the occasional dunking-of-irksome-political-rivals-until-the-bubbles-stopped.

Each building is about three storeys high, all sandstone and marble and great vaunting pillars. There are gargoyles too; snarling lions and something that looks a bit like a griffin. The walls themselves are covered in bas relief figures; muscular peasants working the fields, an Iraqi soldier cradling a small child, and so on. There have been British soldiers living in the Palace for nearly four years by this point, so naturally every single one of these figures also sports a gigantic felt-tip penis, and the occasional speech bubble either proclaiming their profound love for Manchester City, or helpfully informing some archaeologist of the distant future that, 'I am a pedo' (*sic*).

The Palace was once the site of the British consulate, but all the Foreign Office staff were evacuated weeks ago. This was something of a double-edged sword for the infantry battlegroup based here. On the one hand there'd be no more ogling the sole British female civilian for a hundred miles. On the other, at least they wouldn't be getting brassed up[50] escorting the water truck that refilled the Foreign Office swimming pool anymore. You can't blame the diplomats for leaving. Even the infantry are starting to get twitchy; six lots of incoming a day is enough to make the grizzliest of veterans a bit skittish. We've been reading the intelligence summaries for months in Shaibah, of course, but they don't tell nearly the whole story.

AT 1943D BASRA PALACE CAME UNDER ATTACK FROM 11 X ROUNDS OF IDF (11 IMPACTS HEARD). 0 INJURIES sounds alright on the face of it. But it doesn't tell you anything about the Warrior commander flat on his face on the tank park while shrapnel cuts down the palm tree next to him. Or the clerk who is a foot away from oblivion when the shockwave knocks a half-ton gargoyle off the building she's just run into.

We are mortared twice within an hour of arriving. It is all very close.

At least we're not sleeping in breeze-block-tent-tombs like in the Shatt. Instead, B Squadron are accommodated in the upstairs ballroom (because what kind of hopeless peasant only has a downstairs ballroom?) of the residence which once belonged to Uday. He was the eldest and by some distance maddest of the Hussein boys, and had been all set to inherit the family gig until a nicely judged assassination attempt by Shia resistance fighters in

1996 saw him shot seventeen times and semi-disabled. Judging by the décor, he'd clearly pointed at the page titled 'Maniacal-Dictator-Chic' in the swatch book, then hired the same interior designer who'd done Hugh Hefner's private jet.

If only walls could talk, I think. Uday might have been an irredeemable psychopath – he'd used to routinely feed enemies to his pet lions, and once stabbed his father's personal food taster to death with an electric carving knife for disrespecting his mum (take note, Dillon . . .) – but he'd certainly known how to throw a party. It feels as though if you closed your eyes and concentrated hard enough you could almost still catch the faint whiff of Cohiba cigars in the air (not to mention that of huge piles of Charlie and the odd decomposing food taster).

I wonder if Uday ever imagined there'd be a time when his crib would be full of dozing British soldiers. Or that Buxton would lie quietly, his hands as ever on a leisurely safari around the front of his pants, behind the same wooden lattices where once he'd kept a rotating team of sultry concubines.

Probably not.

Sunday, 29 October 2006 – al Qibla

We leave the Palace for al Qibla as dawn is breaking. The focus of this pulse will be on refurbishing a local school, so most of the squadron are stagging on with the engineers. Third Troop, Jonty tells me, will be keeping an eye on the local police. Al Qibla PD are responsible for more roadside corpses than a Tijuana cartel, and while officers in other districts might be turning a blind eye to JAM IDF teams, only in al Qibla are they letting them set up the mortars in the station car park. There's reliable intelligence that if they're left to their own devices, they're going to give all their weapons to JAM for the day and make themselves scarce. We are to stick to them like glue.

We haven't even reached al Qibla when the CO, busy setting up his headquarters somewhere on the district's outskirts, reports that he's in contact. I'm impressed; it's not even eight o'clock yet and JAM are already up and about and trying to kill colonels. I hope for the CO's sake he can sort it out soon; he's due a media visit at some point this morning and it's hard enough making the 'hearts and minds' spiel sound convincing even without an enemy machine-gunner systematically brassing up your interview.

We arrive in al Qibla to a sea of sullen faces and park the Snatches up by the school we'll be refurbishing. Up close the district is even worse than I've been expecting; all single-storey breeze-block houses and dirt roads. The ditches are choked with rubbish. The crowd is mostly young men and children, and they're hanging back, staring at us from alleyways and side streets.

I know why; the only time they normally see British soldiers is when we're busy turning their neighbourhood into 1980s Beirut. So we can hardly expect them to start cheering and hanging flower garlands round our necks just because we've turned up with some tins of paint and a few rakes this time. The PWRR – it's C Company and Darth again – fan out in their Warriors to form a loose cordon, then hunker down in their turrets to see what JAM have planned.

After confirming, for the eleventh time, that we are not to let the fuckers out of our sight, Jonty dispatches Third Troop down the road to the police station to do some joint patrols. We've got an interpreter with us called Omar whom we've borrowed from the pool at Shaibah. On the way to al Qibla, the boys have been blathering away at him as usual and taking the piss out of the Man City shirt he's wearing, but Omar hasn't so much as cracked a smile. In fact, he's a picture of misery. When we arrive at the police station, he pulls on a ragged balaclava before getting out of the Snatch, and the penny drops. This isn't some back of beyond village in Maysan; this is Iraq's second city. And if Omar is some-how recognised then he's a dead man, no matter where he's from. His family too.

By this point, the militia death squads in Basra are openly going from house to house looking for 'collaborators' to kill, and interpreters are top of the list. JAM recently managed to get seventeen of them in one go when they stopped a bus bringing them back into the city after a training course in Shaibah. They'd tied the driver to his steering wheel then shot his passengers in the head by the side of the road. The bodies had been left all over the city as a warning.

Al Qibla police station lies next to a reeking patch of waste ground, which appears to be serving as a fly tip for half of Basra. It's already a hive of activity when we arrive, with a mixed crowd of RMP and Iraqi police standing around in the courtyard shouting at one another. It appears that the RMP have turned up to carry out a snap inspection and their Iraqi opposite numbers are busy throwing six kinds of fit about it. They must have something (or someone) pretty special hidden in their cellar.

I'm not keen to hang around; the atmosphere in the courtyard is febrile to say the least, and Iraqis can be quite quick to go for a gun when they're wound up, without worrying overmuch about the consequences. During the QRH's last tour, the chief of police in Maysan had so annoyed the provincial governor during an argument that the governor pulled out his Makarov mid-sentence and shot him in the head. Which is certainly one way of showing that you think the meeting has gone on too long.

The courtyard scene here shows all the signs of turning into the *Gunfight at the O.K. Corral* the very next time someone gets poked in the chest, so when I see a squad car rolling gently towards the front gate, I don't waste any time.

Jogging over with Omar, I announce to the scowling pair inside the car that we'll join them on patrol – assuming, of course, that that was why they'd been quietly trying to leave? There is a long pause, and they both give me the kind of looks which suggest they wouldn't mind in the slightest if I joined al Qibla's weekly tally of roadside corpses. Then the driver spits disgustedly and nods. Not that he's got much choice; while we've been talking, Sgt Mason, who never misses a thing, has neatly boxed them in with a pair of Snatches.

We begin to drive around the noxious streets, watching as al Qibla's Finest carry out the kind of community policing that would send the *Daily Mail* comments section into raptures. Ears are cuffed, batons applied to the backs of legs, and at one point a donkey cart is almost run off the road after its driver fails to get out of the way fast enough. Not that he realistically could have; the police are driving like there's a camel spider loose in the car, and even we are hard pressed to keep up (which is probably the point). In theory I should be intervening; and I will, if it ever looks like it's about to go full Rodney King. But you have to pick your battles. They would probably think I was quite mad.

After all, it's not like Iraq has ever known anything different; policing by consent has never really been a thing *anywhere* in the Middle East. Not least because while we were debating the Peelian principles and designing funny-shaped police helmets – and this isn't a dig, just a statement of fact – most of this region were still living in goat-hair tents and wondering where the next camel-raiding party would come from. It's the same mistake we're making with the whole 'free and fair parliamentary democracy' concept, which is still showing precisely zero sign of being a thing here; we can't just expect the Iraqis to magic themselves to the same place in five years that took us five hundred.

After about an hour, our new pals indicate that they think they've done enough policing for one day. Very possibly for the rest of this year. Frankly I am minded to agree; the heat has given me a thumping headache and their habit of mashing at the siren button like a toddler with an activity table is kicking it into high gear. We're due to report back to Jonty for our next tasking soon anyway. I tell Omar to let them know they can go, then watch as they pull an outrageous U-turn and shoot off down the street scattering pedestrians like skittles.

We'll do another twenty minutes, I reason, then head back to the school. Now that Starsky and Hutch have departed, we can move like a proper patrol again; the boys dismount and we set off up the road at walking pace.

The Army puts a lot of faith in what it calls 'atmospherics'. And it's forever peppering you with snappy little bits of advice like, 'If There's Doubt There's No Doubt', or 'Look for the Absence of the Normal and the Presence of the Abnormal'. But really it's just your gut; the same instinct which told your ancient ancestors that it was time to finish this conversation at the top of the baobab tree instead of underneath it. And my gut feels fine; the shops are open, there are people fixing cars by the side of the road, and I can see children chasing each other in and out of alleyways.

Which makes it all the more surprising when a five-round burst of AK fire splits the morning air.

My first reaction is to freeze stock still, and stare stupidly in the direction of the shots. Then, recalling that the relevant battle drill for small arms fire is 'take cover' not 'audition for a spot as a living statue in Covent Garden', I drop inelegantly to the floor behind my Snatch. I look around me, wide-eyed. The boys have got themselves into cover too, their weapons in their shoulders.

I fumble for the radio handset and babble a quick report to Squadron HQ, hoping my voice isn't as shrill in real life as it is in my head. Then I peer gingerly over the bonnet. I'm not sure what I'm expecting to see. In training it's normally a Land Rover with orange mine tape all over it to signify enemy. Or a bored-looking squaddie in fancy dress hanging obligingly out of a top-floor window.

Not this time. In fact everything seems exactly the same as it did thirty seconds ago, save that everyone in the street is now staring at us. They don't appear to be particularly worried. Maybe this happens a lot.

Despite what Hollywood would like you to believe, in any contact the first thing most soldiers do isn't to stick a shaving mirror to their bayonet with chewing gum so they can spot the sniper in the reflection. Instead, what most soldiers do is sit back down for a bit while they try to work out where the fuck that lot just came from. It's often all but impossible; after all, the world is very big.

I'm told the Americans have a clever piece of kit called Boomerang, which uses microphones to give you the exact bearing and range to whoever's shooting at your Humvee. We have more chance of being issued a Fabergé egg than getting our hands on one of those, so instead we just do what the British Army always does and run a quick straw poll. Together the troop conclude that the firing point was up the street somewhere, probably near the next junction about 150 yards away. But apart from that, helpfully no one has a 'fucking clue, boss'.

This complicates things. If I knew where the gunman was, I could start getting us into depth; sending a few of the boys to move behind the little fucker, while the rest of us flush him out from wherever he's hiding. But since I don't know, it only leaves us two options. We can treat the gunman like a sketchy-looking teenager flicking chips at people on the top deck of the bus, and just try to rise above it. Or we can drive in the general direction of the firing point and hope for the best.

Frankly, I can't think of anything I'd rather do than pretend none of this is happening. But it doesn't feel as if ignoring sustained bursts of AK fire is quite in the spirit of the 'Basra Security Plan'. Besides, I've already radioed in a report to Jonty. I clear my throat and try to sound as though I know what I'm doing.

'Right, listen in, boys. If you're not made ready[51] then do it now. We'll head up to that junction in the Snatches. Sgt Mason, you stick with me. Cpl Robbins, you box round one block in case anyone bugs out, but for fuck's sake be careful. And if it does all kick off, make sure you can see what you're shooting at. Questions?'

There are none; it's a pretty basic plan. As I cock my weapon for the very first time all tour, it occurs to me that this is finally it. In thirty seconds or less we are almost certainly going to be in a proper firefight. I notice that I'm swallowing compulsively. Getting mortared isn't exactly a day at Alton Towers, but I am fairly sure that I am going to hate this more. For one thing I'm actually going to have to *do* something.

Soldiers often talk about the sense of powerlessness they feel under IDF; the fact that you just have to lie there and take it until someone else decides it's over. Which is true enough. But I'd also bet there are more than a few young officers who'd swap a mortar barrage for a gun battle any day of the week. Because for all that a gun battle is your chance to take the fight to the enemy, to be the master of your own destiny and all the rest of it, it's an equally good chance to *completely fuck everything up and get one of your soldiers killed*. After all none of us – even Sgt Mason – have ever really been in a full-blown firefight before. If I have a brainfart and order Womack to run across fifty yards of open ground, then chances are he will. And if he gets cut in half by a burst of 7.62mm halfway across, then that's all on me.

As we accelerate towards the junction in the Snatches I try to wrestle these thoughts out of my mind, lest I ruin the troop's first ever proper firefight by being spectacularly sick all over the dashboard. There is another burst of gunfire; much closer now. Frantically I scan the rooftops around the junction, looking for the muzzle flash. Nothing. Where the fucking fuck are they? Were they even shooting at us, or are we about to blunder into the middle of somebody else's contact? We are twenty yards short of the junction. Decision time.

'Stop here, Griff. All callsigns, debus. We'll do the last bit on foot.'

No sense in blundering out into the middle of a four-way junction in the Snatches; if there's an RPG gunner around, I'm not about to give him the target of his life. Griffiths swings the Snatch to the side of the road and brakes hard. I leap out just as another burst rends the air.

Fuck me. He must be fifty yards away. But he couldn't have been shooting at us. If anything it sounds like he's round the corner, on the road that leads off to the right. I half run, half scuttle forwards, then flatten myself against the wall of the last shop before the junction. I've stopped wanting to be sick. In fact I'm feeling something like a savage kind of joy. Whoever it is must be taking on another patrol. And we've got the fucker stone cold.

I take a deep breath and flick my safety catch to fire. Technically, when you go around a corner with enemy on the other side of it you're supposed to 'slice the pie'; moving in a slow circle using the corner as your pivot point. What you're not supposed to do is poke your head abruptly round the corner like the policeman in a Punch and Judy show, and stare boggle-eyed towards where you think your gunman might be. But it's exactly what I do. So much for 'the training just kicking in'; mine always seems to end up all over the pavement at the first sniff of adrenaline.

There is a gunman. In fact there's three of them, each one brandishing an AK-47. Unusually for JAM militiamen though, who tend to favour a more subdued black pyjamas and chest webbing combo, these ones are wearing shiny suits and ruffle shirts that wouldn't look out of place on a Jackson 5 backing singer. They're also standing next to a pair of Toyota Corollas covered in flowers and ribbons. Even as I watch, the one closest to me raises an AK-47 into the air and lets off an exuberant five-round burst into the sky. Behind me I hear Griffiths sigh with relief. We've been contacted by a wedding party.

For a nation where they're not exactly short of ways to get killed, the Iraqis have a strange fascination with firing their guns straight up in the air. It doesn't take much to kick them off either; births, weddings, exam results, even football matches (apparently the fusillades after their last Asian Cup win were so enthusiastic that half a dozen locals were killed in Baghdad alone). It's not that I don't understand the attraction – I've been to enough weddings where a thirty-round burst of 7.62mm into the ceiling would have been the best bit of the whole day – but you have to wonder at the thought process. Particularly for these characters, who clearly haven't let the fact that Basra is currently crawling with skittish, trigger-happy squaddies stop them from having it large.

A few seconds later they notice us standing open-mouthed on the corner. They wave and smile, gesturing apologetically as if to say, 'Big day – what can you do, eh?' We wave back, grimly, and watch as they pile into the Toyotas and drive off, presumably to spend the rest of the afternoon throwing hand grenades at one another at the reception. Then we clamber back into the Snatches and go and see what Jonty's got for us next.

Not much as it turns out. The crowd around the school has gone from ugly to positively hideous, and the riot kit's come out. All the engineers have managed to do is whitewash half of the perimeter wall; getting a smooth coat is tricky at the best of times, let alone with 500 people trying to knock you out with bits of paving stone. Installing the playground equipment they've brought with them looks like it'll be a task for another day too; the General has decided that it's a little bit incongruous to do reconstruction projects for the same people you're simultaneously battering with three-foot wooden batons. He is pausing the pulse for today.

So we form up behind the Warriors and drive back to the Palace for another night of lying on the floor of Uday's upstairs ball-room in our body armour.

26
Leila

Monday, 30 October 2006 – al Qibla

The next day we're back at the school, like maniacal Jehovah's Witnesses who just won't get the message. And presumably on the off chance that al Qibla's locals have all simultaneously changed their minds about us overnight. We get our answer within thirty seconds of arriving when a chunk of breeze block the size of an Edam cheese comes whistling out of the clear blue sky and hits Sgt Mason directly in the face.

We gather round and inspect the impressive gash on his forehead. It looks painful, but on the bright side it'll need stitches, and our insurance pays out for stitches. And it's not as if he was exactly Michelangelo's David even before the breeze block. Like the canny veteran he is, Sgt Mason immediately goes at the cut with his Leatherman to see if he can eke out an extra stitch or two (they're worth about fifty quid each) and spends the rest of the day walking around al Qibla like something out of the prom scene in *Carrie*.

While the engineers resignedly put on their helmets and unpack their paintbrushes, I take Third Troop on a clearance patrol. We've been driving for five minutes or so when the engine in my Snatch begins to cough. That's not unusual – this one sounds like Dot Cotton at anything over ten miles an hour – but the stricken look on Griffiths's face is. We coast to a halt and he sighs heavily.

'Er, boss . . . I think we . . . might have run out of fuel,' he says carefully.

I stare at him, aghast.

'How the fuck have we run out of fuel?' I splutter (it's important, when under pressure, to show your men that you're part of the solution, not part of the problem).

'Well, the fuel gauge has been fucked for ages,' says Griffiths, miserably, 'so I've just made sure to fill it regularly, like. But I think I must have forgotten . . . a couple of times. And I didn't notice . . .'

'. . . because the fucking fuel gauge is fucked,' I finish for him. 'For fuck's *sake*, Griff.'

This is something of a bind. We aren't carrying jerrycans and neither is anyone else in the squadron. We could tow my Snatch, but if anyone took us on we'd be in real trouble. More pertinently, Jonty would want to know what had happened. Fuel is technically the driver's responsibility, but running out of diesel in the middle of Basra wouldn't exactly make me employee of the month either. No, we'd have to get fuel from one of the other Snatches. But how?

Then I see the stall by the side of the road. It looks like a typical one-man household goods operation; piles of plastic tubs, boxes of soap powder, and assorted crockery, all covered in a thin patina of dust. But it's the coil of hose that catches my eye. It's hot pink for some reason, but it's not like that matters. It's the answer to our problem. We'll siphon some diesel out of one of the other Snatches, pour it into mine, and Bouraq's your uncle, we'll be back on the road with no one any the wiser.

I jump out and walk briskly over to the stall. We don't have an interpreter with us, but it's not like this is going to be a long conversation.

'*Salaam!*' I say, smiling. 'Er . . . I'm afraid I'm going to have to borrow your hose.' I point at the coil. 'Run out of diesel. Because my driver's a fucking idiot,' I add, for the benefit of Griffiths, who is already unscrewing the fuel cap.

In retrospect, I could have been more circumspect; you don't need to have gone to Harvard Business School to know that you don't start a negotiation by telling the other side that you're a bit fucked without them. Particularly when you're talking to an Iraqi shopkeeper, most of whom could give Alan Sugar a run for his money when it comes to dealmaking.

The shopkeeper's eyes narrow. He looks at Griffiths, then back at me, then places his hand protectively over the hose.

'*Bakhsheesh?*'[52] he says enquiringly.

'What? No. No bakhsheesh,' I reply. 'Just want to borrow. Bo-rr-ow. Then give back.'

The shopkeeper considers this.

'*La. Bakhsheesh,*' he says, a lot more confidently this time.

I grind my teeth and suppress the urge to launch into my version of the boys' favourite polemic: 'It's-their-fucking-country-so-why-aren't-they-fucking-well-interested-in-fucking-helping-us.' It wouldn't do any good. And anyway I already know the answer: 'Probably-because-we-just-pitched-up-at-the-border-with-an-armoured-division-and-proceeded-to-total-their-whole-society-without-anything-close-to-a-plan-for-after-the-war.'

Instead I take a deep breath and try to smile winningly.

'Jesus *Christ*. Alright, how much?'

He understood that alright.

'*Miya.*' One hundred. It's practically nothing.

'Fine. One hundred. Miya. Miya dinar.'

'*La, la. Dular.*'

'One hundred *dollars*? Are you insane? I'm not giving you one hundred dollars! It's a bit of fucking hose!' I cluck, outraged.

'One hundred dollar,' the shopkeeper says firmly, ignoring my chicken impression.

'I'll give you five, and fuck all more.'

The key to haggling is knowing your BATNA, or Best Alternative To a Negotiated Agreement; what you will do if you have to walk away from the deal. For Basra's answer to John D. Rockefeller, it's pretty simple; continue to sit quietly in the sun by the side of the road flogging the occasional soap packet or washing-up bowl.

For me the BATNA is less attractive; die horribly in a hail of gunfire because I'm being towed by a vehicle that has all the torque of a Matchbox car, or admit to Jonty that I've set off into Basra City with about a Coke can's worth of diesel in my Snatch. Which is probably why five minutes later I find myself clutching a short length of hot-pink hosepipe that has just cost me eighty US dollars.

As far as the boys are concerned it's *Monty Python* meets *Saturday Night Live*. And when I accidentally swallow during the siphoning process and collapse gagging on my hands and knees, they sound as if they're about to give themselves a collective hernia. But Jonty will be none the wiser. And on the bright side – not that I'll be able to appreciate this until I've got the taste of diesel out of my mouth – it's probably one of the more impactful purchases I'll ever make; eighty dollars might well have been a month's wages for that shopkeeper.

By the time we get back to the school it's clear that the locals have decided to up the ante from yesterday. The hail of paving stones and breeze blocks is more or less blotting out the sun, and the throwers are getting better with practice. Several of the engineers have been cleaned out and most of the rest are now painting the wall from the prone position. They're using the new slides they've unpacked in the playground as makeshift shields.

More worryingly, various shady-looking characters have started popping up on rooftops all around the school. Someone has already had a pop at Brooksie; shortly after we'd left, a round from an unseen gunman hit the side of his Snatch just below the top cover, prompting his entire troop to immediately hightail it out of there, *Wacky Races*-style. Ten minutes later, and in a neat bit of historical revisionism on the battlegroup net, this has become, 'one of my callsigns moving into depth to exploit likely firing points.' Bravo, Jonty.

The word on the street – the one which is currently covered in half bricks and semi-conscious Royal Engineers – is that we'll soon be pausing today's pulse too.

I head off to find Jonty. Ahead of me is a Warrior, with a scarlet-faced Darth standing in his turret and shouting. He's busy dispatching his dismounts to disperse a group of kids who are throwing stones at him. I'm not sure why; not one of them looks more than seven years old, and it's the grown men – some with slingshots now, I notice – who're doing most of the damage. But Darth is in a deep rage, even for him; someone must have bounced one too many bricks off his helmet, and it's a good thing that he doesn't actually own a planet-annihilating Death Star, because if he did, then al Qibla and everyone in it would be cosmic dust by now.

His dismounts aren't really getting into the spirit of things though. Whatever they've joined the Army for, it clearly isn't to hit children with wooden batons. So instead they're roaring theatrically, mock charging the stone throwers, then watching as they all laugh hysterically and dash for the nearest alleyway. This is evidently winding Darth up to breaking point. But if you can ignore him flinging his arms around like he's headlining a Nuremberg Rally, it's an almost playful scene, in its own way. God knows these kids need a bit of fun in their lives.

As I watch them creeping back from the alleyways and giggling while the dismounts pretend not to notice, I find myself almost smiling. Right up until the point that a five-round burst from one of the rooftops smacks straight into the side of Darth's Warrior, he drops out of sight like he's fallen through a manhole, and the kids scatter in panic. I pelt back to my Snatch, bent almost double. Ten seconds later the call we've all been waiting for comes over the radio.

Time to go home.

Tuesday, 31 October 2006 – al Qibla

Apparently the engineers are determined to finish painting their wall if it kills them. Or indeed one of us. Because we're back at that fucking school for the third day on the trot. Frankly by this point I've had enough; we're going home in just over two weeks, and my appetite for putting my and Third Troop's arses on the line in al Qibla is so low you'd need CERN to measure it.

They don't want us here – there's a clue in the large hostile crowds and repeated volleys of 7.62mm – and it's beyond me why we keep turning up. I'm with Bismarck on this one; if Alsace Lorraine wasn't worth the bones of a single Pomeranian grenadier, then a whitewashed wall and wonky playground sure as shit aren't worth Womack or Greene taking a sniper round through the neck.

Jonty must sense the angst, because he promises this is the last time we'll do this. And for once I actually believe him. He tasks me with more clearance patrols. I'll take it. At least I'll be well away from what's already shaping up to be another long morning watching the engineers trying to be the first men in history to win a gallantry award for installing a see-saw under fire.

I grab Omar and we drive around the area for about fifteen minutes then stop to conduct a quick VCP. We're just about to flag down the first car when a small figure walks straight past me and hops smartly into the back of my Snatch.

As a soldier you have a few options open to you at this point. The first is to yank the intruder bodily out of the vehicle, bundle them to the floor, then ask shrilly what the bloody fuck they're playing at. The second is to turn on your heel and run for it. After all, there's an outside chance your new passenger may be about to push a small button and splatter themselves, you, and anyone else nearby, all over the scenery. The third option is to put your rifle into your shoulder and shoot them directly in the head. It sounds dramatic – this isn't the Sunni Triangle – but I suspect I'd have got away with it.

Suicide bombings are rare down south, but they still happen. Quite apart from the one at Shaibah just before we arrived, there have been two in Basra itself over the summer; including one, oddly enough, at a senior citizens' home (presumably someone had decided they really were going to go out with a bang). So while shooting someone dead for jumping in my Snatch would probably raise eyebrows down here in a way it never would in Baghdad, frankly I'd still fancy my chances in the investigation.

There is however also a fourth option, which is the one I eventually opt for; you gawp for a moment, then fling open both back doors on your Snatch and say, 'Er . . . look!' in aggrieved tones. Not the most soldierly course of action, but then again I'm clearly not much of a soldier. As evidenced by the fact that I now appear to have a small Iraqi woman sitting proprietorially in the back of my command vehicle.

Even before I've closed my mouth, she looks at me and I forget all about suicide bombers. Her eyes are wide with fright and she is motioning furiously for me to shut the doors. For want of any better ideas I clamber inside and sit on the small bench seat opposite her, pulling the doors closed behind me. Then I clear my throat.

'Now, listen – can you understand me? – you CANNOT. BE. IN. THIS. VEHICLE. IT. IS. VERY. DANGEROUS. FOR. YOU,' I begin. I am using the classic 'Engaging With The Natives' voice, with which the British Army once built a whole Empire. ('WE'RE. GOING. TO. NEED. TO. TAKE. A. LOOK. AT. YOUR. DIAMOND. MINES.')

'Of course I understand you,' she replies quickly. 'I was three years at the American University in Cairo. And I know it is dangerous. So don't open the doors again.'

I gawp again. This is the first Iraqi woman I've heard speak in the entire tour. In fact it's the first Iraqi woman anyone in B Squadron's heard speak. Probably in the battlegroup too. More to the point, until now the only English I've ever heard from the locals – interpreters aside – is a token 'lovely jubbly' or 'welly good', or variations on a theme of 'gimme lightstick/pen/sweet/ gun'. But this woman speaks like a newsreader. She's dressed in a black *abaya* and *hijab*, like most of Basra's women by this point, and looks to be in her early forties.

As I continue to stare she takes off the *hijab*, revealing a head of glossy auburn hair. Ladies' styling is a closed book to me – written in Ancient Greek, inside a locked safe, wrapped in chains, at the bottom of the Mariana Trench – but that haircut looks Western. I nod dumbly.

'That is better. It is too hot for the *abaya*, but we all must wear them now, or there will be trouble with the militias. They beat women, you know,' she says, matter-of-factly.

'Right. Yes. Er . . . listen, what is it that you want? I mean, you're not really supposed to be in here . . .'

'Yes, I know. But I could not just talk to you in the street. People are watching. And I have important information. You should write this down,' she says pointedly.

As I scrabble for my notebook she begins to talk. Her name is Leila, she says, and she's not from al Qibla; she's from Gzaiza district, in the north of the city. She lives there with her son and daughter, fifteen and thirteen respectively. Her husband is 'not around' anymore; she doesn't elaborate and I don't ask. Gzaiza has never been a good area, she tells me, and it's getting worse. There are no jobs, no security, and the militias are becoming ever more influential. She knows this because one of the militia commanders lives in the house next to hers. And he has started to come round to visit. She stops for a moment, and to my sudden horror I realise that she has quietly begun to cry.

'He says he is looking for fighters,' she says miserably. 'And Hassan, my son, he wants to go with him. They will pay him, he says, and we need the money. And he is right, we do need it. I cannot even afford to buy school materials for the children, sometimes.'

'I see. Have you been to see the police about this?' I say, realising even as the words leave my mouth what an irredeemable idiot I am.

'The militias *are* the police,' replies Leila, fixing me with a tearful stare. 'You must know this. You were the ones who gave them the uniforms.'

I nod. She's right, of course. I have a feeling I know what's coming next. But I ask the question anyway.

'What is it that you'd like us to do about it?'

'I want you to kill him,' she says coldly. She has stopped crying. 'I know you do night raids; we see your tanks all the time. You must come to Gzaiza and go to this man's house. He will fight you, and when he does, you can kill him.'

It makes sense. Presumably young Hassan would be a lot less keen on joining up if he woke up one morning to see his new pal splayed all over the front garden courtesy of the PWRR Recce Platoon. I feel a sneaking admiration for Leila. There can't be too many women who'd order a hit on their neighbour as calmly as if they were arranging an Ocado delivery. Or maybe there are; a mother's love and all that. But we're the British Army, not the Five Families; I'm pretty sure we're not supposed to do assassinations to order.

'I see. Well, I can certainly take your information. And I will make sure it gets to the right people. But you understand that I cannot guarantee that we will come to his house. And if we do come, it will be to arrest this man, not to kill him,' I say.

'If you arrest him, he will just be released again,' says Leila wearily. 'The judges are scared of the militias too. You kill people all the time. Why not this man?'

This is more familiar territory. We've got a Line To Take on the primacy of Iraqi law and how we can't just go round offing people at random. I start reeling off what I can remember from the card but I don't even get halfway.

'What law?' interrupts Leila. 'Sharia? There is no law now, not since you came. You have put maniacs in uniforms, you understand that? Sadrists, and Badr Brigade, and thugs. Life under Saddam was difficult, sometimes, but at least we had a life. At least I could go out at night. At least I did not have to wear the *abaya*,' she says, plucking at the material contemptuously.

I don't say anything. None of this is news exactly; we all know how Basra is for women, at least in an abstract kind of way. They've gone from having secular freedoms that were once the envy of women across the region, to a kind of quasi-theocracy where there isn't a day goes by that someone doesn't get shaved, stoned, kidnapped or even murdered for having the gall to wear make-up in the streets, or go to work in an office. But it's the first time I've heard it from someone who's living it. And it suddenly doesn't feel very abstract anymore.

'Yes, life was difficult with Saddam,' Leila continues. 'But I could work, and feed my family. And there were no militias to take my son. I was an engineer. You know that the bridges in Basra, every single one was built by a woman engineer?'

She sighs and looks at me. I didn't know that, but it also doesn't surprise me. The Ba'athists might have had their faults, but they were instituting six months' paid maternity leave while women in the West were still having their arses pinched in the name of 'banter'.

'Thank you for your information, Leila. I promise we will do our best,' I say. It sounds pathetic, even to me.

She sighs again and nods slightly. Then she pulls the *hijab* back over her hair and looks meaningfully towards the rear doors of the Snatch.

'Wait one moment,' I say. Speaking into my PRR, I explain what's going on to Sgt Mason. He doesn't need me to spell it out; even as I pop my head out of the roof, he and Buxton have stopped a passing minibus taxi on the far side of the road and are loudly inviting the occupants to get out and bring their ID cards with them. A small crowd of spectators have already started to gather.

Nodding to Leila, I open the doors. She drops lightly to the ground and starts walking briskly back the way she came. The last I see of her is a small black figure trotting around a corner. On her way back to Gzaiza, and Hassan.

We're pulled back to the Palace about an hour later. And this time it's clear that the al Qibla pulse really is over. The crowd, who've been flirting with a riot for two days now, throw caution to the wind and go full *28 Days Later*. The police are nowhere to be seen. Which is a shame, because they've got much more robust public order drills than we're allowed; they basically just shoot at the riot until it ceases being one.

This riot is much less impressed by plastic shields and wooden sticks, so they mob the Snatches and we have to drop a dozen of the ringleaders with baton guns to clear our path out. Quite the finish for an operation that was supposed to be about building consent. It doesn't feel like they'll be colouring al Qibla green on Jonty's big wall map any time soon. Still, at least the engineers finished painting their wall, and by the looks of it got a couple of slides up in the playground too.

Back at the Palace, I pass Leila's information to the intelligence cell. But I'm not hopeful; no one's about to launch a strike op into Basra off the back of single source, uncorroborated information written on a grimy piece of notebook paper. But maybe it'll help fill in a piece of the jigsaw somewhere. I hope so anyway; what Leila did to get it to us was hideous with risk.

Later on, back in Uday's ballroom, I wonder what she'll make of it if – as seems almost certain – we never do come to Gzaiza. Will she lie in bed, night after night, wondering if this might finally be the moment where the British Army actually does something, and saves her Hassan from life in a JAM mortar crew? Or after a while will she just lose hope, and notch it up as yet another let-down in the long litany of disappointment we've visited on Basra ever since we've arrived? Either way, I hope Hassan doesn't join the militias. But I'm not sure I'd blame him if he did.

Wednesday, 1 November 2006 – Basra Palace / al Qibla

After a final night in the Palace, during which it transpires that JAM may have a sniper on the riverbank opposite, meaning everyone will be leopard crawling to breakfast until they catch him – we head back to Shaibah. Our route takes us back through al Qibla and past the school. Someone has graffitied down the full length of the newly whitewashed wall. I stare at the looping, foot-high Arabic script, and ask Omar what it says.

'Fuck your sister's pussy. Iraq is for the Iraqis.'

Right.[53]

27

SITREP

Thursday, 9 November 2006 – Shaibah

And just like that there's only a week left to push. The RIP (Relief in Place, not the other one) is in full swing and Shaibah is bursting at the seams with troops. Half of them with deep tans, battered boots and a smirk they can barely wipe off their faces; the other half self-conscious in their pristine combats, nervousness written all over them, and still carrying the extra stone of good eating from pre-tour leave that'll drop off them in days when they get to the Palace or the Shatt.

They're right to be nervous. If Basra was restless when we arrived then it's *Götterdämmerung* now. And JAM aren't stupid; they know there are novices in town, and are determined to put them on the back foot before they can settle in. They sent their first message at the Old State Buildings three days ago. A nineteen-year-old private soldier who'd been in Iraq for all of a week climbed into a sangar for his first ever stag, and was shot square in the chest by a sniper ten minutes later. They took his body out on the same helicopter that was still bringing his mates in to start their tour.

Our own replacements have arrived too. They're from the Royal Tank Regiment, which is useful since I suspect Basra's going to need a lot of Challenger 2 over the next few months. Jonty tells us to take them on a familiarisation patrol in the local area. We're prepping our kit when the SQMS comes over; he needs to box up the squadron's ammunition for handover and wants to collect all but twenty rounds per man. Apparently doing it like this will really help him make a good head start on the admin.

Once we've confirmed that the SQMS is not, in fact, fucking joking, I counter that *not* doing it like this will really help Third Troop avoid being wiped out to the last man if we get into a fire-fight carrying less ammunition than would come with a Roy Rogers cap gun. We agree to differ on the relative importance of efficient administration vs. not dying in an ambush because some-one's locked all your bullets in a shipping container, and Third Troop keep their ammunition.

It sounds mental, but it's just the Army being the Army really; apparently Wellington was still getting memos from Horseguards on how many tent-poles and ox-carts he had while they were storming the breach at Badajoz. It's also part of the same strange inversion of priorities which means we're spending days maniac-ally cleaning every nook and cranny in Tiger Lines before we hand it over, while a couple of miles away Basra continues to slide ever more irretrievably into the abyss. 'Sorry about the raging insurgency down town, lads. But on the bright side, look; you could eat your dinner off the floor in the ablutions.'

We mount up in the Snatches with the tankies in the back and head from Shaibah up to the Air Station, then round the outskirts of the city. I try to suppress a smile as I watch their heads swivelling urgently from left to right as they try to take it all in. That was Godders and me once. When we're finished, we take the cross-country route back to Shaibah; it's slow, it throws the guys in the back around like maraca beads, and even a month ago we wouldn't have thought twice about using the roads. But there's no sense in taking chances when JAM are working hard to catch out the new boys.

Unfortunately, it also means that when the first tankie shits himself spectacularly – an early casualty of D&V (*diarrhoea and vomiting*) – it isn't long before someone else bounces off the inside of the Snatch and lands in the result. They in turn immediately gag, then hurl all over themselves, which causes someone else to hurl, and so on and so on, until the back of the Snatch resembles the inside of an incredibly niche underground Berlin fetish club.

We can't stop, despite the SQMS's conviction that southern Iraq is basically just like the Cotswolds, so the tankies are sliding around in their own fluids like Fun House contestants for a good twenty minutes. When we eventually get back to Shaibah we have to wash it all out with a hose, and the tankies can barely stand up.

The realisation that we're so very near the end seems to have provoked mixed emotions in the boys. On the one hand they're gagging to get out of this place; from the chatter in Third Troop's tent, the first night out back in Sennelager is going to be like the Vikings going ashore at Lindisfarne. On the other, I sense that they already know they'll miss it – or at least parts of it – when it's over.

I know I will. When you're sitting on the roof of Uday's palace with the late afternoon sun on your back, watching the fishermen in their skiffs, or gazing at the Plough a hundred miles from anywhere on the Iranian border, it's hard to ignore the voice saying, *Remember this, because you probably won't get to do it ever again.*

Mostly though – as evidenced by the white-faced, shit-smeared tankies staggering dazedly back to their accommodation – we're cautious. There isn't a Snatch unit anywhere else in southern Iraq who have got away with it the way we have. And no one wants to get whacked just before the curtain comes down.

Sunday, 12 November 2006 – Shaibah

We've handed over Tiger Lines to the tankies and moved back into the RSOI accommodation where we first stayed when we got to Shaibah. There's not much to do anymore – we officially stopped being the Force Reserve at 00.01 this morning – so I wander over to the internet Portakabin to see if there's a spare computer. My parents know our tour's basically over, but they'll still be glad to get an email which says in black and white that their son will be back in Germany in a couple of days. When I get there it's locked, a big laminated Op MINIMISE[54] sign on the door. JAM have hit one of our boats on the Shatt, says the grey-haired PWRR colour sergeant sat smoking on the step.

They've done more than hit it; they've fired 100lb of HME (*home-made explosive*) packed with nails into the top of it. It happened while the boat was passing slowly below a low bridge. Someone must have crossed under the same span one time too many and JAM had noticed. Four of the crew were killed instantly, the other three grievously wounded. One is now blind. The river – which until now has always been the safe-ish option; a less risky way of transiting Basra if you don't fancy two hours listening to 7.62mm pinging off your Warrior – is now closed to all movement.

They're going to work out exactly what happened, explains Jonty, but it'll probably stay that way. He doesn't need to point out the sick irony; this tour started with another 'safe-ish' option which suddenly wasn't anymore, when JAM blew a Lynx out of the sky over Basra. And it's finishing with this; a boatful of dead and dying soldiers, drifting slowly on the current down the Shatt.

I cannot wait to get out of this fucking place.

Monday, 13 November 2006 – Shaibah

At orders this evening, Jonty announces that we'll be going on a strike op tomorrow night.

For a moment we just stare at him. If it's some kind of gag it's not a particularly funny one. But Jonty's never been much of a one for jokes, and particularly not when it comes to ops. No one says anything. Then in a tight voice, Mike asks whether this isn't one for the tankies, the new Force Reserve, who're supposed to have taken over two days ago. I mean, we haven't even got any vehicles anymore, he explains helplessly (as if Jonty doesn't know full well). And we've handed back all our ammunition.

Jonty – because he is Jonty – meets our eyes with his. Then he quietly explains that the General doesn't think the tankies are up to it. They've barely been out of the front gate yet, and they're certainly not ready for a battlegroup operation at night. He wants us.

I suddenly notice that my nails are digging deep into my palms. I don't give a fuck whether the tankies aren't up to it, I scream inside; it's their fucking *turn*. We've done our bit, and now someone else can drive into Basra in the dark and mix it up with fucking JAM. I'm blind with rage at the basic, primal, playroom *unfairness* of it all, and for a moment I wonder if I might actually just burst into tears. But I don't, of course.

I just sit there dully while Jonty tells us that – two days before we're supposed to fly out of here for ever – we'll be taking Recce Platoon back into al Qibla, to lift a JAM bombmaker.

Wednesday, 15 November 2006

At 150130CNOV06 FORCE RESERVE launched OP COBRA, a detain-and-search operation on five buildings and four associated targets in the AL QIBLA district. Between 0201C and 0211C the target buildings were struck. The search of three of the target buildings was complete by 0230C with nothing of significance found. At 0224C a call-sign (at A3) was contacted by SAF, resulting in one T3 casualty (GSW to the leg) and one dead BRAVO (B227) and the detention of one male (possibly the brother of B227). An Iraqi female also received an abdominal wound. IRT was requested for both the T3 casualty and the Iraqi T1 female casualty; the latter was declared dead at the HLS by the RMO at 0312C. (SITREP 5583B)

That is how they report it in the daily SITREP; a dry little paragraph describing what the Force Reserve got up to last night, neatly summarised, like all good staff work, in as few bare sentences as possible. Then it would have been on to the next item on the agenda; the latest political situation in Basra, progress on the RIP in the Shatt, or a note about the change of contractor for the laundry service at Shaibah. But it doesn't tell the whole story, that little paragraph.

It doesn't, for example, talk about the taut expressions on the boys' faces as they prepped weapons that we'd told them were already being loaded onto an aircraft for the flight home. Or the sick feeling in my stomach as we knelt by the Snatches in the darkness, watching Recce Platoon stack up outside the door of the breeze-block hut where the bombmaker was supposed to live, while shadows darted about the rooftops all around us.

It mentions the SAF (*small arms fire*) contact in passing, that's true. But it leaves out the detail. Like how, when Recce Platoon finally put the door in, the target was just standing there, a yard inside the house, with his AK-47 held firmly at the hip.

Or how the cover man is telling the medics he still can't understand how he's alive, with nothing more than a graze on his calf – which isn't even really bleeding that much, look – after that fucker back there fired a full magazine at him from five yards away.

Or the eruption of red tracer when half of Recce Platoon returned fire back into the hut, which ricocheted in every direction imaginable and sent Third Troop sprawling in the dust outside. Or Steve's horrifying scream over the radio that he was in contact, and needed help.

And it tells you about what happened to the people in the hut. But it doesn't tell you the who, or the why, or the how. It doesn't explain that the Iraqi female with the abdominal wound was the target's mother, gut shot by her own son as he was spun round by Recce Platoon's bullets with his finger still on the trigger.

It doesn't tell you how he was dead before he hit the ground, but that Recce Platoon tried to get his mother out; lifting the small body into the back of a Warrior, with her other son crying next to her, and racing for the main road and a helicopter. Or how, when the helicopter finally lifted off, thundering away back to Shaibah and the hospital, the medic just looked up from the patch of bloodied sand where he'd been treating her, and slowly shook his head.

The next day, we flew home.

Epilogue

And with that, the tour was over. For some reason we didn't go to Cyprus to decompress; instead it was straight back to Sennelager, where the CO had four trucks full of lager driven onto the parade square, confined the entire battlegroup to camp for three nights, then left everyone to it.

We didn't leave the Officers' Mess much for the next few days – we weren't idiots – but from the cheering, singing, and the occasional sounds of furniture being lobbed out of an upstairs window, it seemed to do the trick. I expect it'd be frowned on nowadays, because I don't remember having a single session with the Padre, and the boys' version of group therapy appeared to involve inserting rolled-up newspapers in each other's sphincters and setting fire to them.

But it worked. Scores were settled, air was cleared, and difficult feelings discussed with the kind of blunt honesty you only really ever find at the end of a shared 24-pack of Carling Black Label. More to the point, by the time we were eventually allowed out into Sennelager, we were all so broken by three full days of suicidal boozing that the entire battlegroup was probably back in bed by half ten.

For me, it was back to the UK not long after that. I'd joined the QRH for the tour, but I was never a permanent part of their world. Whatever they went on to do next, it wouldn't be with me. I said my goodbyes to Third Troop on the same tank park I'd first met them, a whole lifetime ago. I thanked them for their hard work, for keeping going – even in the tough times – and for never, ever letting me down (at least, not when it mattered).

And I told them they should be proud of themselves. Because they really should have. There was a lot more I wanted to say. I wanted to thank them for doing everything their nation had asked of them, for less than you'd pay a traffic warden. And I wanted to tell them how much they meant to me. But I'm not sure it would have landed. And anyway, they knew, I think.

Before I left, Sgt Mason took me to one side. We shook hands, and he told me I'd been alright. For a fucking Rupert, that is. I just smiled and thanked him. I meant it. At that moment you could have stuck all your degree certificates and your diplomas right up where Third Troop put rolled-up newspapers. Then I walked off the tank park and into a minibus that would take me to the airport.

I never saw any of them again. But they're on the wall of my study as I write this, in a picture we took by the Land Rovers on that two-day patrol out to the border in Maysan. To give them their real names now: Stevie, Hammy, Oz, Jay, Mikey, Middie, Bear, Donters, Dill, Kenny, Vargs, Chic, Beggers, Higgie and Wee Mac.

I never did go back to teaching in the end. I'd have missed having a baton gun and six-foot shield too much. Instead, after a stint in the Civil Service, as well as two more operational tours (in Afghanistan this time, which is a different story), I eventually ended up a management consultant. I have a wonderful wife and two small children, and live in a quiet suburb at the end of the Northern Line.

I am also now, of course, exactly the kind of seat-polishing dweeb who my 23-year-old self – oozing testosterone and wander-lust – would have regarded with something approaching horror. But it's probably about right for forty-two, and I can't pretend I'm not happy.

My feelings on Iraq and the tour, even nineteen years down the line, are still a mixed bag. When it comes to the war itself, it's pretty clear where the consensus lies; the whole thing was an ocean-going disaster, and it should never have happened. Saddam's regime was brutal, repressive, and an affront to civilisation, but at some point you have to put your practical head on and think about the Leilas and the Hassans of this world.

It's sometimes tempting to treat principles – the lofty stuff; democracy and equality and perfect freedom – as if they're the only things that really matter. Well, not for me; I'd venture that 200,000 dead civilians, 3 million displaced, a shattered infrastructure, endemic sectarian division, ISIS, and all the endless rest of it, is nowhere near a price worth paying, no matter how shiny your ideals. As Leila told me in the back of that Snatch in al Qibla once, life before the war might have been difficult, but at least they had a life.

As for my part in the whole mess, about the only thing I can say for sure is that my being there didn't make Iraq worse. Not much of a return for seven months of your life. But then again it was a war, not a Duke of Edinburgh's award. That isn't to say, by the way, that Iraq didn't *get* worse while we were there; it did, by almost every metric, and the tours after ours were brutal. It's more that I don't think it was because of anything we – by which I mean my own small gang of B Squadron and Third Troop – did or failed to do. Everything they sent our way we did, to the best of our abilities. And we'd have done more if they'd asked.

But they didn't ask. Because long before we even arrived it had stopped being about winning (whatever that would have meant), or actually doing something about the locals' problems; it was about getting out with as little fuss as possible and leaving the whole sorry mess to the Iraqis. It was unforgiveable, and a stain on the Army and our nation that we shouldn't let those responsible ever blot out.

That probably sounds a lot like kicking the responsibility upstairs – a kind of light-touch *'befehl ist befehl'* Nuremberg defence. So be it. Life's not a film, and you can't just storm into the General's HQ like Peter O'Toole in *Lawrence of Arabia* to point out where he's going wrong and how you're going to fix it; they'll just sack you and send you home. But if you break it, you own it. And we broke Basra. I just hope those generals and politicians who let the city drift into chaos in 2006 – and then abandoned it to the militias in the middle of the night less than a year later – realise what they did. Twenty-five British servicemen and women died on our tour; it sure as shit wasn't much of a return for their lives.

But for all that I still sometimes get angry about the ineptitude, and the let-downs, and the sheer waste of it all, when I look back on that tour my overwhelming feeling is still one of gratitude. In the first instance, of course, I'm grateful that I'm still here. That I'm not sitting in a wheelchair because an EFP took my legs. Or struggling to remember my kids' names because there's still a chunk of 107mm rocket in my brain. Enough people are.

And I'm grateful for having been in that place, at that time, and for being able to see what I saw. Never again will I lie on the bonnet of a Land Rover on the Iran–Iraq border, looking up at a canopy of brilliant stars which seems like it goes on for ever. Or swim in a desert tributary, listening to the boys whooping as they throw off their body armour and helmets and leap into the glittering water.

Or watch the sun rise over the Central Marshes, with the reed warblers slowly waking up on the tarmac road in front of me, where they've been sitting all night trying to keep warm, safe in the knowledge that no cars ever come this way. You can't recreate it, not with a million pounds and air miles to anywhere in the world. Because even if you could get there, it wouldn't be the same.

But much more than all that, I'm grateful for the boys. For showing me, every single day for seven months, what selflessness really means.

Not long after I got home, they published the New Year's Honours list; the usual mixed bag of nonagenarian lollipop ladies, eminent scientists and random celebs. One of the celebs was some youth TV presenter, who it was widely thought had been bunged her MBE for soft-soaping Blair in an interview where she'd spent most of the time asking penetrating questions about his favourite cologne and what he did for his wife's birthday – rather than the small matter of the raging bin fire he'd helped to light in Iraq.

All of a sudden and quite without warning (I was reading about it in the paper on the tube at the time), I burst into tears. For some reason I just couldn't stop thinking about the boys. And how when I'd told them there was a helicopter down in the city, surrounded by hostile crowds, and that we'd probably be going in, they'd just nodded quietly and carried on clipping the visors to their helmets. Or how even when JAM were blowing people up on the daily, they'd climb out of their Snatches without a word to clear a VP and help get a convoy through to someone who needed it.

Or how when we'd been mortared and rocketed to hell and back in CAN, and Mr Kite told them there were wounded out there in the darkness, Womack and Buxton had simply picked up their medics' kits and run out into the night to help treat people they had never even met.

There would be no MBEs for them. But they were the best men I would ever know. They were John 15:13,[55] through and through.

Acknowledgements

It's something of a truism that any author of a book about an operational tour really ought to start this bit by acknowledging the people who kept them alive to write it. So to Third Troop, B Squadron, The Queen's Royal Hussars – thank you, lads. And sorry about the minefield thing. To my fellow troop leaders, for bearing with a clueless STAB, and for seven months of relentless, belt-fed 'morale'. And to the unflappable, methodical, anti-Flashman 'Jonty', for making sure we all got through it. No wonder they made you a brigadier.

More broadly, of course, our own tour would all have been for nothing were it not for the boys with the funny shaped berets and avant-garde approach to weapon handling. So to 2/4/10, 3/4/10, and everyone else who's still out there risking their necks to finish something you didn't start, thank you for staying in the fight.

Closer to home, I am indebted to Charlie Campbell for taking a punt on a management consultant who thought he could write. Rupert Lancaster and Lucy Buxton at Hodder & Stoughton have been exceptional; patient, encouraging, and surprisingly tolerant of my attempts to 'assist' the copy-editing process via the medium of PowerPoint. I am also grateful to Barry Johnston for his meticulous eye, which has produced a much more readable book – with many fewer subordinate clauses – than would otherwise have been the case.

Every nervous, greenhorn writer needs a first reader, to reassure them that their work shows spectacular promise and that it's all going to be OK. Or alternatively that the opening is a bit crap, but that she quite likes the rest of it. Quite how I managed to land Xandra Bingley as confidante-cum-agony-aunt-cum-editor is beyond me, but without her this book wouldn't have happened. You selflessly distilled a professional lifetime's worth of experience into guidance even I could understand, and somehow made it all seem like fun. I could not have been luckier.

To my mother and father, without whom *I* wouldn't have happened, thank you for the lifetime of love. It's only now, as a parent myself, that I realise quite what it must have been like watching your favourite child go off to war. And sorry about all the filth and swearing – I promise it was the other boys, not me. To Carey, who didn't make it into the book because frankly I think we've all heard just about enough on you by this point . . . you were then, and still are now, a much better sister than I deserve.

To Benjie and Orla, if anyone ever asks how long the book took, my default answer is always 'about two paternity leaves'. Whole chapters of *The Accidental Soldier* were written while one or other of you lay farting (we're allowed to say it if it's used in proper context) gently in your sleep, strapped to my chest. So thank you for your prodigious newborn power napping. And for making every day since you arrived such a boundless joy.

Finally, to Marianne: the 'Quentin bloody Blake, with a full-time job, two children, and – by the way – a grown adult to pick up after . . .' who produced the wonderful illustrations you see at the start of every chapter. But much more importantly, the one who makes it all worthwhile. Thank you for everything.

Notes

1 The code name for operations in Iraq.
2 The Army's way of saying tea with milk but no sugar. In other words, 'white nun', based on Andrews' seminal performance in *The Sound of Music*. If you've seen *Sister Act* you can probably guess what a 'Whoopi Goldberg' got you.
3 Much later, in a contemplative frame of mind, I would go on to test this analogy with Sgt Mason. He rejected it out of hand, pointing out that in his view our dynamic was much more that of great white shark and remora fish. ('You know, that useless twat who just latches on then spends all day blowing bubbles and getting carried.') Charming.
4 A mixed unit of armour and infantry, of about 1,000 personnel.
5 A paramilitary organisation loyal to Saddam Hussein.
6 US Navy Special Forces.
7 Engagement with the enemy.
8 He was dead right; I was. And Jonty is a brigadier now, which just goes to show.
9 A four-engined propeller transport aircraft.
10 The RAF's affectionate nickname for the Army; thought to be derived from their dim view of our personal hygiene; 'Everywhere the Army goes, the pong goes.'
11 A medium-lift helicopter.
12 Collapsible wire-mesh containers covered in heavy duty fabric liner, and then filled with sand or soil to provide protection from blast.
13 Rear Echelon Mother Fuckers.
14 Indirect Fire from mortars, rockets, artillery, and so on.
15 Chemical glow sticks used for marking things at night.
16 An unkind nickname for young officers.
17 Where the bombmakers link up the detonators to multiple IEDs. Like a child's daisy chain. Except with more exploding Land Rovers.
18 A twin-engined utility helicopter.
19 A company-sized outpost in the heart of Basra City.

20 About 12–15 soldiers.

21 The Army has three main grades of triage: T1 priority (cannot wait); casualties with life, limb or sight-threatening injuries. T2 priority (can wait); casualties with serious injuries that require treatment within 2 hours. T3 priority (must wait); casualties whose injuries can safely wait for up to 4 hours before treatment.

22 A derogatory term for the locals, of unknown derivation.

23 The designated period after which most unexploded rounds should probably have gone off.

24 Nickname for the Intelligence Corps, due to their cypress green berets. And general sliminess.

25 Pre-approved statements on everything from our overall mission in Iraq and the primacy of Iraqi law, to the treatment of detainees.

26 At least up until the point – about three months after we'd gone home – when a Hercules touched down and was abruptly blown off the runway by a forty-foot string of IEDs.

27 Small guns firing PVC canisters about an inch and a half wide, used for riot control.

28 Intellectually impaired; derived from Gaelic football players in Ireland bemusedly watching soccer players using their heads to play.

29 Moving in an irregular, unpredictable pattern, i.e., making yourself a 'hard target'.

30 Quick Reaction Force, who are on standby 24hrs a day to be the first on scene if something happens.

31 Imaginary lines on a map, each with its own codeword agreed in advance with the ops room.

32 Very tired.

33 The motion of your sphincter as you realise you're very alone in a very unfriendly part of the world.

34 Fields of fire for their weapons.

35 'Let's go' or 'Come on'.

36 Saddam Hussein, Taha Yassin Ramadan and Tariq Aziz are lounging on the balcony of one of Saddam's palaces when a flock of geese flies over. 'Ramadan, shoot the geese,' Saddam says. The vice president lifts his AK-47 and empties a clip into the sky, but doesn't hit a single goose. 'You try, Tariq,' Saddam says. The deputy prime minister fires and misses as well. 'Damn, I have to do everything around here,' Saddam says. He fires five rounds in the air. None of the birds fall. There's an awkward silence. Then Tariq Aziz points at the receding flock and says, 'My God, would you look at that! Dead birds flying!' I know . . .

37 Period of duty or guard.

38 Lining up outside the target's door, ready for entry.

39 Individuals observed running away from the objective.

40 'God is the greatest.'

41 I have since discovered that Chris de Burgh is one of the biggest artists in Iran; apparently it's something to do with his 'conservative haircut and clear lyrics'. Which is a double-edged compliment whatever way you cut it.

42 A piece of paper with the names, Army numbers, and blood groups for everyone on your patrol.

43 Ex-SAS, who are based in the town.

44 I was right, too.

45 Firing your weapon without intending to.

46 The name allegedly originates from an incident in Hartlepool during the Napoleonic Wars, when a French ship was wrecked off the coast. The only survivor was a monkey, wearing a French uniform and a red handkerchief on his head, who was presumably someone's pet. On finding the monkey some locals decided to hold an impromptu 'trial' on the beach; since the monkey was unable to answer their questions (and because they had seen neither a monkey nor a Frenchman before), they concluded that the monkey must therefore be a French spy. As such, it was duly sentenced to death and hanged on the beach by the local attending Provost Marshals, the forerunners of the RMP. I can *totally* believe it.

47 'De-eyed'. I'll admit to having to look that one up.

48 A brightly coloured truck used by the locals, usually featuring elaborate floral patterns or calligraphy, and often a real work of art.

49 Which he did; he was shot dead on the objective at the end of a quite spectacular gunfight.

50 Shot at very intensely.

51 If you don't have a round in the chamber of your weapon, ready to fire.

52 Tipping (or in some cases bribery).

53 Two days later someone turned the slides round and used them as launch rails for a rocket attack on Basra Palace.

54 MINIMISE was called whenever there was a serious incident in theatre. The Army immediately cut off personal communications to stop any news getting back to the UK before families could be informed.

55 'Greater love hath no man than this, that he lay down his life for his friends.'